MIXED RACE LITERATURE

Mixed Race Literature

Edited with an Introduction by

JONATHAN BRENNAN

STANFORD UNIVERSITY PRESS

Stanford, California 2002

Stanford University Press
Stanford, California
©2002 by the Board of Trustees of the
Leland Stanford Junior University
Printed in the United States of America

Library of Congress Cataloging-in-Publication Data

Mixed race literature / edited with an introduction by Jonathan Brennan.
    p. cm.
    Includes index.
    ISBN 0-8047- 3639-1 (alk. paper) — ISBN 0-8047- 3640-5 (pbk. : alk. paper)
    1. American literature—Minority authors—History and criticism.
2. Racially mixed people in literature.   3. Ethnic relations in literature.
4. Race relations in literature. 5. Minorities in literature. 6. Ethnicity in
literature. I. Brennan, Jonathan.

PS153.M56M59   2002
810.9'920693—dc21   2001055146

This book is printed on acid-free, archival-quality paper.

Original printing 2002

Last figure below indicates year of this printing:
11 10 09 08 07 06 05 04 03 02

Typeset at Stanford University Press in 10/13 Galliard

A mi esposa, Natalia. Mi fe, mi luz, mi amor.

Contents

Preface

I am grateful for the support of the many family members who deeply enrich my life. I would like to thank my wife, Natalia, for many years of happiness, for her commitment and collaboration in the work we do together, and for sustaining us both during countless hours of research and writing. I am sustained beyond measure by my children, Carmen Alicia and Liam Rafael, who laugh like geckos, love like lions, and truly appreciate reading a good book. I am grateful to my parents for their support, to my younger brother for his courage, and to my older brother, despite his absence, for the gift of hope. Thank you Susannah and Ken for taking good care of my family, and Maria Dolores por las hierbas y el fu-fu tan fuerte. Y a usted, Titi Carmen Brennan, un abrazo y dos besos. Fernando, te quiero mucho, tio. Y pa' mi suegra, Carmen Rita Menéndez Nuñez Tolivar, pues, me das de todo.

I am also appreciative of the support of faculty, staff, and students at U.C. Berkeley, especially Professor Hertha Dawn Sweet Wong. Thank you, Hertha, for your many careful readings of my work, and for company on the road we walk together. Thanks also to Professors Carlos Muñoz Jr., Waldo E. Martin Jr., Robert Pinsky, John Bishop, and Carolyn Dinshaw. I am indebted to the late Professor Barbara Christian for her constant support and encouragement. Barbara, thank you for your thoughtful questions, your many letters, and your island wisdom. I hope they have *bacalao* (salt cod) in heaven and hot pepper sauce so you can doctor it up.

I would like to thank some of my friends, mentors, and leaders: Siobhan Duffy (mo chara), Rosetta, Steve, Sharene, Dorrie, Rabbi Bender, Donnelle and Wendy, Neil Russack, Manouso and Rita, Robert Allen, Rosemary, John, Claire and Nora, Ito, Piti y Marta, Rossi and Dorian, Kamika, Rob (big music) and Michelle, Joannie Parker, Skip, Samuel Lind de Loiza Aldea, JoeSam., Mrs. Hinda Heller (and Simon), Qa'id, Big Chief Andrew Justin, Tony and John, and of course my Armenian second family: Laura, Eddie, Andre, and Eric.

I am constantly challenged by the ideas, insights, and soul-searching of my students, and I am grateful that they allow me the opportunity to teach.

My big band of musical support includes: the late greats—Tito Puente, John McCormack, Ismael Rivera, Canario, Cortijo, Billie Holiday, and Mon Rivera—and the still moving Celia Cruz, Gloria Estefan, The Chieftains, the Pogues, Stevie Wonder, the Neville Brothers (and all of the Mardi Gras Indians), and all practitioners of the plena, bomba, reel, and jig.

Everything in this world sits on the shoulders of our ancestors: Tomas, Michael, Mary, R. J., Frederick Douglass, Black Elk, Okah Tubbee, Nat Turner, John Brown, William Wells Brown, Coyote, J. D. Green (trickster extraordinaire), Harriet Jacobs, Mark Twain, James Joyce, and the souls of Ireland, Panama, and Puerto Rico.

I would like to thank the contributors to the volume for their hard work, numerous revisions, and supportive dialogue. I also thank the editors and staff at Stanford University Press: especially Laura Comay, Helen Tartar, Nathan MacBrien, and the readers who contributed to the shaping of this volume. I am honored to edit this volume of essays and heartened by the strong interest in this field. Thank you to all of the people who forwarded proposals, suggestions, leads, advice, warnings, and guidance.

Negotiating the field of mixed race studies can be tricky. Only a millipede has more toes to step on. My advice to the reader is as follows: remember who you are, make no assumptions, and listen carefully. In *Black Indians*, author William Loren Katz recalls the words used to describe African-European-Native American frontiersman Edward Rose: "cunning as a prairie wolf." Try it; it worked for Rose.

J.B.

Contributors

SANDRA BARINGER is a lecturer at the University of California, Riverside. She has published essays in the *American Indian Culture and Research Journal* and *Studies in American Indian Literature*, and most recently an essay in *FemSpec* on Silko's *Almanac of the Dead*. Her current book project deals with discourses of persecution and prosecution in late-twentieth-century fiction and law enforcement.

JONATHAN BRENNAN teaches African American and Native American literature at Mission College in Santa Clara, California. He holds an M.A. in English and a Ph.D. in Ethnic Studies from the University of California, Berkeley. He is the editor of *When Brer Rabbit Meets Coyote: African-Native American Literature* (forthcoming, University of Illinois Press) and author of essays on African-Native American literature in *A/B Autobiography Studies* and the *Oxford Companion to African American Literature*.

MARTHA J. CUTTER is an Associate Professor at Kent State University, where she teaches classes on Ethnic Literature, African American Literature, and Women's Literature. Her book, *Unruly Tongue: Identity and Voice in American Women's Fiction, 1850–1930*, was published by the University of Mississippi Press in 1999, and she is currently at work on a book on multilingualism in contemporary ethnic literature. She has published articles in *American Literature*, *Criticism*, *Women's Studies*, *African American Literature*, *Callaloo*, *MELUS*, and many other journals.

WEI MING DARIOTIS is an Assistant Professor in the Department of Asian American Studies in the College of Ethnic Studies at San Francisco State University. She teaches courses in Asians of Mixed Heritage, Asian American Literature and Culture, and Asian American Gender Issues.

Since 1999, Dariotis has facilitated the San Francisco Chapter of Hapa Issues Forum, and she is the Faculty Advisor of the Hapa Club at SFSU. As a member of the Advisory Board of Kearny Street Workshop, the oldest ongoing Asian American arts organization, she acts as a curator for both performing and visual arts, and is herself a visual artist and creative writer.

MICHELE JANETTE is an Assistant Professor of English at Kansas State University, where she teaches courses in Asian American Literature, Women's Literature, Contemporary American Literature, and Vietnamese Literature in Translation. She is currently creating an anthology of Vietnamese American literature in English, and has published articles on the novels of Toni Morrison, Maxine Hong Kingston, and Lan Cao, as well as interviews with Maxine Hong Kingston and le thi diem thuy.

ISABELLE THUY PELAUD is a graduate student in Ethnic Studies at the University of California, Berkeley, writing a doctoral dissertation on Vietnamese American narratives and identity politics. She is active in the promotion and production of Vietnamese American cultural work. She initially left France as a young adult to live with her Vietnamese American refugee family in Orange County. Her essays have been published in *Making More Waves* and *Tilting the Continent*.

PATRICIA RILEY, a poet and writer of Cherokee and Irish descent, is an Assistant Professor of English at the University of Idaho, where she teaches courses in Native American and other ethnic literatures. She is the editor of *Growing Up Native American*, an anthology of fiction and nonfiction. She has published articles in *Fiction International* and in collections of essays such as *Understanding Others: Cultural and Cross-Cultural Studies and the Teaching of Literature* and *Our Voices: Essays in Culture, Ethnicity and Communication*. Her poetry has appeared in *Northeast Indian Quarterly* and *Studies in American Indian Literature*, and her short fiction has been included in *Earth Song, Sky Spirit: An Anthology of Native American Fiction*, and *Blue Dawn, Red Earth: New Native American Storytellers*.

WERNER SOLLORS (http://www.fas.harvard.edu/~amciv/faculty/sollors.shtlml) teaches Afro-American Studies and English at Harvard University. Most recently he published *Neither Black Nor White Yet Both: Thematic Explorations of Interracial Literature* (1999) and edited *Multilingual America: Transnationalism, Ethnicity and the Languages of America* (1998),

Interracialism: Black-White Intermarriage in American History, Literature and Law (2000), *The Life Stories of Undistinguished Americans* (expanded edition 2000), *The Multilingual Anthology of American Literature* (co-edited 2000), and the Norton Critical Edition of *Olaudah Equiano* (2000). His electronic publications include "From 'English-Only' to 'English-Plus'" in American Studies *Interroads* website at http://www.georgetown. edu/crossroads/interroads/sollors1.html and "Americans All!" at http:// www.nyupress.nyu.edu/americansall.html.

ALICE TEPUNGA SOMERVILLE, Māori (Te Atiawa)/Pākehā, has an M.A. (1st class honors) from the University of Auckland, Aotearoa/New Zealand, and is now studying for her Ph.D. in English at Cornell University. She has taught at the University of Auckland and Massey University, working specifically with Māori students at the former, and NESB (non–English speaking background) students at the latter. She also established the Kaitautoko position at University of Auckland's Centre for Professional Development. In 1999, she published *Ngā Take Atawhai*, a report about the provision of learning support for Māori tertiary students through Massey's Student Learning Centre, and has poetry in a forthcoming volume of Polynesian writing. Her current research focuses on developing critical approaches to indigenous literature.

HERTHA D. SWEET WONG, Associate Professor of English at the University of California, Berkeley, is the author/editor of numerous works on autobiography and Native American literatures, including: *(Post)ethnicity and Its Discontents: A Reader, Louise Erdrich: A Casebook* (2000), and *Sending My Heart Back Across the Years: Tradition and Innovation in Native American Autobiography* (1992). She is currently writing a book on visual autobiography.

And so when she asked me, "What part Indian are you?"
I said, "I think it is my heart."

Inez Petersen (*As We Are Now* 86)

Introduction

> When I am East, my heart is West. When I am West, my
> heart is East.
> —Sui Sin Far, "Leaves from the Mental Portfolio of an Eurasian"

One of the seminal works of early-twentieth-century fiction in the canon of African American (and American) literature is the novel *Cane* (1923), by Jean Toomer. *Cane*, often acknowledged as the first African American modernist novel, exerted a strong influence both on Toomer's contemporaries and on later generations of African American writers. Henry Louis Gates argues that *Cane* was an important forerunner in the African American literary tradition due to its complex form and multiple literary strategies:

> Not only are tropes such as repetition, catachesis, parataxis and chiasmus and modes of mimesis used by Toomer but his work serves as a critical literary influence on writers in the African American tradition such as Sterling Brown, Zora Neale Hurston, Ralph Ellison, and Toni Morrison.[1]

Yet in 1930, Toomer refuses James Weldon Johnson permission to publish his work in the *Book of American Negro Poetry* and writes to Nancy Cunard, editing the anthology *Negro*, that "though I am interested in and deeply value the Negro, I am not a Negro" (Gates 205). Toomer's stance creates a dilemma for critics of African American literature: Was Toomer an African American writer, despite his denial that he was a Negro? Was Toomer passing as European American? Is *Cane* an African American text?

In fact, there are no easy answers to the question as to whether Toomer was African American or European American. The problem, however, lies not in the answer, but in the question. Toomer was not *either* African American or European American but *both* African American and European American, and Native American as well. Like other mixed race writers, he refused to allow himself to be corralled into a singular identity, because he experienced himself through multiple identities. In an essay on mixed race writer Hum-ishu-ma (Mourning Dove), Carol Roh Spaulding cites the mixed blood protagonist of Mourning Dove's novel, *Cogewea* (1927), in her description of the limitations imposed on mixed race Indians by both Native Americans and European Americans: "We despised breeds are in a zone of our own and when we break from the corral erected about us we meet up with trouble."[2] Roh Spaulding argues that this corral, despite its limitations, proves to be "a freely chosen space beyond the reservation and the white man's world" (106), a site where Cogewea and her half-blood husband, Jim, have an opportunity to exist beyond the constraints of racial designations, in a liminal state that promises opportunity in place of tragedy.

In spite of the potential liberation that movement beyond racial designation can bring, as Cogewea states, "we meet up with trouble." Because most mixed race people have been categorized according to the prevailing mode of hypodescent, a policy that assigns mixed race individuals to the race that has been saddled with the lowest social status, any attempts to move beyond racial proscription have traditionally been viewed as a threat to already threatened communities. In *Who is Black?* F. James Davis discusses both African American acceptance and rejection of the one-drop rule, and examines the situation of a former student discussing her identity in a panel on racial discrimination:

> "I am part French, part Cherokee Indian, part Filipino and part black. Our family taught us to be aware of all of these groups, and just to be ourselves." ... As this panelist tried to describe her feelings of group marginality, a young black woman student (who appeared to be about half white, biologically) raised her hand and asserted strongly, "You don't have any problem. You are black." There was a murmur of approval and nodding of heads, especially among the black students, but the panelist replied softly, "No. No. Not just black. I am the other things too. All of them."[3]

Davis also notes that in a discussion following the class, some of his African American students were "frustrated and disturbed by this questioning of the one-drop rule, which had provided them with a clear guide to their own group identity"; some students accused the (openly) mixed race student of attempting to "deny her race" (134). In fact, for many mixed race members of marginalized communities, their attempts to assert a mixed race identity are often met with concern or derision because the marginalized community believes (often rightly) that it cannot afford to lose additional members in the face of centuries of sustained genocide (or allow unknown potential members to join), and that because the vast majority of the members of Native American and African American communities are of mixed race, such an assertion might lead to the disintegration of their communities (and/or nations), and to a disruption or dissolution of their cultural traditions, social fabric, and political power.

But note Davis's student's response to the offer of community extended by the other student: "Not just black. I am the other things too." She did not try to deny her African American heritage but to assert her other affiliations as well, to occupy multiple spaces, and this is precisely what Toomer often attempted to do when challenged to define his identity as either black or white. In response to the question posed by Claude Barnett of the Associated Negro Press, "are you Negroid?" Toomer responded that "the true and complete answer is one of some complexity and for this reason perhaps it will not be seen and accepted until after I am dead"; he goes on to recall his African American grandfather and acknowledge that he (Toomer) had "peeped behind the veil ... and my deepest impulse to literature ... is the direct result of what I saw."[4] He also argues that "insofar as the old folk-songs, syncopated rhythms, the rich sweet taste of dark-skinned life, insofar as these are Negro, I am, body and soul, negroid" (Gates 205). Toomer believed that "in time, in its social phase, my art will aid in giving the Negro to himself" (196).

Toomer refused to observe established racial categories, despite the strong hold they maintain over most Americans, and insisted on both cultural affiliations and a complex identity, yet this complexity does not deny African American heritage; in fact, Toomer clearly celebrates his "deepest impulse to literature" and his cultural roots, believes that he writes for the benefit of an African American community, and claims his Negro soul quite openly. An assertion of multiple identities does not entail a destruction of all identities, but an insistence on the right to claim one's true self. Toomer claims this self when he also acknowledges the influence of "the entire body of contemporary literature" (205), not just African American literature, and when he writes himself as "an American with Negro blood in his veins" (205). Toomer insisted upon an American identity alongside his others, to achieve a "spiritual fusion" (204) of racial selves, and to argue as well that America's future was one of mixed race. About his poem "The First American" Toomer wrote, "In America, we are in the process of forming a new race. ... I was one of the first conscious members of this race" (201). With a conscious stance as a mixed race writer, he records the reality of America's mixed race population, arguing that the corral reserved for mixed race subjects might also promise the opportunity to expand the restricted definitions of race.

In spite of Toomer's proclamations, we again meet up with "trouble" in the form of resistance or skepticism. Henry Louis Gates (one of many in a long line of critics) notes Toomer's marriages to "two white women" (208), and posits that Toomer's racial assertions were oscillations between Toomer's "black and his erased black self" (209), maintaining that, in a "rhetorical gesture" (205), Toomer has denied his African American heritage. Gates goes on to argue that "Toomer's was a gesture of racial castration, which, if not silencing his voice literally, then at least transformed his deep black bass into a false soprano. Toomer did not want so much to be white as most of us, like his fellow 'colored of more than ordinary mental grasp,' would have it; rather he sought to be racially indeterminate, which Johnson suggests to be the nature of the castrato" (208).

In response to these strong accusations of racial abandonment, I would argue that Toomer is only one of many writers to have published successful work early in his career and struggled throughout the rest to find his writing voice, or to find a receptive audience for his later writing (if that was indeed his intention). Gates assigns this struggle to Toomer's refusal to be racially "determined," thereby rewriting the mixed race writer, Toomer, precisely in the emplotment of the tragic mulatto that Toomer sought to avoid, representing his tragic literary fate as stemming from his choice to follow a (European?) false soprano rather than an (African?) deep bass literary voice. Gates's argument raises many issues, including his accusations of Toomer's "passing" through marrying white women (arguments leveled against Frederick Douglass and many other mixed race writers as well), a romanticized trumpeting of African American culture/literary tradition over European American culture/literary tradition (an unlikely argument when set beside Toomer's French, Dutch, Welsh, German, and Jewish ancestries) coupled with a gendered analysis of Toomer's literary intentions (soprano versus bass) that assigns the mixed race writer, following a long tradition, apparently negative female characteristics, and that even suggests a self-lynching through castration. Gates also assumes that Toomer refused a single racial categorization only after *Cane* was written (which he did not), and he reinforces the old and prevailing myth that mixed race writers are indeed mulatto (from mules) and thus sterile (castrato), lacking a definitive writing voice.

I do not mean to single out Gates, for in spite of these shortcomings he also provides in his essay an often deep, nuanced, and penetrating reading of Toomer's writing, but I do intend to point out issues in his criticism that represent arguments made by numerous critics about mixed race writers and mixed race writing. I would also argue, and I believe that Gates would agree, that one of the richest facets of *Cane* indeed stems from Toomer's conscious mixed race writing; as Rudolph P. Byrd argues, "hybridity and innovation are the defining features of the artist as well as the classic he produced."[5] Even Gates acknowledges its "multiple forms and shifting points of consciousness ... its very ambiguity, of structure and of densely metaphorical lyricism, that continues to compel such a diversity of discursive responses, as do few texts in the American canon."[6] Finally, one critic, William Stanley Brathwaite in the *Crisis* in 1924, argued for Toomer's importance as a Negro writer but, ironically, simultaneously acknowledged Toomer first and foremost as a writer, a position that Toomer himself would likely have noted with pleasure:

> It's a mere accident that birth or association has thrown him into contact with the life that he has written about. He would write just as well, just as poignantly, just as transmutingly, about the peasants of Russia, or the peasants of Ireland, had experience but given him knowledge of their existence. (Gates 199)

Even though Gates and many other literary critics acknowledge the rhetorical nature (rather than the reality) of race,[7] he is clearly disappointed that Toomer "abandons the race" in a "rhetorical gesture" (200). But, of course, race already is a rhetorical gesture, a social rather than strictly biologically defined category, and to insist that Toomer uphold the one-drop rule, that he adhere to rhetorical restrictions on inscribing his true self into his books, that he pretend to recognize the empty rhetorical gesture of racial assignation, certainly dooms a mixed race writer to a tragic fate, and fulfills Toomer's predictions that he would not be understood, even accepted, until after his death. I would argue that mixed race writers should not have to live out their writerly lives in an arena of misunderstanding, fenced in a half-breed corral awaiting the literary fate of the much maligned tragic mulatto, the treacherous half-breed, or the conflicted Eurasian, and so, in this collection of essays, we attempt to provide both a context for understanding this work and a critical apparatus for critiquing this literature.

This collection of essays attempts to both map and respond to some portion of the rapidly emerging fields of mixed race literatures, including African-European, Native-European, Eurasian, African-Asian, and Native-African American literature as well as other non-American literatures. Mixed race (multiple heritage/culturally hybrid) literatures are defined in this collection as texts written by authors who represent multiple cultural and literary traditions. These authors are, in many cases, culturally mixed race themselves, and in other cases are attempting to represent a mixed race subjectivity in their literary text. Although there have been sporadic studies on individual traditions and authors (yet rarely in a mixed race context), the ubiquity of centuries of mixed race experience, the current demographic/social trends (in the direction of intermarriage) in the United States, and the growing interest in mixed race texts clearly demonstrate the need for studies that will assist scholars and other interested readers in gaining both a comprehensive and comparative knowledge of these literary traditions, from sixteenth-century writers to contemporary playwrights and novelists. These studies will assist scholars and students to engage a wide variety of mixed race literatures and critical approaches and to situate these literatures in relation to existing fields of literary inquiry.

This collection focuses on theorizing mixed race literatures and not on theories of race nor theories of mixed race, but it is impossible to address the mixed race literary traditions without inquiring into the history, politics, and cultures of mixed race traditions in the United States. Taking one step back from this position, it is also important to address the creation and conception of the idea of "race," without which, one imagines, the idea of "mixed race" wouldn't exist. It is questionable whether race really exists: in an essay in *"Race," Writing, and Difference,* Anthony Appiah argues that research into the human genetic constitution at chromosome loci must lead one to the conclusion that "race is relatively unimportant in explaining biological differences between people."[8] In other words, the biological concept of race is very tenuous, in spite of the enormous social and political implications of the various meanings with which race has been burdened. As Appiah argues in *In My Father's House: Africa in the Philosophy of Culture,* "the truth is that there are no races: there is nothing in the world that can do all we ask race to do for us."[9] Yet it is these social constructions of race that have attempted to define the communities encircling mixed race writers, and these writers often grapple with the ramifications and the meanings of these definitions in their writing. Despite the fragility, hostility, or vulnerability of racial terminology, the metaphor of race and mixed race is invoked and engaged by many mixed race writers.

In *Race and Mixed Race*, Naomi Zack argues that her intention is to use the words "race," "mixed race," "black," "white," "mulatto," "quadroon," and so on as an anthropologist might use the words "'untouchable,' 'berdache,' 'totem,' 'shamin'—the words are used to describe what is going on in a culture, in order to understand that culture" and she defines her stance as a "critical, philosophical, anthropological ... [and historical] analysis."[10] Because the gaze of an anthropologist usually comes from *outside* these communities, and as all of us are both inside and outside the wide variety of "racial" communities, the anthropologist model could be coupled here with the gaze of an inside observer who already "understands" his or her culture. Regardless, I will argue for the acknowledgment of the common usage of racial definitions without arguing for their correctness, and suggest that once one enters the territory of race, one must simultaneously suspend belief (because even though the consequences of racism exist, race exists only as a false biological and social construct), acknowledge the powerful grasp that race often maintains over us, and work actively to continually challenge our beliefs. I will suggest that an exploration of the world of mixed race identity both reinforces these essential categories of race and also provides one of the best opportunities to see the limitations and absurdity of racial categories. For example, in Frederick Douglass's *Narrative of the Life of Frederick Douglass*, he addresses the existence of numerous mulatto (African-European) slaves on the plantations and reasons that the slave owners' attempts at scriptural argument (that God cursed Ham and thus Africans are doomed to enslavement) is bound to collapse:

> It is nevertheless plain that a very different looking class of people are springing up at the south, and are now held in slavery, from those originally brought to this country from Africa. ... if the lineal descendants of Ham are alone to be scripturally enslaved, it is certain that slavery at the south must soon become unscriptural; for thousands are ushered into the world, annually, who like myself, owe their existence to white fathers, and those fathers most frequently their own masters.[11]

As Douglass acknowledges his own mixed race identity, he also points out the imminent collapse of the dichotomous racial categories of black and white, prefiguring both Jean Toomer's "new race" of mixed race people and Toomer's conscious mixed race subjectivity, although the horrors detailed in Douglass's slave narrative make it terrifyingly clear that the social categories and hierarchies of race (Douglass writes these as class/caste) have not yet collapsed. Douglass also co-opts the authority of biblical interpretation, reinterpreting the slaveholders' scripturally assigned arguments in favor of enslavement, underlain by distinct racial categories, with an argument more akin to Toomer's notion of a racial "spiritual fusion." It is also clear that Douglass is calling attention to the power that literacy and scriptural interpretation hold to construct notions of race, notions that literary readings have an opportunity to refashion and reinterpret (especially through the recognition of mixed race spaces) due to the literary and not biological nature of race.

Douglass's overturning of racially coded arguments, an act of trickster reversal, acknowledges both the literary nature and linguistic embedding of race. Many mixed race literary texts serve as trickster narratives, overturning and undermining our fixed expectations of identity and appropriate behavior. In an essay on "Trickster Discourse" in *Narrative Chance*, Gerald Vizenor argues that the trickster is "a semiotic sign; not cultural material or discovered elements that are recomposed to endorse invented models in social science" and that trickster narratives should be read not in terms of social science theories, as an anthropological exploration of minority cultures, but with an "emphasis" on semiotics and with a "consciousness of signs in literature (signs, myths and metaphors)."[12] These mixed race trickster narratives should not be read simply as cultural objects, reflections of multiple underlying cultural manifestations, as *true* books of mixed identity, but as literary works employing literary strategies such as metaphor and myth-making, as true *books* of mixed identity. Any mixed race identity is always negotiated, manipulated, represented, and subject to multiple shifts in meaning; in other words, the lives of mixed race subjects are perfect candidates for a literary rather than a literal reading.

In fact, in *The Race Concept*, Michael Banton and Jonathan Harwood argue that the first written record of the use of the term "race" was in an early-sixteenth-century poem and that this term was used for centuries primarily in a "literary sense" rather than as a strict determinant of social/economic status.[13] Whether the term race was being used or not, it is clear that the concept was in existence as early as the sixteenth century as the English and other Europeans confronted Africans, Native Americans, the Irish, and other colonial subjects who they argued were "racially" distinct; for our purposes the critical issue is the invocation of a "literary sense" and the location of its usage, in a poem, for a literary sense of race is what should underlie an exploration of mixed race. Vizenor notes that

the trickster is a "sign" and that Jacques Lacan has arg
should not "cling to the illusion that the signifier answers t
of representing the signified, or better, that the signifier ha
its existence in the name of any signification whatsoever."[
gests that the trickster is real in the act of literary imaginat
thus I argue that we should set aside our belief that mixed race can be
consistently defined outside an act of literature and turn to literary works
for an exploration of the relationship between signifier and signified.
Gates has maintained that "'race' is a metaphor for something else and
not an essence or a thing in itself, apart from its creation by an act of language," and I believe that the literary text, poem or prose, the site for
metaphor, is the act of language that encodes social meanings of race and
mixed race and challenges them as well.[15] Although Appiah utilizes genetic research to build his arguments around race, he turns to a work of
literature, W. E. B. Du Bois's second autobiography, *Dusk of Dawn*, in
order to explicate them; the literary rather than biological implications of
mixed race are what I would like to explore although, again, I do not believe these implications are always separate from the political and social
effects of racial terminology.

Another one of the "metaphor[s] for something else" is culture, and
since literature cannot be located in biological terms, I would argue that
the term mixed race serve as a metaphor for cultural hybridity, the merging of more than one stream of cultural/literary tradition. Anthony Appiah states that "talk of race is particularly distressing for those of us who
take culture seriously. ... communities of meaning, shading variously into
each other in the rich structure of the social world [are] the province not
of biology but of hermeneutic understanding," and thus my attempt in
this collection is to enter the shaded provinces of mixed race hermeneutic
understanding.[16] Still, in spite of my use of the term mixed race, I would
like to use it only to define a wide category of inquiry, to engage the
reader with a widely encompassing term as an open door leading to its
own redefinition, so at every opportunity I will advocate a much more
specific terminology for mixed race literary traditions such as African-
Native American, French-Vietnamese, African-Choctaw, or Chippewa-
Chinese American literatures.[17] These categories must most often be defined culturally and not racially, in that one is grounded in a culturally
(and not racially) defined literary tradition, although within this context
issues of racial categorization and racism arise as well and are engaged in
the literary text. In *Africans and Native Americans*, Jack Forbes discusses

an ancient Roman definition of hybrid (*hibrida*) that is essentially nonra-
cialized, *hibrida* meaning the offspring of a native citizen and foreigner, a
definition that focuses on political or cultural mergings, and this comes
closest to the sense in which I would like to use hybrid, rather than as a
genetic distinction.[18] The process of literary hybridization, the merging of
multiple streams of literary traditions, the call and response between multiple oral traditions, and the representation of multiple identities are some
of the processes that define mixed race literatures, the literary works that
arise from the shaded provinces of Appiah's "communities of meaning."

Spiritual Fusions

The creation of mixed race communities in the Americas has roots
that reach back centuries. Scholars Jack Forbes (*Africans and Native
Americans*) and F. James Davis (*Who is Black?*) both note mixing between
Africans, Europeans, and Native Americans that occurred before the
widespread establishment of American colonies, and although there has
been little research into the cultural exchange that must have accompanied these social interactions, there is an abundance of evidence documenting such interaction and exchange during and following the American colonial period.[19] In fact, in 1526, many years before English colonies
were established in North America, Spaniard Lucas Vásquez de Ayllón
brought one hundred African slaves and five hundred Spanish colonists to
the east coast of North America (near South Carolina):

> Determined to succeed, Ayllón drove his people until they came to a great
> river, which was probably the Pee Dee. Selecting a location in a low, marshy
> area, Ayllón ordered his band to set up camp. He paused to name his settle-
> ment "San Miguel de Gualdape." When he ordered the Africans to begin
> building homes, he launched black slavery in the United States.[20]

After the African slaves revolted and escaped to a neighboring Native nation, the Spanish colonists returned to Haiti, leaving behind an African-
Native American community.[21] There are numerous other historical interactions that led to African-Native American communities, including the
widespread enslavement of Native Americans alongside Africans, the African-Native American maroon nations of escaped Indian and African
slaves, the enslavement of Africans and African-Native Americans by
some members of Native American nations, and the extensive interactions between free African Americans and Native Americans in segre-

gated "colored" communities throughout New England, the Southeast, and the western United States.

Paralleling the growth of African-Native American communities were those of African-Europeans. In *Who is Black?* Davis cites Joel Williamson (author of *New People: Miscegenation and Mulattoes in the United States*) in arguing that "the first extensive mixing was in the seventeenth century in the Chesapeake area of the colonies of Maryland and Virginia, between white indentured servants and slave and free blacks."[22] Davis also cites statistics from a body of studies that state that "between one fifth and one fourth of the genes of the American black population are from white ancestors," and that "at least three fourths of all people defined as American blacks have some white ancestry" (21). Historically, numerous leaders of the African American community have been African-European Americans, including Adam Clayton Powell Jr., Walter White (former president of the NAACP), and A. Phillip Randolph, president of the Brotherhood of Sleeping Car Porters.

There are as well a large number of European-Native Americans, and many who have played a substantial role in their nation's politics, such as Cherokee leader John Ross and Osage leader John Joseph Mathews. In "Blood Quantum," Terry P. Wilson argues that "no more knotty issue preoccupies Indian America than that of identity," and that the tribal membership "process hinges heavily on blood quantum, or the degree of Indian ancestry expressed in fractions such as one-fourth or three-eighths."[23] In fact, most Native Americans are mixed bloods (the 1910 census reported "full-blood" Indians at 46.3 percent); the process of hybridization began centuries ago and continues today.[24] In *American Indian Ethnic Renewal*, Joane Nagel notes that the intermarriage rate of Native Americans with non–Native Americans is higher than 50 percent, clearly leading quickly to a situation where the vast majority of Native Americans are mixed blood (and only partially racially Indian), and where the measurement of Indian blood quantum cannot possibly be the determining factor in tribal affiliation; cultural and political affiliations are likely to become the prevailing factors in determining "Indianness."[25]

There are also Asian-Native Americans, especially in California, where, as Terry Wilson notes, there are "many instances of Filipino-Native American mixed bloods, mostly in California, but virtually no scholarly or popular notice. The same is true of other Asian-Native American mixed bloods."[26] While editing an autobiography by a Chinese American elder several years ago, I heard numerous stories of Chinese miners escaping racist legislation and physical violence by joining Native communities and/or passing as Native American. These Asian-Indian interactions have made their way into several works of Asian American literature, including Sky Lee's *Disappearing Moon Cafe* (1990) and Shawn Wong's *Homebase* (1979).

African-Asian and European-Asian interactions have been common, both in the United States and abroad, but especially as a result of the numerous wars fought by the United States in Asian countries, which resulted in Amerasian populations both in these Asian countries and emigrating to the United States. Substantial numbers of U.S. servicemen had children with Japanese, Chinese, and Korean mothers, many of whom immigrated into the United States:

> The large U.S. military presence in Asia from 1945–1965 is a key factor in explaining most of this spousal immigration to the United States. The occupation of Japan became the major network for post-war Japanese immigration to the United States. Thousands of Chinese entered under the War Brides Act, while others married American citizens after the act expired in 1952. ... most of the 17,000 Korean immigrants who came to the United States from 1950–1965 were wives of U.S. military personnel.[27]

The population of Vietnamese Amerasians was estimated at 30,000 in 1975 at the end of the Vietnam war, including large numbers of European-Amerasians and African-Amerasians who were singled out for humiliation with the use of words such as *con lai* (half-breed), *my lai* (American mix), or *my den* (black American); large numbers of these Vietnamese Amerasians came to the United States under the Amerasian Homecoming Act (1987).[28]

Japanese Amerasians often use the term *haafu* (half) to self-identify as mixed race. One Japanese "Afroasian man who lived in North Carolina for three years described his experience: It was awful. We were 'niggers.' Then, we were 'Japs.' Then, we were 'Chinks.' I finally got so mad that I went, 'make up your minds.' So they settled with 'Nigger.'"[29] A large community of African-Chinese and European-Chinese Americans has roots in the 1,200 Chinese agricultural laborers who arrived in the Mississippi Delta in the late nineteenth century and followed a model of hypergamy, "the tendency for males to marry 'down,' females 'up' in a social system."[30] Partially due to a nearly all-male work force in the late nineteenth century (Chinese men were nearly 93 percent of the Chinese American population in 1870),[31] partially as a result of the immigration restrictions of the 1882 Chinese Exclusion Act, and partially as a result of the antimiscegenation laws prohibiting African/European, Indian/European, and Asian/European marriages, some Chinese men married African American women. Filipino men found themselves in a similar situation; the unmarried men outnumbered unmarried females twenty-three to one in 1930, and thus they found themselves often marrying African American or Native American women, although some married European American women in spite of the prohibition, or traveled to Utah where interracial marriage was not outlawed.[32] In *Who is Black?* Davis notes Roi Ottley's observation of the "frequency of intermarriage between Chinese Americans and blacks in Harlem" (126).[33]

There is every indication that there will be growing numbers of Amerasians in the United States, for of the two million interracial households with children recorded in the 1980 census, "the largest proportion live in Asian-White households."[34] The rate of interracial marriage measured in Los Angeles county in 1977 among Asian Americans was as follows: Japanese 60 percent, Chinese 50 percent, and Korean 34 percent.[35]

There are, of course, an enormous number of mixed race populations outside the United States, particularly throughout Latin America, and as well in every country in the world, but their examination is outside the purview of this particular study. But because this collection includes two essays on mixed race writing outside the United States, one on French-Vietnamese writer Kim Lefevre, and another on the Maori-Pakeha literary tradition in Aotearoa/New Zealand, a brief examination of these groups is in order.

The Vietnamese Eurasian population in Vietnam was estimated at 25,000 in 1954, and significant numbers left to take advantage of the French offer of citizenship and education. One Vietnamese Eurasian notes the cultural and political interactions that took place: "Most of my Eurasian friends went to France to study. They wrote back home to their mothers about their life in France. And some, after getting their French citizenship, brought their Vietnamese mothers to France."[36]

A different set of political circumstances led to the development of a mixed race Maori-Pakeha population. The Maori are the indigenous people of New Zealand and the Pakeha are the European (English, Irish, and Scottish) immigrants. A 1966 study noted that more than 50 percent of Maori marriage partners choose a Pakeha partner.[37] In *Mapping the Language of Racism*, Margaret Wetherell and Jonathan Potter document the "racial formulation" of Maori people by Pakeha New Zealanders, including arguments centered around mixed race identity:

> The Maori isn't a leader, uh I think that the Maori that is leading in this way probably has a lot of Pakeha blood. Cause there are no pure-bred Maoris in New Zealand and that probably, you know, that's the reason why ...
>
> ... alright we have a lot of intermarriage, I mean none of the Maoris are pure, and um they have a racial trait, a characteristic that I don't know whether it's going to be dominant or not, but they're basically a lazy people.[38]

In much the same way that mixed race subjects are discussed in the United States, mixed Maori-Pakeha are assigned negative and enduring "dominant" traits stemming from their non-European identity, and are simultaneously assigned positive traits that are argued to arise from their Pakeha "blood." Mixed Maori-Pakeha writers find themselves attempting to write their way out from under a barrage of mistruth and misrepresentation, while negotiating dual identities and grievous cultural misunderstandings.

The language of racial hybridity that has developed in New Zealand in response to the rise of mixed race subjects has many parallels to the vocabulary of (racial) hybridity that developed in the United States, in many cases a language in the purview of colonial power that attempted to define an enormous number of mixed race variations. Forbes cites a nineteenth-century court case that utilized an "expert" witness in racial mixing:

> In 1859, a North Carolina court called in a planter as an expert who could distinguish between the "descendants of a negro and a white person, and the descendants of a negro and an Indian." He could also, allegedly, differentiate between a pure African and a "white cross" or an "Indian cross." Unfortunately, most of us today lack that kind of certain expertise, whatever phenotypical features are seized upon as evidence providing "proof."[39]

In *Africans and Native Americans*, Forbes also documents an extensive pattern of racial terminology in English, Spanish, Dutch, German, Arabic, Portuguese, and other languages, terms such as "griffon," "half blood," "half-breed," "mulatto," "mustee," "mamaluco," "mestizo," "branco," and "Indian-Negro," and there are hundreds of additional markers in mixed race terminology such as quadroon, octoroon, Eurasian, Amerasian, Hapa, Afro-Asian, and Haafu; the language of hybridity continues to grow and change. Ultimately, Forbes's research reminds us that we cannot rely on a static state of meaning for mixed race terminology because it is region, language, and time-period specific. For example, "mulatto" has been used interchangeably as a marker for African-Europeans, European-Natives, and African-Native Americans, and its multiple shifts in meaning require the researcher to ground his or her subject in a particular cultural and political setting before attempting an analysis of the subject's historical position using mixed race terminology alone. Not surprisingly, the attempts to circumscribe mixed race subjects have also provoked literary responses from mixed race writers who respond to the use of mixed race vocabulary that is used to restrict their opportunities (acts of linguistic domination) with attempts to create new linguistic ground on which to stand.

In spite of the patterns of extensive categorization of mixed race subjects, leading to the development of a complex and elaborate racial classification system, there was a simultaneous push to erase mixed race identity, a policy that established patterns of mis-remembering that continue today. The practice was based both on hypodescent, the assignment of racial (and social) identity based on the lowest category on the racial hierarchy that was a portion of one's identity, as well as on the repercussions stemming from the development of racial categories.

Since the establishment of European colonial rule and the creation of the institution of slavery, it has been a widespread policy, authorized by the "one-drop rule," to classify those with any perceivable or arguable African American heritage as "black," thus attempting to negate the wide variety of mixed racial and cultural identities in the United States. The institution of slavery constantly undermined any enduring recognition of mixed identities when the slave owners insisted that everyone be classified as either "white" or "colored," and those that were colored were enslaved. The acknowledgment of the subtlety of various racial and cultural mixtures threatened to undermine the basic dichotomy of slavery; in particular, it threatened the potential for maximum profitability. In order for the slave owners to classify as many potential slaves as possible, it worked to their advantage to inscribe the slaves into "blackness," and thus most African-Native Americans and European-African Americans were recognized by the institution of slavery as African Americans (black) only.[40]

Once the slaves were trapped in the system of slavery, however, the various subtleties of both African and Native American identities, and those of African-Native Americans and African-European Americans, were often recognized. Slave owners, although engaging in an argument that condensed all Africans into "Negroes," often deliberately separated those Africans who came from the same nations from each other in order to destroy alliances and communication. Their actions made it clear that they recognized all too well the various cultures, languages, and nations that composed this so-called "Negro" heritage. Slave owners also recognized differences between Native American slaves and African slaves, engaging in a variety of arguments about their perceived differences and their best use within the slave labor force. They also recognized both European-African and African-Native American slaves, identifying them variously as mustees or mulattoes, yet disallowing the potential meaning of these identifications, a part Native American or European American identity, when such an identity might interfere with plantation profits by increasing claims to freedom.[41]

Furthermore, European colonists and European Americans recognized (at least initially), in some cases, an obligation to Native Americans as a result of the treaty process conducted between England, Spain, France, or the United States and the numerous Native American nations. Although the United States has ignored or misconstrued much of the treaty process, it was clearly in the best interests of European Americans to reclassify Native Americans as African Americans. In this way the United States leadership erased potential financial obligations stemming from treaties and inscribed instead a new race of slaves on whose labor they could profit tremendously. As a result, they wrote a false racial narrative that erased African-Native American identity.

The mis-reporting of mixed race identity established in the colonial period continues today. The experience of the Japanese Afroasian man in North Carolina who was identified primarily by others as "nigger" reminds us that the pattern of hypodescent, outright racism, and the one-drop rule are still practiced in determining social privilege. Despite Frederick Douglass's or Jean Toomer's nineteenth- or twentieth-century pronouncements of a new mixed race, and despite the existence of numerous mixed race individuals and communities, there seems to be little room in the American psyche for the acknowledgment of mixed race identity (most obviously because it threatens established hierarchies), for the recognition of a spiritual fusion. As Zack notes in *Race and Mixed Race*:

> As groups, races are not stable entities. In Melville J. Herskovits's often-quoted words, "Two human groups never meet but they mingle their blood." And of course this has always been the case in the United States. But due to the alchemy of American racism, no new race ever results.[42]

Despite the continuing practice of mis-recognition, the body of literary works by mixed race writers stands as a testimony to their existence, and as a repudiation of false racial narratives. The growing body of mixed race scholarship testifies to its (slowly) increasing acceptance and importance.

Mixed Race Scholarship

Much of the discussion on mixed race identity and literature is being developed in the growing field of "mixed race studies," perhaps beginning with studies such as Edward Reuter's *The Mulatto in the United States* (1918), and with more recent development by scholars such as Joel Williamson (*New People*), F. James Davis (*Who is Black?*), Paul Spickard (*Mixed Blood: Intermarriage and Ethnic Identity in Twentieth-Century America*), Gloria Anzaldúa (*Borderlands/La Frontera: The New Mestiza*), Maria Root (*Racially Mixed People in America*), Lise Funderburg (*Black, White, Other*) and Naomi Zack (*Race and Mixed Race, American Mixed Race*). In response to other scholarly fields that often ultimately prove hostile to the idea of mixed race by insisting on a reductive reading of multiple identities, the field of mixed race studies is developing a framework for the discussion of contemporary multiple identities and for the analysis of the historical development of these identities in a sociological and psychological framework, which can be quite useful in informing an analysis of mixed race literatures.

Because it is crucial for literature scholars to engage the numerous mixed race American literature texts as hybrid literatures that reflect acts of cultural merging, it is essential for scholars to understand the prevailing issues in the field of mixed race studies to inform their critiques of this body of American literature. There is a growing body of mixed race literary criticism that attempts to do so. Because the fields of both African American and Native American literary study are significantly marked by the work of mixed race writers, and by work that attempts to represent a mixed race subjectivity, critics in these fields have sometimes grappled with mixed race issues in their analyses. There have certainly been many studies of writers who are mixed race, and even studies of mixed race subjectivity in writing, some of which discuss mulatto, half-blood, or Eurasian identity, but very few of these studies have demonstrated a sustained analysis of the writer's text within a mixed race tradition, choosing instead to explore the mixed race writer's role within a single literary tradition. There are some exceptions, studies that have focused on mixed race traditions. In the 1970s, William J. Scheick published a study of literary representations of mixed race Indians entitled *The Half Blood: A Cultural Symbol in 19th-Century American Fiction*. Scheick examines the depictions of half bloods in nineteenth-century popular prose fiction, argues for a set of "unique characteristics" of mixed race Indian subjects in literature, and concludes his study by comparing mulatto and half-blood literary representations. Judith Berzon published a study of the European-African mulatto in literature in 1978 (*Neither White nor Black: The Mulatto Character in American Fiction*), and Werner Sollors recently (1997) published a fascinating and very thorough study of African-European interracial literature (*Neither White Nor Black Yet Both*) in which he explores the origins of interracial themes, images, and texts, the resonance of the biblical curse of Ham, racial terminologies and taxonomies, and issues of the tragic mulatto and passing in literary and critical texts. Samira Kawash published *Dislocating the Color Line: Identity, Hybridity, and Singularity in African American Literature* (1997) as an interrogation of the color line between black and white and an exploration of the geographies of literary productions that negotiate the color line, such as the writings of Charles Chesnutt, James Weldon Johnson, Zora Neale Hurston, and Nella Larsen.

Several collections of personal and political essays focus on mixed race writers. *As We Are Now: Mixblood Essays on Race and Identity* (1997), edited by William S. Penn, focuses on the perspectives of nonreservation or urban mixed blood Indians. *Miscegenation Blues* (1994), edited by Carol Camper, is a collection of mixed race women's writing. *Cross Addressing: Resistance Literature and Cultural Borders* (1996), edited by John C. Hawley, includes essays on American and international mixed race writing, and focuses "not upon what some would describe as the *universal* deracination of our age so much as it is upon those whose 'hybridized' biology or shifting locale forces their ironic confrontation not only with uprootedness but also with *rootedness*, generally in two cultures."[43]

Yet book-length studies are scarce, monographs even more so, and much of the mixed race writing dialogue still unfolds within articles and unpublished dissertations. Because the foundation for a mixed race framework has yet to be substantially transported to literary studies and has yet to inform the critical approach of most scholars who research and write about mixed race texts, and because of a subsequent lack of a critical language to address mixed race literature, those critiquing literature in this field have either had to build a new critical position from which to evaluate these texts, or ascribe the complexity of these hybrid texts to a single tradition, often misinterpreting the merging traditions that underlie the hybrid texts. For instance, because most literature scholars tend to follow distinct racial categories while explicating literary texts, and because they also often follow the long-established one-drop rule, writers of mixed heritage who are part African are examined in the light of an African American literary, cultural, and social tradition. In part, this is correct. Many of them do belong to an African American community, and if they are simultaneously members of other communities, this does not deny them their claim to an African American community. Yet in order to really understand the tradition from which these writers create their literary works, one must also examine their parallel heritage without denying either one.

For instance, both Olivia Ward Bush-Banks and Ann Plato, authors included in the Schomburg Library of Nineteenth-Century Black Women Writers series, were African-Native American writers.[44] Plato published one volume of poetry and essays, some of which speak to the European colonization of both Africans and Native Americans, and another that addresses her Indian father, apparently a seaman. Bush-Banks, an African–Montauk Indian American, wrote *Indian Trails; or, Trail of the Montauk* in 1920, a play that utilizes "character roles matching Algonquian social and cultural patterns and names that correspond to the *r* Algonquian dialect traditionally existing between eastern Long Island and southeastern New England."[45] Bush-Banks also attended the tribal pow-wows and other meetings, and she was the Montauk tribal historian; she clearly demonstrated what Bernice Guillaume argues was a "*conscious* immersion in an Algonquian heritage" (6). Bush-Banks also lived in Harlem, was active politically in the African American community, was especially involved in literary and dramatic circles in the Harlem Renaissance, and dedicated her first published work to her African American community. Both her sketches in black dialect, *Aunt Viney's Sketches* (completed at least a decade before Langston Hughes's Simple columns) and her racial (African American) uplift poetry reflect her active engagement in an African American world, an engagement that did not preclude her work in Montauk politics and literature as well. In recognition of these facts, Guillaume argues that Bush-Banks's African and Montauk Indian identities led to a "sensibility that challenges traditional ethnic categorization and that clouds an objective understanding and analysis of her use of tone, meaning, and figurative language" (3–4). In other words, without an understanding of and active engagement in both of Bush-Banks's literary and cultural traditions, any analysis of Bush-Banks's literature is likely to misread the fundamental literary aspects of her work.

Yet Bernice Guillaume, perhaps because she is an African–Montauk Indian herself, adopted an unusual position in beginning her introduction to Bush-Banks's collected writings with the question, "How would one characterize an African Indian?" (3). Most critics, regardless of the facts at hand, fail to recognize the significance of a writer's multiple literary heritage, and would follow the one-drop rule in assigning an identity and literary heritage to a part-African American. In spite of Guillaume's introduction, series editor Henry Louis Gates, a very perceptive literary critic, argues in his foreword that the women in this series were "Americans who were, at once, black *and* female," acknowledging the importance of examining their literary works in a tradition marked by distinct, parallel identities, but discusses exclusively an African American women's identity and literary tradition.[46] If we are able to understand these texts as both distinctly African American *and* African American *women's* texts, can we not understand them as distinctly African American *and* Native American texts? I suspect that, if we don't, we run the risk of misunderstanding both the authors and their literary works, of failing to uncover layers of meaning, cultural, historical, and political, that are crucial to understanding the author's text. As Guillaume argues in her introduction, Bush-Banks "embraced and consciously cultivated her dual sensibility," and it seems clear, in interpreting these mixed race literary works, that the task ahead of us is to do no less.[47]

Mixed Race Writing

It appears obvious that Olivia Ward Bush-Banks is an African–Native American writer, a mixed race writer. Yet how does one define a mixed race writer? How does one define a mixed race text? There are again, as with the issue of Toomer's identity, no easy answers, although there are themes and literary strategies that often inform mixed race texts, including narratives of passing, formations of new racial space, multiple naming, redefining and challenging racial categories, gendered racial crossings, grappling with the tragic mulatto, and the appearance of the tragic trickster.

Are all writers of mixed race, mixed race writers? Must writers proclaim their mixed race identity for us to consider them mixed race writers?

Toomer clearly adopted the position of a deliberate, conscious mixed race writer, both as a literary strategy and in his decisions regarding his public and private identity. Like Toomer, Sui Sin Far defines herself as Eurasian, particularly in her autobiographical "Leaves from the Mental Portfolio of an Eurasian" where, as Carol Roh Spaulding argues, Sui Sin Far "insists on her doubleness, on her identity as an Eurasian, even when she could easily pass for white."[48] The Cuban poet Nicolás Guillén argues in his "Prologue" to *Sóngoro cosongo* that "The African injection in [Cuba] is so profound, and in our well-irrigated social hydrography so many bloodlines crisscross that one would have to be a miniaturist to unravel that hieroglyph," and as translator Vera Kutzinski asserts, "almost all aspects of Guillén's poetry, formal and thematic, are deeply rooted in the cross-cultural imagination of the Caribbean—*mestizaje*, as he himself calls it."[49]

Yet not all mixed race writers insist on their doubleness, their *mestizaje*. Okah Tubbee, an African-Choctaw autobiographer, deliberately developed a Choctaw textual identity, suppressing the African American identity, especially in the edition of his autobiography published after the passage of the Fugitive Slave Act. Because Tubbee was an escaped slave, he likely hoped to avoid recapture by rewriting himself exclusively as Indian, a Choctaw who had been kidnapped as a child and stolen into slavery. His autobiography, however, contains elements from both Native American and African American literary traditions, thus revealing itself as a mixed race text.[50] Tubbee's text, which utilizes a literary strategy that cloaks a portion of the writer's identity, engages in a form of passing (although in Tubbee's case not the traditional transformation into whiteness) that characterizes many mixed race texts.

Other mixed race writers have not openly claimed their multiple identities for a variety of reasons. As I have already noted, the prevailing notions of race in the United States require these writers to choose one identity, thus erasing others that they might assume. Many writers, particularly those with African ancestry, have been denied the opportunity to choose how they wish to be identified. Instead, they have been assigned an African American identity. For mixed race Native American writers, if enrolled members of Indian nations, the decision to assume another identity alongside an Indian identity can endanger their tribal enrollment, their place in their community, and their political and legal status. Still, enrolled Indians are sometimes more secure in their identity than urban (nonreservation) mixed blood Indians, and this security can allow more open claims of mixed race identity.

Other mixed race writers problematize their identities in fascinating ways. In her autobiography, *Dust Tracks on a Road*, Zora Neale Hurston "maintain[s] that I have been a Negro three times—a Negro baby, a Negro girl, and a Negro woman," a clear statement of her identity.[51] But at other times, both in her life and in her autobiography, Hurston insists that she was "sick of the subject" of racial identity and politics and, in the (initially unpublished) final chapter of her autobiography, adopts a position of refusing to acknowledge race, arguing that "all clumps of people turn out to be individuals on close inspection," and insisting on "less race consciousness."[52] Samira Kawash argues that Zora Neale Hurston "repudiates race consciousness, insisting that the race line cannot hold all the varied interests and particularities of any people."[53] This oscillation between claiming one or more of their multiple identities and opting out of rigid and inaccurate racial categories is typical of many mixed race writers, sometimes as a literary strategy and other times as a strategy of performance that allows them to negotiate their liminal status in a deeply racialized world.

But among Hurston's choices in claiming an identity, she did not limit herself to either a Negro identity or no racial identity at all. During a trip to Honduras in 1947, Hurston mailed a letter acknowledging her mixed race status, an assumption of identity that proved an advantage in her anthropological endeavors. Hurston writes that "[being] what they call here a Mestizo (mixed blood), I am getting hold of some signs and symbols through the advantage of blood."[54] In a portion of her autobiography, Hurston also claims (and rejects) her mixed race identity:

> I see no benefits in excusing my looks by claiming to be half Indian. In fact, I boast that I am the only Negro in the United States whose grandmother on my mother's side was *not* an Indian chief. Neither did I descend from George Washington, Thomas Jefferson, or any other Governor of a Southern state. I see no need to manufacture me a legend to beat the facts. I do not coyly admit to a touch of the tarbrush to my Indian and white ancestry. You can consider me Old Tar-Brush in person if you want to. I am a mixed blood, it is true, but I differ from the party line in that I consider it neither an honor nor a shame.[55]

Although acknowledging the truth of her mixed blood identity, even claiming both an African American and a mixed blood identity, Hurston is careful to argue that she does not view her multiple identities as an opportunity to pass out of African American heritage, and she (typically) rejects racial politics surrounding mixed race just as she does the racial politics surrounding categories of race. Kawash argues that Hurston's stance leads the reader (albeit reluctantly) along a path of inquiry that I argue exists in many mixed race texts:

> Indeed, the trouble with Hurston is that she troubles the received notions of race, identity and community on which the politics of racial collectivism (in Hurston's day and in our own) are based. Hurston forces us to rethink race, identity and community—a project far more complex than the simple disavowal of race or the abandonment of community.[56]

As Kawash notes, Hurston's position is not an erasure of race but instead a challenge to narrate the "facts" of racial identities in place of the prevailing "legends," a challenge posed by many mixed race writers in their texts.

These same challenges can sometimes be posed in mixed race texts, some of which have been written by mixed race writers and others not, but more often (at least until very recently) these texts are marked by the appearance of the tragic mulatto (or half-breed or Eurasian), whose identity is always deeply conflicted, most often leading not to a new challenge to racial categories, but to a reinforcement of the legitimacy of existing categories through the death of the mixed race protagonist. Roh Spaulding argues that in the representation of mixed race subjectivity, there are a number of characteristics these texts hold in common:

> First, mixed race is founded in the experience of marginality; second, mixed race characters are always negatively defined (neither "white" nor "raced"); third, the characters serve a kind of barometric function, revealing the racial tensions embedded in the text; and last, mixed race protagonists come to a crisis point in the narrative when they are forced to confront in some manner their indeterminate racial status.[57]

The literary depictions of tragically mixed race subjects follow a common trajectory, leading to "discoveries" and interrogations of racial identity, and often resulting in the death of the mixed race subject.

In response to the limitations imposed on mixed race subjects, and in an attempt to overturn or escape such restrictions, mixed race texts are also marked by the appearance of tricksters and trickery. Paul Radin argues that "Trickster is at one and the same time creator and destroyer, giver and negator, he who dupes others and who is always duped himself," thus describing the struggle of the mixed race protagonist, the victim of racial trickery and tragic treachery, often under attack by both worlds they inhabit, and equally the instigator, troubling the still waters of racial determinacy.[58] Because mixed writers are not adequately served by fixed identities, there is often a constant evolution of identity that occurs in their texts, an exploration of appropriate spaces in which to exist and a trickster role undertaken by a narrator who struggles to survive in the liminal spaces between races. The narrator conceals, creates, and revises facts, particularly concerning the origins of the mixed race narrator. Zora Neale Hurston claimed multiple birth dates (1898, 1899, 1900, 1901, 1902, 1903) according to her autobiographer Robert Hemenway,[59] while Okah Tubbee created a fictionalized father from Choctaw chief Moshulatubbee to bolster his Choctaw identity.[60] The traditional trickster narratives are often marked by identity transformations undergone by trickster figures (into animals), such as in the Winnebago trickster cycle when the Trickster transforms himself into a deer,[61] or in the Assiniboine trickster myth, where Sitconski transforms himself into a moose.[62] These transformations appear in many mixed race texts when characters pass between worlds, assume new identities, or cast off old identities. Just as Henry Louis Gates notes that the Yoruba trickster, Esu-Elegbara, has legs of two different lengths because he walks in two worlds, human and divine, so too do mixed race characters inhabit dual spheres, parallel worlds where any insistence solely on humanity negates their divinity and any insistence solely on divinity negates their humanity.[63]

Just as one of the hallmarks of many trickster traditions is the trickster's constant shifts in identity, mixed race texts are also marked by these transformations in identity, particularly in names, race, and gender. A tradition of both successive naming, the adoption of new names at a critical juncture in life, and multiple naming, the acquisition and use of multiple naming, takes place in mixed race texts by authors such as Sui Sin Far, Onoto Watanna, Long Lance, William Wells Brown, and Okah Tubbee.[64] William Andrews argues that the writer William Wells Brown had "two literary personas, two performing selves," William W. Brown, the narrator of the autobiography, and Sandford, the name under which Brown was known as a slave. In fact, these multiple selves are at odds with the antislavery aims of the slave narrative and, as Andrews argues, William W. Brown "generally presides over the narrative, posing as its exclusive namer, but Sandford's subversion of the reputation of Brown prevents the latter's ever taking full and sole possession."[65]

Chief Buffalo Child Long Lance, most likely Catawba-African-European American, underwent numerous transformations, beginning his life as Sylvester Long before being given the name Sylvester Long Lance at

Carlisle Indian School, where he claimed Eastern Cherokee identity. He was adopted by the Blood Indians and given a new name, Buffalo Child, eventually promoting himself to Chief Buffalo Child Long Lance, perhaps much as "he promoted himself from sergeant to captain" when he embellished his World War I military experiences.[66] Long Lance, who wrote what was intended to be a fictional account of a Blood Indian boyhood (published by *Cosmopolitan* as his autobiography), claims five names in a chapter on Indian naming: Chief Buffalo Child, Night Traveler, Spotted Calf, Holds Fire, and Long Lance. The English-Chinese writer Edith Eaton took the name Sui Sin Far in publishing her literary works, while her sister, Winnifred Eaton, used the name Onoto Watanna and published "Japanese" romance novels. Okah Tubbee was known early in life as both Warner McCary and James Warner, assumed the name Okah Tubbee upon his escape from slavery, and was consequently and variously known as William McCary, Cary, William Chubbee, Okah Chubbee, William McChubby, William McChoubby, William McChobby, Dr. Okah Tubbee, Dr. O.K. Tubbee, Council Chief Wah Bah Goosh, and Chief Okah Tubbee.[67] Much like the Sandford of William Wells Brown's narrative, Tubbee's trickster identities require the reader to frequently reconsider the role of the narrator and test the reader's ability to discern either truth or falsehood. Tubbee's arsenal of names, accompanied by numerous performing selves (musician, Choctaw leader, doctor), was a strategy that usually kept him one step ahead of his pursuers. William Andrews argues that "for more than a brief moment, Sandford liberates the narrative from William W. Brown's moral control and proceeds to celebrate himself as a trickster instead of a truth-teller,"[68] and similarly Tubbee's trickster narrator intercedes when he risks his free status by publishing a broadside in the local newspaper antagonizing a man, Alexander McNab, who had decried Dr. Okah Tubbee as a quack. The broadside, rather than being an exercise in moral argumentation, taunts his accuser and reclaims his newly assumed trickster healer identity:

> Of late I've been shamefully (M') Nab'D at
> and cruelly held up to view
> I'm now like a target to shoot at;
> shoot on till your honors get through
> Whenever the battle is over
> Call at 15, on Victoria Street
> You'll find me quite snug in my clover
> FRIENDS or FOES I'll be happy to meet.[69]

Finally, Andrews also argues that Sandford prevents the narrative from "becoming the literary chattel of William W. Brown,"[70] and Tubbee's multiple identities serve a similar function, supporting his escape from slavery and his claim to liberty through maintaining literary freedom. The multiple or successive names of these mixed race writers allow them to assert control under oppressive situations, staying one step ahead of those who would supply both their names and their fates, to create multifaceted identities that come closer to representing their mixed race selves, and to write themselves their own destinies.

The frequent shifts in names and racial identity are sometimes accompanied by gender transformations. These transformations occur in traditional trickster tales as well as in mixed race trickster narratives. In one portion of Radin's summary of the Assiniboine trickster myth, "Sitconski travels in female garments, and is married by a young man," and in the Winnebago myth, Wakdjunkaga transforms himself into a woman, marries the chief's son, and becomes pregnant.[71] In William Wells Brown's *Clotel*, Clotel passes as a white man in order to rescue her daughter, simultaneously crossing borders of race and gender. Harriet Jacobs crosses the same, dressing as a sailor (and blackening her face to appear more African American) in narrating her escape from slavery.[72] In William and Ellen Craft's slave narrative, *Running a Thousand Miles for Freedom*, Ellen Craft passes as a white male master with her husband, William, passing as her slave. Hazel Carby notes that Frances Harper, mixed race author of the mixed race text entitled *Iola Leroy: Or; Shadows Uplifted*, was accused of passing as both black and female: "She was so articulate and engaging as a public speaker, audiences concluded that she couldn't possibly be a black woman. Some even speculated that she must be a man, while others reasoned [!] that she was painted to look black."[73] Racialized gender crossings also occur in Mark Twain's *Pudd'nhead Wilson* and Sui Sin Far's *Mrs. Spring Fragrance*, and of course these crossings of conventional gender boundaries upset readers' expectations in much the same way as racial crossings. Anticipating the readers' uneasiness over gendered racial crossing, William Craft felt the need to reassure the readers of their slave narrative that Ellen Craft's assumption of these identities was only temporary: "My wife had no ambition whatever to assume this disguise, and would not have done so had it been possible to obtain our liberty by more simple means."[74] Yet disruptions of traditional borders, once begun, are difficult to contain, and are clearly linked in the Crafts' argument to overturning restrictions on freedom, a challenge faced by many writers in the mixed race tradition.

Mixed Race Writers

There are many parallel traditions of mixed race writing that have developed in the United States, including African-European, European-Native, African-Asian, and European-Asian American literatures. The earliest African-Native American literatures were mixed folktales and mythologies. Because they often lived side by side on plantations or socialized and intermarried off the plantations, African Americans and Native Americans exchanged folktale traditions to create new African-Native folktales and mythology; an African-Seminole creation myth accounts for the existence of both Africans and Native Americans, and there is a large body of African-Native folklore among nations such as the Cherokee, Creek, Natchez, Hitchiti, Seminole, Potowatomi, Alabama, and Koasati.

Two of the earliest African-Native American writers were Paul Cuffe (1759–1817), Wampanoag-African American, and William Apess (1798–?), Pequot-African American. Cuffe's journals and letters discuss his sea travels, trading, and voyages to Sierra Leone and include arguments against the African slave trade. Apess, a civil rights advocate and preacher, published two autobiographies, a sermon, political essays, and a eulogy of King Philip. In the mid-nineteenth century, both Okah Tubbee (1810–?), an African-Choctaw, and James Beckwourth (1798–1866), African-European-Crow, published autobiographies. Tubbee's narrative contains elements of both African American slave narratives and nineteenth-century Indian autobiographies,[75] and Beckwourth narrates portions of his autobiography drawing from traditional Crow coup tales.[76] The young poet Joseph Seamon Cotter Jr. (1895–1919), African-European-Native American, published a book of poetry, *Band of Gideon* (1918), and sonnets in the A.M.E. Zion Quarterly Review, and his work includes the poem "The Mulatto to His Critics," which acknowledges his multiple heritages of "Red Man, Black Man, Briton, Celt and Scot."[77]

Alice Walker (1944–) and Clarence Major (1936–) are both African-Cherokee. In *Meridian* (1976), *The Color Purple* (1982), and *Living By The Word* (1988), Walker historicizes African-Cherokee culture and elaborates on the reasons for its denial, draws from African-Cherokee folklore, and examines the relationship between African American and Native American culture, history, and civil rights. Clarence Major belongs to an African-Cherokee family and community from Atlanta, Georgia. In two novels, *Such Was The Season* (1987) and *Painted Turtle: Woman with Guitar* (1988), and in a book of poetry, *Some Observations of a Stranger at Zuni in the Latter Part of the Century* (1989), Major explores African-Native American identity, family, and community. *Painted Turtle* focuses on the negotiation of identity, belonging, and insider/outsider politics.

The politics of insider/outsider have been frequently explored by many European-Native American mixed blood writers as well, including Hum-ishu-ma (Mourning Dove), who wrote what was likely the first novel by a Native American woman, *Cogewea: The Half-Blood*; Israel Folsom, a Choctaw-European poet and historian; John Lynch Adair and John Rollin Ridge, both Cherokee-European poets; the famous poet and journalist Alexander Posey (European-Creek-Chickasaw), author of the humorous Fux Fixico letters series; and Pauline Johnson (English-Mohawk), who published "A Red Girl's Reasoning" as her first work of fiction in 1893 and a collection entitled *Moccasin Maker* in 1913.[78]

In the twentieth century, D'Arcy McNickle, whose mother was Cree (Metís) and father European-American, published the well-known *The Surrounded* in 1936, a novel with a mixed blood protagonist, and which, like his last novel, *Wind from an Enemy Sky* (1978), raises issues of communication and conflict between Indian and non-Indian beliefs. Osage John Joseph Mathews published *Wah'Kon Tah* (1932) and *Sundown* (1934). The latter features Challenge Windzer as the main character, whose traditionalist mother is full-blood and whose mixed blood father has closer cultural ties to European Americans; Windzer is comfortable in neither Osage nor European American culture, and lives out a destructive fate.

Among the best-known contemporary European-Native American authors are N. Scott Momaday, Kiowa-Cherokee-European American (author of *House Made of Dawn*, which won the Pulitzer prize in 1969), Leslie Marmon Silko, Laguna-Mexican-European (author of *Ceremony*, *Storyteller*, and *Almanac of the Dead*), and Gerald Vizenor, who consistently explores the issues of crossbloods in literary works such as *The Trickster of Liberty, Griever: An American Monkey King in China*, and *The Heirs of Columbus*. One of the most prolific novelists is Louise Erdrich, German-Chippewa, author of two works of poetry and numerous novels, including *Love Medicine*, *Tracks*, and *The Beet Queen*, in which she explores the dynamics of liminal identities. Other authors include scholar/writer Paula Gunn Allen (Laguna-Sioux-Lebanese) and poets Linda Hogan (Chickasaw-European American), author of *Eclipse* (1983) and many other works, and Jim Barnes (Choctaw-Welsh), author of several books of poetry, including *The American Book of the Dead* (1982).

Much like the mixed blood European-Native American tradition, a significant portion of writers often critiqued in the African American literary tradition have been African-European Americans. Many of the writers of nineteenth-century slave narratives were African-European or African-Native-European Americans, including such well-known authors as Frederick Douglass, Harriet Jacobs, William Wells Brown, and Henry Bibb. William Wells Brown's slave narrative (1847) begins with his declaration of the facts of his mixed blood birth:

> I was born in Lexington, Ky. The man who stole me as soon as I was born, recorded the births of all the infants which he claimed to be born his property, in a book which he kept for that purpose. My mother's name was Elizabeth … My father's name, as I learned from my mother, was George Higgins. He was a white man, a relative of my master, and connected with some of the first families in Kentucky.[79]

Frederick Douglass, whose mother was African-Native American, problematizes his identity while critiquing the rationale for his enslavement, recording his mixed birth in the first pages of his autobiography:

> My father was a white man. He was admitted to be such by all I ever heard speak of my parentage. The opinion was also whispered that my master was my father; but of the correctness of this opinion, I know nothing; the means of knowing was withheld from me.[80]

Charles Chesnutt published short stories and novels at the turn of the century, beginning his career with the publication of "The Goophered Grapevine," a conjure story told by Uncle Julius McAdoo, later published in his first short story collection, *The Conjure Woman* (1899). His second short story collection, *The Wife of His Youth and Other Stories of the Color Line* (1899), as well as his first novel, *The House Behind the Cedars* (1900), focuses on mixed race issues such as passing and miscegenation.

During the Harlem Renaissance, many of the leading writers were mixed race, including Zora Neale Hurston (African-Native-European American), Langston Hughes (African-French-Cherokee-European American), Jean Toomer (African-Native-European American), and Nella Larsen (African-Danish American). Hurston, trained by Franz Boas as an anthropologist, was the author of numerous works, including a volume of folklore, *Mules and Men* (1935), essays, plays, short stories, and four novels, including *Jonah's Gourd Vine* (1934) and *Their Eyes Were Watching God* (1937). Langston Hughes is also appropriately discussed as an African-Native American literary figure, since he was raised primarily by his maternal grandmother, Mary Sampson Patterson, the granddaughter of a French trader and a Cherokee woman, who served as a major influence on his writing imagination through her constant storytelling, though he sometimes also viewed himself according to the terms of the reigning white-black racial paradigm.[81] Hughes published essays, plays, poems, children's books, short stories, and a novel, including works such as *The Weary Blues* (1926), *The Ways of White Folks* (1934), and *Mulatto*, a play that opened on Broadway in 1935. Jean Toomer, discussed earlier in this essay, published one novel, *Cane* (1923), which is an acclaimed modernist, experimental novel in three parts comprised of sketches, poetry, and drama with a shifting narratorial structure and an interrogation of race, slavery, and sexuality. Toomer's later works were strongly infused with the philosophy of Russian mystic Georgei Gurdjieff, and Toomer's later work represents a challenge for many because he both published a classic work that has been situated in the field of African American literature and was simultaneously forthright about his identity as an American of mixed race, not just an African American. Larsen published two major novels, *Quicksand* (1928) and *Passing* (1929), which focus on mixed race women, identity struggles, and crossing color lines. Larsen was awarded a Guggenheim fellowship in 1930, and in the next decade made many attempts to write and publish additional works, but her writing faltered and, in financial difficulty, she returned to work as a nurse and never published again.

As in the African-European American tradition, many Asian-European and Asian-African American writers have had a substantial impact on their literary fields. Edith and Winnifred Eaton were the children of English painter Edward Eaton and his Chinese wife Grace Trefusis. Edith Eaton would become the writer Sui Sin Far, and Winnifred used the Japanese pen name Onoto Watanna. Sui Sin Far published a collection of stories, *Mrs. Spring Fragrance* (1912), and Onoto Watanna numerous romance novels like *A Japanese Nightingale* (1901). Han Suyin (Rosalie Chou), Belgian-Chinese, first published the autobiographical *Destination Chungking* (1942) before writing and publishing nearly a dozen more books. Hazel Lin, French-Chinese, was a doctor and also published an autobiography and four novels, including *The Physicians* (1951). Diana Chang, Irish-Chinese American poet and novelist, published her first novel, *Frontiers of Love*, in 1956. Sadakichi Hartmann, a German-Japanese American poet and playwright, was the author of *Passport to Immortality* (1927) and *Buddha, Confucius, Christ* (1971). Velina

Hasu Houston, African-Japanese-Native American, is a playwright and author of the *American Dreams* trilogy, *Asa Ga Kimashita (Morning Has Broken)*, *American Dreams*, and *Tea*, and situates her work squarely in a mixed race tradition, exploring mixed marriages and multiple ethnic identities.

Mixed Race Subjectivity

Houston's *American Dreams* trilogy is a more recent example of the creation of mixed race subjects in literary works, including drama, but such an undertaking has a long tradition, and has been engaged by both mixed race and non–mixed race writers. African-Native American subjects have appeared in numerous American texts. The first recorded dramatist of African descent in America went by the last name of Brown and his play, *The Drama of King Shotaway* (1823), focused on Joseph Chatoyer (King Shotaway), the leader of the Black Carib Indian nation on Saint Vincent.[82] During the reconstruction era, Albery Whitman wrote an epic poem in Spenserian stanzas entitled *Twasinta's Seminoles* (1885), which narrates the events of the Seminole Black Indian struggle against the United States military. The tradition of exploring the Black Indian subject extends into the literature of contemporary writers such as Alice Walker's *Meridian* (1976) and *Living by the Word* (1988), Nettie Jones's *Mischief Makers* (1989), Leslie Marmon Silko's *Almanac of the Dead* (1991), and Louise Erdrich and Michael Dorris's *A Yellow Raft in Blue Water* (1987), portraying the African-Native American character Rayona.

In the first chapter of Elaine Kim's study of Asian American literature, she explores the prevailing images of a variety of Asian American groups embedded in American literature by writers from outside these communities. John Marquand's Mr. Moto novels, Sax Rohmer's Fu Manchu novels, and Earl Derr Biggers's Charlie Chan novels created stereotypes of Chinese and other Asian Americans. Kim notes that stereotypes of Eurasian subjects in much of American literature are often applauded for their attributed "white" characteristics and accused of a racial reversion to purported "Asian" values:

> When a Eurasian girl longs for freedom, she is "white at heart." When a mixed-blood boy is cruel to animals, it is because he has "inherited his callousness from his stoic Eastern blood." A war is waged in the blood of the Eurasian in Achmed Abdullah's short story, "A Simple Act of Piety": "the Chinese blood in her veins, shrewd, patient, scotched the violence of her pas-

sion, her American impulse to clamor loudly for right and justice and fairness." The Eurasian character in Irwin's *Seed of the Sun* is tortured by the feeling that "the dragon's tail of the Orient [is] fastened to the goat's head of Europe" in his being: "All the time the European in me is striving to butt forward, the dragon's tail is curling around some ancient tradition and pulling me back."[83]

Carol Roh Spaulding notes the role of the "enchanted fox woman of the province of Fukui" in Winnifred Eaton's romance novel *Tama* (1910), an "outcast" of the citizenry of Fukui, as well as the Eurasian brother and sister, Hyacinth and Koma, in Eaton's *Heart of Hyacinth* (1903).[84] In her autobiographical "Leaves from the Mental Portfolio of an Eurasian," Sui Sin Far posits herself as a mixed race subject who consciously maintains a mixed race identity as Eurasian despite the pressure to choose either a European American or Chinese identity. The Eurasian protagonists in Han Suyin's *A Many Splendored Thing* (1952) or *The Crippled Tree* (1965) tend to function in contradistinction to the tragic mixed race characters so common in many literary works; Elaine Kim notes that the protagonists "are not particularly restless; they neither wish to be dead nor white ... no wars are waged in their veins."[85] Finally, contemporary writers such as playwright Velina Hasu Houston in her *American Dreams* trilogy, Shawn Wong in *Homebase* (1979), short story writer Mei Mei Evans in "Gussuk" (1989), and Sky Moon Lee in *Disappearing Moon Cafe* (1990) feature characters who embody an African-Native, Eurasian, and/or Chinese-Native American subjectivity.

In writing about African-European Americans, the figure of the mulatto/a has been widely discussed. In the nineteenth century, writers such as Harriet Wilson, William Wells Brown, Frances Ellen Watkins Harper, and Pauline E. Hopkins utilized the figure of the mulatta (or quadroon or octoroon), sometimes tragic and sometimes not. Harriet Wilson's *Our Nig* (1859), likely the first novel published by an African-European American in the United States, is the story of Frado, whose mother was white and father black, and whose circumstances mirror those of Wilson herself. William Wells Brown's *Clotel* (1853) was first published in the United States as the serialized *The Beautiful Quadroon: A Romance of American Slavery Founded on Fact* (1860–61). Clotel is a fictionalized offspring of the well-known relationship between Thomas Jefferson and Sally Hemmings, and she is sold into slavery, escapes, and eventually suffers a tragic death fleeing from the men who wish to recapture her. In Frances E. W. Harper's novel *Iola Leroy* (1892), the protagonist was enslaved when her

African heritage was revealed upon the death of her European American father.

In the early twentieth century, Pauline E. Hopkins published *Contending Forces: A Romance Illustrative of Negro Life North and South* (1900), and in the next several years three more novels, *Hagar's Daughter: A Story of Southern Caste Prejudice*, *Winona*, and *Of One Blood, or the Hidden Self*; these four novels all explore issues of mulatta/o, quadroon, and octoroon identity and taken together form an important body of mixed race writing that captures the evolving relationship between fiction and the tragic mulatto/a theme. James Weldon Johnson's *The Autobiography of an Ex-Colored Man* was first published anonymously in 1912 and later claimed by Johnson. In his only novel, Johnson, the poet, lyricist, editor, lawyer, and composer of the Negro National Anthem, develops an African-European American narrator who moves alternately through African American and European American worlds, finally deciding to pass as European American in response to a lynching; he marries and raises a white family in New York. Nella Larsen's *Quicksand* (1928) is the story of African Danish American Helga Crane, rejected by her Danish American family, embraced by both middle-class African American culture and by her Danish family in Denmark. Larsen's second novel, *Passing* (1929), explores the lives of Irene Redfield and Clare Kendry, two African-European American women, one of whom lives in a middle-class African American world (except for occasional brief forays into a European American identity) and the other as European American, married to a man who has no idea she is partially African American.

The African-European American subject continues to be explored in contemporary novels, including Charles Johnson's *Oxherding Tale* (1982), whose main character, the son of a European American slave owner and an African American slave, passes into European American society, and Toni Morrison's *The Bluest Eye* (1970), with West Indian mulatto Elihue Whitcomb, also known as Soaphead Church, who tricks Pecola Breedlove into believing that her eyes have been transformed into blue eyes.

The figure of the European-Native American mixed blood is as frequent in American literature as that of the European-African American mulatto. Hum-ishu-ma, likely the first Native American woman to write a novel, made the focus of her work *Cogewea: The Half-Blood* (1927) a young woman of European-Native ancestry who must decide between two suitors, Densmore, a conniving European American man, and Jim, another half blood like herself. From the first page, she raises her central concern of exploring half-blood identity: "The features were rather prominent and well defined. The rich olive complexion, the grave pensive countenance, proclaimed a proud descent from the only true American—the Indian. Of mixed blood, was Cogewea; a 'breed'!—the socially ostracized of two races."[86] Emily Pauline Johnson, whose father was Mohawk and mother English, wrote short stories and poetry, among them "A Red Girl's Reasoning" (1893), a story later published in *Moccasin Maker* (1913), Johnson's collection of (mostly) short stories with a central focus on mixed blood women; the mixed race protagonist, Christine, facing cultural conflicts, decides to return to her Indian nation. Johnson's early work includes the poem "A Cry from an Indian Wife," which was "based on the first mixed blood rebellion (1869–1870), led by Louis Riel, against the Canadian government."[87] In the 1930s, D'Arcy McNickle, whose mother was Cree and father white, published *The Surrounded* (1936), a novel whose protagonist, a Flathead-Spanish man named Archilde Leon, returns to the Flathead reservation and struggles to reconcile traditional and off-reservation ideas and values. Lynn Riggs, author of *Green Grow the Lilacs* (1931), the basis for the musical *Oklahoma* (1943), published *The Cherokee Night* (1936), which focuses on Oklahoma Cherokee mixed bloods in the early twentieth century.

Contemporary writers who have explored mixed blood identity include N. Scott Momaday, Leslie Marmon Silko, James Welch, Janet Campbell Hale, and Gerald Vizenor. In Momaday's *House Made of Dawn* (1968), the main character, Abel, is a mixed blood veteran in search of healing and cultural reunification. In Silko's *Ceremony* (1977), the mixed blood Tayo is also a war veteran, wracked by emotional anguish, who returns to his Indian roots to find his ritual healing. James Welch's *The Death of Jim Loney* (1979) depicts a half-blood character who attempts to retrieve his past, searching for a connection to his European American father and Native American mother. Janet Campbell Hale, author of *The Jailing of Cecilia Capture* (1985), explores the dilemma of the mixed race protagonist Cecilia, who, like many other mixed blood subjects, attempts to resolve cultural conflicts between Indian and European American culture. Finally, Gerald Vizenor, discussed earlier, is perhaps the contemporary writer who most relentlessly explores the mixed race subject, particularly in his literary works, *The Trickster of Liberty* (1988), *Landfill Meditation: Crossblood Stories* (1991), and *The Heirs of Columbus* (1991).

Contributors' Essays

The essays by the contributors explore numerous categories of inquiry, from visual stereotypes to performance, gender, history, community, and transnational spaces. Some of the essays use existing theories of ethnic literatures to explore mixed race traditions. Others draw from cross-cultural literary theories to shed new light on mixed race writing, while still others develop new literary theories to explore both mixed race literary traditions and individual texts. I selected essays for this collection that represent a wide variety of critical approaches and traditions, hoping to represent the range of opportunities available in the exploration of mixed race literature. I have purposely not drawn widely from the most prolific bodies of scholarship on mixed race writing, African-European American (mulatto/a) and Chicano/Latino, for a number of reasons, but most particularly because these fields have been explored frequently, because the traditional focus on black/white interactions too often limits our ability to see beyond such binaries, and because many Chicano/Latino literatures are often approached from the onset of their interrogation as hybrid literatures representing a fusion of traditions. I still believe that such literatures are an essential component in developing our understanding of mixed race traditions (for mestizo/a theories are often essential tools in exploring other mixed race traditions), and that a more specific focus (in many cases) on the interplay of their fused elements is a worthwhile investigation, but for my current purposes they are outside of the purview of this collection.

The essays I have selected include works that address writers and literatures from both within and outside the United States. In my research on Native American literatures I have often discovered that traditional boundaries of genre and historical period (for example, autobiography and transcendentalism) do not easily lend themselves to understanding traditions that are often both historically parallel to and culturally outside of European American literatures. Geography occupies much of the same ground, and as political boundaries are frequently drawn and redrawn, communities of speakers/writers continue their practices despite shifting national lines, or continue by straddling such lines. As some of the contributors have argued, the transnational spaces occupied by many mixed race writers can often fall outside our existing categories of inquiry, and beyond political (but well within literary) spaces and boundaries. Critics can use approaches applied to American mixed race writers to interrogate such traditions outside the United States, and simultaneously, writers exploring these "outside" traditions have developed tools that can help to illuminate American mixed race traditions as well. The issues of merging literary traditions and mixed race subjectivity, in light of increasing globalization and cultural hybridity, will become more and more critical in our understanding of culture and literature, both in the United States and the rest of the world, addressing what Werner Sollors calls the "largely unrecognized scope of interracial literature." Carol Roh Spaulding, in a reading of Momo, an Algerian-Vietnamese-Turkish literary subject in Leila Sebbar's *Le Chinois vert d'afrique*, argues that mixed race literatures from outside the United States offer new readings on racial formation in the United States, and offer new possibilities of mixed race identity formation, and I would agree, adding that the intersection of these racial formulations and literary texts represents an important field of literary inquiry for Americanists and other literary specialists. Finally, the inclusion of such "international" essays on mixed race should also help nudge readers from the myopia of American models of inventions of race and ethnicity and American literary hybridity.

The approaches in these international essays provide readers new ways to understand American mixed race literatures. For instance, an American expatriate literary tradition (often representing a revolving door of relocation and return, impelling the production of popular travel and anthropological narratives, both for "Native American" and "African American" writers) was frequently peopled by mixed race writers from these communities, such as Frederick Douglass, Langston Hughes, Paul Cuffe, William Wells Brown, George Copway, Okah Tubbee, Gerald Vizenor, Nella Larsen, and Zora Neale Hurston, among others. Because American mixed race narrators found themselves already oscillating between nations, whether that be African America and European America, North and South, the United States and Canada (especially for slaves), or Native America and European America, their narratives present an interesting parallel to that of Lefevre's *Metisse Blanche* illuminated by Pelaud in her essay. The "transnational space" she explores represents a liminal condition, "caught chronically astride borders," interrogated by numerous mixed race American writers, and Pelaud argues that Lefevre has created a transnational space serving as a site for the expatriate resolution of national origins complicated by mixed race identity.

While in this Introduction I have explored a number of roles adopted by writers in the mixed race literary tradition, the initial essay in the collection, by Patricia Riley, argues that a critical role of the mixed blood Indian writer is one of interpretation and mythmaking. The writer often translates between cultures, interprets for all sides, and negotiates between communities. Riley raises issues of audience, publishing demands, new literary strategies, and the role of spiritual traditions. Like Gates's discussion of Esu-Elegbara, walking in both worlds, Riley draws on the mythical Cherokee Wild Boy or Orphan, whose very essence is of mixed origins, and also notes that the Lakota term for mixed race is *iyeska*, a word that signifies a connection between the human and divine worlds. She argues that many mixed blood Indian writers have adopted the role of the Cherokee Wild Boy, creating new mythic traditions by disordering traditional boundaries. In closing, Riley argues that Leslie Marmon Silko, the author of *Ceremony*, has "purchased a contemporary mythic space for mixed bloods everywhere," precisely the space that our inquiry into mixed race writing demands.

It is a virtual mythic space, a raced cyberspace, that Werner Sollors explores in his essay on the visual representations of Mark Twain's mixed race African-European American character, Roxy. The literary representation of mixed blood subjects has often been the purview of European American authors, such as Mark Twain, Bret Harte, and Herman Melville, and these literary illustrations reveal the tensions inherent in racial classification, literary ethnic representations, and hypodescent. Just as the political and social realities of this racial coding process lead to enslavement and "social death," these early fictional works form a body of imagery that inevitably culminates in a tragic characterization resulting in the mixed race subject's death.[88] This is a potent characterization with which later mixed race writers grapple in order to chart a different trajectory for both their liminal characters and themselves. Sollors discusses both the literary and more importantly the visual illustrations by Edward Windsor Kemble, now posted on the web, which accompany works by Mark Twain and Paul Laurence Dunbar, and the literary and artistic portrayals of race and mixed race. Sollors argues that the racial choices made by Kemble in representing Roxy tell a tale that is at odds with the arguments made by Twain in *Pudd'nhead Wilson*, and that undermines Twain's attempts to challenge racial assumptions through posing a mixed race subject, but that they are quite in line with prevailing American beliefs concerning African-European Americans, miscegenation, and the one-drop rule. Such beliefs reinforce a racial dichotomy in the United States that deplores racial ambiguity and posits dichotomous identity.

Sollors, however, asks of the novel and its illustrators the same persistent questions that Twain pursued (echoing Shelley Fisher Fishkin's "Was Huck Black?"): Was Roxy black? Was Mark Twain black? Was Jim white? Every question has as its premise the insistence on exploring the middle ground of ambiguity, the "mythic space for mixed bloods."

In her essay on African-Native-Japanese American writer Velina Hasu Houston's trilogy of plays, Michele Janette argues that Houston's positioning of her plays in "the overlappings of multiple ethnicity" provokes responses from directors and audiences that mimic the limitations posed by an insistence on nonambiguity: the plays are not "Japanese" or "African American" enough. Characterizing Houston's play *American Dreams* as a "drama of immigrant miscegenation," Janette employs Chicana literary theory, Edward Said's notions of Orientalism, and playwright David Henry Hwang's plays to build her argument that the play moves from racial conflict to gendered alliances. She sets Houston's work in opposition to Israel Zangwill's racially charged 1909 play *The Melting Pot* and the 1967 film *Guess Who's Coming to Dinner*, insisting that Houston's work overturns the notion of social progress concerning both race and gender, and redefines immigrant space not as a gentle oscillation between cultural traditions but as a struggle in *la frontera* for identity, historical interpretation, and connection.

Another *frontera*, also the site of strained relations and failed love, is the subject of Sandra Baringer's essay on Diana Chang's *The Frontiers of Love*, where this struggle, through Chang's appropriation of American romantic fiction, plays itself out in the frontiers of an occupied Shanghai. Marked by conflicting racial and national identities, the mixed blood characters negotiate issues of desire, subjectivity, and exploitation, according to Baringer, and she further argues that Chang engages in an exploration of the "dynamics of masochism in the context of both gender and mixed racial identity." Baringer also explores spatial constructs and definitions of home, theorizing that "transcendental moments" create a textual space to explore both the frontiers of love and the boundaries of home.

These transcendental moments are also an opportunity for the definition of textual transnational spaces that serve expatriate mixed race writers. In her essay, Isabelle Pelaud examines Kim Lefevre's *Mettise Blanche*, arguing that Lefevre's work contests colonial representations of Viet Nam, grapples with linguistic dominance, and ultimately resurrects a textual memory of Viet Nam that "serves as a hyphen bridging multiple identities." Pelaud asserts that Lefevre has assumed, even "forged," a transnational space that connects expatriate communities of Viet-Kieu with their Vietnamese origins, and that such spaces allow for the formation of new identities, beyond national boundaries, which neatly coincide with the textual space Lefevre must create for her mixed race French-Vietnamese identity. Although Lefevre's autobiographical texts have previously been read as representational, providing "accurate" accounts of Eurasian identity and an essentialization of the "metisse" leading to a tragic textual ambivalence, Pelaud insists that such interrogations of Lefevre's mixed race text must not overlook issues of French colonialism, class structure, and patriarchy, which primarily account for such textual ambivalence. In fact, she argues, such identities are continually revised, subject to shifting political winds.

The revision of identity and the cross-border movements of transnational subjects are also explored in Martha Cutter's essay on the writing of Sui Sin Far, "Smuggling Across the Borders of Race, Gender, and Sexuality: Sui Sin Far's *Mrs. Spring Fragrance*." Among the many issues to examine when exploring gender, sexuality, and mixed race writing is the relationship between circumscribing women's political power and the mixed race subject's sense of belonging. As Janette notes in Houston's *American Dreams*, men in the community often serve the function of policing identity, and I would argue that such policings are often extended to varied expressions of sexuality and to suppressing the attempted political and literary expressions of mixed race women and their children. Female mixed race narrators negotiate their role in their ethnic communities and in their nation, frequently crossing racial, gender, and sexual borders. Cutter argues that names and naming practices in *Mrs. Spring Fragrance* interrogate racial, gender, and sexual norms and ultimately serve to destabilize them, and that the destabilization in mixed race writing in fact opens new textual spaces for crossing sexual and gender borders. Rather than inscribing identity, naming in Sui Sin Far's text serves to "un-write" or "de-script" assumed categories of identity. Ultimately, the "sutures" (borders) revealed through exploring the textual stitching of naming practices and identity formation offer significant possibilities of identity formation outside traditional boundaries.

Hertha Wong's essay on African-Native American subjectivity moves outside both traditional academic boundaries and geographic boundaries, drawing from "spatial metaphors for transcultural contact" such as contact zones, border/lands, and boundary cultures to locate a site of grounded place for both African Americans and Native Americans. Wong suggests that such homelands, where the terrain is storied, can be the literary site for the reparation of "*dis*placement," and she examines both mapping and storytelling in Louise Erdrich and Michael Dorris's *A Yellow Raft in Blue Water*, a novel that includes an African-Native American mixed blood subject, Rayona, and a complication of the frequent portrayal of a "Native mixed blood protagonist being torn between two worlds." Rayona has grown up not on the reservation, but in a major city, and her "return" is to a reservation she has only visited once before. Erdrich and Dorris's novel offers both "problems and possibilities" for a mixed race subject searching for home, and Rayona's move to a geographic space affords her the opportunity to create a social space through storytelling, and, as Wong argues, a transformation from "being a victim of untold, partially told or mistold stories to being a speaker of her own experience."

Wei Ming Dariotis also theorizes the formation of a new space, discovered in the "fissures" and "cracks" in identity, the "go-between places" where mixed race subjects serve not as a bridge between cultures but as mirrors that can promote the development of a "kin-aesthetic" between Native and Asian American literatures and peoples. In "Developing a Kin-Aesthetic: Multiraciality and Kinship in Asian and Native North American Literature," Dariotis posits a process of recognition between "ethnic minorities" that is facilitated by mixed race subjects, and that provides the "possibility for new alliances." She argues that Tayo, a mixed blood character in Leslie Marmon Silko's *Ceremony*, sets in motion much of the novel's action through his (mis)recognition of a Japanese soldier as his Uncle Josiah; in fact, Dariotis argues, such a kin-aesthetic recognition is made possible not through an alliance of color but through the interpretive mirror of a mixed race subject. Dariotis also theorizes such moments of Chinese-Native American kin-aesthetic recognition, and the promotion of new alliances, through mixed race subjects in Shawn Wong's *Homebase*, Gerald Vizenor's *Griever: An American Monkey King in China*, and Sky Lee's novel *Disappearing Moon Café*. She finally argues that "transracial and transnational kinship alliances are ... revolutionary" in their resolution of fragmentation, and that the relations between mixed race and "monoracial" family members function as a metaphor, holding up a mirror to American society.

The final essay also offers a metaphor for healing, through the Maori *marae*, the symbolic space that stands in front of a meetinghouse. Alice

TePunga Somerville attempts to construct a literary framework for an understanding of Maori-Pakeha writing, drawing from Aotearoa/New Zealand history and opening a waharoa/gateway that also serves as a metaphor for the mixed race literary experience. She begins with a discussion of the te taiapa/fence that surrounds the courtyard, obscuring vision and restricting movement between social/cultural spaces, linking it with the country's colonial history of Maori and ultimately Pakeha (European) settlement. TePunga Somerville explores first the Maori oral tradition, and then the proliferation of both newer technologies that underlie written traditions as well as the Pakeha literary tradition. She discusses issues of mixed race identity, identifies a Maori-Pakeha writing tradition, and critiques the existing body of scholarship on this literary tradition. Finally, TePunga Somerville proposes a new approach that reflects and protects the mixed race tradition. Rather than following a Western academic framework, or countering by proposing an indigenous Maori approach, TePunga Somerville argues that "specific modes of Western academic thinking and of Maori thinking *both* need to be present in a central way to any new method of analysis." She builds this approach on a paradigm for Maori physical/spiritual well-being that consists of four walls, tinana, hinengaro, whanau, and wairua, categories that also embody the Western concepts of body, self-identity, community, and spirituality. TePunga Somerville proposes that mixed race Maori-Pakeha literature should be explored through a multistranded critical approach, and that the waharoa/gateway that makes mixed race writing accessible should be supported by strong posts built from the merging traditions, which will allow one to see the carved korupe/lintel that resides at the top of the gateway, the site of mixed race writing.

Conclusion: The Mixed Race Tragic Trickster

In response to TePunga Somerville's proposal that any interrogation of mixed race traditions be supported by the posts of multiple traditions, I would like to conclude the discussion of mixed race literature with an invocation to the trickster. Like Esu-Elegbara, walking in both worlds, or *iyeska*, a figure from the human and divine worlds, the trickster often embodies the diverging/merging traditions of mixed race worlds. Because one of the most compelling figures in mixed race writing has been that of the trickster figure, I will end by examining the many roles that this figure has played in mixed race writing, and by extending an invitation to the trickster to teach us how to walk in both worlds. One writer who exemplified this trickster tradition was Chief Buffalo Child Long Lance, born Sylvester Long (African-European-Native American-Catawba), who performed in a Wild West show, was educated at Carlisle Indian School (as a declared Cherokee Indian), was a decorated war hero in the Canadian military, and had a career as a journalist writing on Native American affairs in Canada, covering issues of Native American civil rights. Eventually, Long Lance would publish an "autobiography," a fictional/historical work of his life as a Blood Indian. Although he had been adopted into the Blood nation as an adult, and given the name Buffalo Child Long Lance by the Blood Indians, Long Lance did not grow up as a Blood Indian and could certainly not have written accurately about his life as a youth before the reservation period; in fact, he had intended as a historical work for youth a work that *Cosmopolitan* magazine insisted on publishing as his autobiography. Yet why was Long Lance's identity changing in this manner? Native American nations have traditionally adopted new members, and his new name to mark this transition was also a Native tradition,[89] but it appears that Long Lance, like many mixed race writers, adopted not just a new name but also the role of the trickster, as demonstrated both by his fictional autobiography and by his behavior in the city of Calgary:

> In Spring 1922, Long Lance became restless. For months, he had covered city hall; since the previous fall, he had been given no more Indian assignments. So he decided to liven up the municipal meetings with a mock terrorist attack. Donning a mask, he slipped into the council chamber and placed inside the door of the mayor's office a gas inspector's bag that looked suspiciously like a bomb, the fuse attached sputtering sparks. City commissioners and the mayor ran for their lives, the mayor colliding with his secretary in a jammed exit door. One commissioner dived under a table. Another leaped through layers of storm window glass, then jumped ten feet to the ground. Over the next several days, the rival newspaper, the *Albertan*, played this prankster story for its laugh value. But the *Herald* was not amused: Long Lance was summarily fired.[90]

In fact, the role of the trickster has been adopted by numerous mixed race writers, including Long Lance, Okah Tubbee, and Onoto Watanna. Tubbee was an African-Native American who, in the mid-nineteenth century, declared himself a Choctaw Indian in order to bolster his escape from slavery, and in his written autobiography, a collaboration with his wife Laah Ceil, a Mohawk-Delaware Indian, they narrated an identity for

Tubbee that attempted to erase his African ancestry and thus transcend the one-drop rule. Winnifred Eaton, the sister of Edith Eaton (Sui Sin Far), developed a literary persona not of a Chinese-English writer, but as a Japanese American writer instead, writing "Japanese" style romance novels decorated with Japanese calligraphy. In fact, rather than mixed race texts following the tragic emplotment assigned by scholars and readers alike to mulattos, octoroons, Eurasians, and half bloods, their evolution has been from tragedy to trickster, upsetting literary conventions and social expectations of existing traditions, and developing new literary strategies to negotiate the representation of multiple subjectivity.

The prevailing images embedded in American literature of mixed race subjects have demanded a tragic emplotment, a representation of the mixed blood character as morally and physically degenerate and thus leading to a plot structure that insists on the erasure of the mixed race subject. In Cynthia Nakashima's "An Invisible Monster: The Creation and Denial of Mixed-Race People in America," she cites Berzon's study of the mulatto in American fiction in which Berzon argues that the "tragic mulatto" character is often cast as irrational, moody, and completely tormented by his/her "racial disharmony," "clash of blood," and "unstable genetic constitution," "typically dying while still young." Nakashima argues that this description of a multiracial African-European is similar to the description of a mixed Japanese-European in the 1921 book *Kimono*: "A butterfly body with this cosmic war shaking it incessantly. Poor Child! No wonder she seems always tired."[91] In the first chapter of her study, *Asian American Literature*, Elaine Kim argues that "the dilemma of the Eurasian in Anglo-American literature is unresolvable. He must either accept life as it is, with its injustices and inequalities, or he must die. Most of the stories about Eurasians end with the death of the protagonist."[92] Raymond Stedman cites W. H. Emory denouncing Indian half bloods as a "very inferior and syphilitic race" and also notes that the prevailing literary treatment of half bloods tries to represent their "mercurial nature [which] often led to the mixed-blood's early death."[93]

The literary representations of mixed race subjects were both a reflection and a perpetuation of stereotypes surrounding mixed race people. In an interview, Eurasian writer Han Suyin discusses his thoughts about the persistence of these stereotypes surrounding mixed race:

> As a Eurasian, I was always fighting. I am still fighting race prejudice today. I was told by people in the sphere of my young life that I was only good

enough to be a prostitute. This situation made me strong. It was either show strength or go under.... A very important Swiss surgeon once said to me, "All Eurasians are degenerate, syphilitic." I said: "Me, degenerate? Me?" He said that I am the exception. When he was speaking these words, he was hitting the table with his thumb. I told him: "It is not necessary to hit the table." That got him! I was commenting on his bad manners.[94]

Han Suyin, in response to attempts to fix his identity, responds in classic Ellison fashion: "change the joke and slip the yoke," and this survival skill has been demonstrated by numerous mixed race writers struggling under oppressive circumstances. In his study of African American autobiography, William Andrews argues that two autobiographers, Moses Roper (African-European-Native American) and William Wells Brown (African-European), became literary tricksters, capable of manipulating identity and creating literary illusions. According to Andrews, William Wells Brown was "a trickster, a very accomplished one in fact, and he recounts with some pleasure his ruses and manipulations of whites, even though doing so might have risked his audience's respect for him."[95] Brown was capable of fooling both whites and blacks in his attempts to survive his enslavement, and his insistence on narrating this trickster identity in spite of the reader's judgment was a testimony to the importance of using trickster strategies in Brown's life. Andrews also discusses Moses Roper's ability to selectively manipulate portions of his identity in his autobiography and, most importantly, Roper's ability to construct a trickster narrative at the appropriate "autobiographical occasion":

> The Narrative shows that during Roper's several attempts to escape from slavery, he was regularly stopped and required to give an account of himself to suspicious whites. On these autobiographical occasions, Roper learned how to invent an identity and a past for himself that were close enough to the facts so that he could sustain cross-examination yet were free enough with the facts to let him manipulate whites into thinking he was someone to help and sympathize with. Because he was the light-skinned son of a white man and a woman of African and Indian ancestry, Roper could pass himself off as a runaway indentured servant, a cross-breed of white and Indian, not white and black blood.[96]

Perhaps one of the reasons behind the mixed race subjects' appropriation or assumption of the trickster role is their constant struggle to act in response to the enforcement of identity. In essence, the outside actor, slave owner or other oppressive figure, attempts to define the mixed race subject according to hypodescent, placing them at a political or psychological disadvantage, which can be overcome by the mixed race subject's assumption of the trickster role. In their constant struggle to maintain and define identity, they are thrust again and again into the role of trickster in order to overcome tragedy, an observation made by John Roberts in his study of the African trickster in the Americas:

> Therefore, in their portrayal of the animal trickster's world, enslaved Africans justified the trickster's actions on the basis of his constant need to protect his well-being in situations in which his physical survival was always in jeopardy. No matter how many times the trickster secured the makings of a meal from his dupes, or how clever the ruse he used to escape annihilation in a particular tale, he still emerged in his next adventure as the prey of his dupes, a situation which justified his repeatedly acting in any way that protected his survival.[97]

Another trickster tradition can also shed light on the relationship between tragedy and trickery. In his study of Winnebago and other Native American trickster mythology, Paul Radin argues that Winnebago have two categories of prose narrative, *waikan*, the sacred world, and *worak*, the "present workaday world" of human beings, and that although the *worak* story has to end tragically, the narrative world in which the trickster lived (ordinarily), the *waikan*, could not, by definition, have a tragic ending: "that is, the hero could not be represented as dying or being killed except temporarily ... conditioned by the fact that the heroes in a *waikan* were always divine beings."[98] Thus it is in the conversion of their narrative, in the transformation from workaday world to the sacred world of the trickster, in the mixed race writer's adoption of the trickster, that they could move from tragedy to trickster, inscribing a mythic status in place of an anticipated tragic ending.

In an essay on half-breeds and crossbloods in Gerald Vizenor's writing, Betty Louise Bell argues that in *The Heirs of Columbus*, "Vizenor re-creates the 'almost' space of the crossblood as historical and interpretive opportunity. ... in contrast, in his autobiography, *Interior Landscapes*, Vizenor returns to the traditional half-breed space in which the tensions of a divided life inhibit the creation of the energetic, transgressive narrative found in his crossblood stories."[99] One of the most important distinctions between half-breeds and crossbloods is the progression from tragedy to trickery, from tragic to comic, from isolation and repression to liberation and community as argued by Vizenor when he intertwines crossbloods and tricksters almost inextricably in his *Crossbloods: Bone Courts, Bingo and Other Reports*:

Crossbloods hear the bears that roam in trickster stories and the cranes that trim the seasons close to the ear. Crossbloods are a postmodern tribal bloodline, an encounter with racialism, colonial duplicities, sentimental monogenism, and generic cultures. The encounters are comic and communal, rather than tragic and sacrificial; comedies and trickster signatures are liberations; tragedies are simulations, an invented cultural isolation.[100]

Bell maintains that the limitations of the half-breed subjectivity can be overcome by Vizenor when mixed race identity is seen as an opportunity and not a tragic fate. Vizenor overcomes the "invented cultural isolation" with a complex metamorphosis in his novel *Griever: An American Monkey King in China* (1987), when a mixed blood Indian becomes the Chinese trickster, the Monkey King, thus achieving a trickster identification between cultures that works against cultural isolation.

Bell also argues that Vizenor's positioning of crossblood tricksters "between words and dreams. Maybe that was seams," leads to his rejection of "monologic truth" and a championing of "multiple memories, multiple autobiographies, without privileging the truth of one memory over the other."[101] This is precisely what a deliberate mixed race writer must do: reject a monologic racial/cultural identity while balancing multiple memories from multiple cultural and literary traditions. He/she must operate in the seams between fixed cultural/racial identities. Bell finds that the half-breed subject of Vizenor's autobiography, trapped in "silence between two isolated cultures" (187), will find his trickster liberation, a transformation from tragic half-breed into trickster crossblood, only after a visit from the trickster, and that the shift in perception transforms Vizenor's subsequent literary production from a passive half-breed victimization to an active crossblood reappropriation of history.

Mixed race trickster narratives, Bell argues, "transform half-breed divisions into a crossblood dialogic, privileging neither fact nor fiction, neither colonial nor tribal discourse" and such a position, subverting "dominant discourse, brings authority into question" (188). William Andrews notes a similar issue in the trickster narrative of autobiographer J. D. Green in the master's response to Green's trickery:

"You black vagabond, stay on this plantation three months longer, and you will be the master and I the slave." Most likely, Earle [the master] did not fear a literal reversal of the status between his slave and himself, but rather a more generalized threat to order, appointed status and authority embedded in a trickster who refused to stay in his place. When the trickster's activities level hierarchies, dissolve distinctions and reverse roles even temporarily, an alternative modality of social relationship is created. ... under such liminal circumstances, when all social classifications and proprieties are suspended if not reversed, one has the chance to gain fresh insight into the provisional character of those sociocultural institutions that define identity.[102]

It is in the leveling of hierarchies, the dissolution of distinctions, and the suspension of social classifications and sociocultural institutions that mixed race writers stand their best chance of avoiding a tragic fate, and thus their transformation into a tragic trickster can suspend the very categories that perpetuate the marginalization of the mixed race person. In "Trickster Discourse," Vizenor cites Paul Watzlawick's argument that our "construction of reality ... rests on the supposition that the world cannot be chaotic—not because we have any proof for this view, but because chaos would simply be intolerable."[103] In spite of the potential chaos, it may even be that a serious consideration of mixed race writing may help bring about the downfall of racial categorization altogether, a categorization we have so internalized that it has become a part of our unquestioned, unconscious selves. Jung's commentary, "On the Psychology of the Trickster Figure," argues that if we regard the trickster as a parallel aspect of the shadow, it is only through recognition (of the trickster and the shadow), through the "development of consciousness" that one will receive "liberation from imprisonment in ... unconsciousness [bringing] light as well as healing."[104] Most important, both Radin and Jung argue that the Trickster is a reflection of ourselves, that part of ourselves we reject, cast into shadow. As Stanley Diamond argues in the introduction to *The Trickster*, laughing at the trickster (in the circus) "demands the capacity to laugh at oneself, to identify with the reversals and risks of identity that take place before our eyes," so it is perhaps through our recognition and understanding of the mixed race subject that we can best understand ourselves, and can best shine the light of consciousness on the unworkable fixed categories of racial identity and destiny.[105]

In *Neither Black Nor White Yet Both*, Werner Sollors argues that "the time may have come to stop avoiding the interracial theme in literature, to investigate it, and to unpack its semantic fields."[106] Indeed, this time has come, and this unpacking holds the promise of offering new approaches to critiquing literature, a better understanding of existing mixed race texts, a framework for critiquing the rapidly growing literary field of mixed race writing, and a new perspective on the entire body of American literature. The mixed race texts examined in this study have served as boundaries or contact zones between races and cultural groups, and their significance lies both in their ability to develop new and distinct literary forms through the merging of multiple literary traditions and as a critical site from which to theorize the overall formation of the American literary tradition in which ethnic literary traditions merged to produce new bodies of literature.[107] A consideration of the function and significance of mixed race texts within previously defined categories of literary inquiry and as part of a wider body of mixed race literature will define a new way to inform our understanding of the development of American literature, to complicate it in ways that interrogate our notions of race, gender, and cultural formation. The examination of the construction of identity in mixed race autobiographies should shed new light on identity formation and representation in existing fields of American autobiography. The discussion of mixed race literature also offers an opportunity for deeper comparative approaches to what have heretofore been defined as separate literary traditions; mixed race subjects have often served as translators and interpreters of language and culture, and the study of these texts offers scholars an opportunity to posit modes of cultural transmission and exchange that have led to literary innovation in American literature. Finally, because mixed race writers have often been in the forefront of acknowledged literary traditions and movements, an analysis of the apparent "seams" (mixed race writers at the cultural periphery) of what scholars have articulated as seamless and unified literary traditions will engage scholars in a reassessment of the ways in which our notions of literary traditions have been constructed and how these traditions have developed.

I would argue that a "true" postcolonial literary perspective is critical for mixed race literatures precisely because a reliance on traditional theories of racial formation (and on racial categorization established in the colonial period) overlooks cultural transformations and complex structures of identity formation and representation in favor of perpetuating imprecise and reductive racial categorizations of literary traditions, thus overlooking much of the literary and political significance of mixed race texts. Connecting existing scholarly traditions with the developing discourses of mixed race identity, and other multidisciplinary fields, in order to reconceptualize mixed race texts develops a new postcolonial lens through which to view these texts.

These mixed race narratives have created new forms of writing as well as served an essential political function. It is often the case that mixed communities have undergone a phase of submerged identity (similar to that described by Edward Braithwaite) from which the reemergence into a transformed cultural/literary expression was (and is) a critical process in maintaining cultural integrity and autonomy.[108] For the mixed race writer, identity exists in a state of liminality, a site where a mixed race narrator negotiates and transforms identity, yet often the communities in which the writer negotiates attempt to overwrite multiple identities, to maintain limitations on both form and content. This intersection of restrictions on mixed race identity leads to the creation of new literary strategies by the authors and to newly formed syncretic narratives, perhaps even new languages. William Scheick notes an observation by Chandler Gilman in 1836, describing "this [half-blood] language as 'a sort of lingua franca, made up of Indian and English terms grafted onto a stock of most extraordinary French; besides which it contains some terms which cannot be reduced to either language yet withal; it is, perhaps, as poor a dialect as was ever spoken by man, one word often serving a dozen meanings.'"[109] In spite of Gilman's position on the linguistic or social value of a mixed race language, these new languages are a viable site from which to investigate cultural and linguistic transformations in mixed race literatures, and from which to argue the significance of the creation of new languages and literary forms. One of this hybrid language's greatest riches lies in Gilman's primary complaint, in its capacity to hold multiple meanings for concepts we often attempt to restrict to a singular meaning.

The examination of hybrid languages, as well as the issues of merging literary traditions and mixed race subjectivity, in light of increasing globalization and cultural hybridity, will become more and more critical in our understanding of culture and literature, both in the United States and the rest of the world, addressing what Sollors calls the "largely unrecognized scope of interracial literature."[110] In fact, scholarship on mixed race identity and writing outside the United States demonstrates some fascinating parallels to the development and unfolding of cultural and racial hybridity in the United States. For example, in Wetherell and Potter's *Mapping the Language of Racism*, the arguments created by Pakeha colonists surrounding mixed race Maori people are strikingly similar to those made about mixed African or Native Americans: "The Maori isn't a leader ... the Maori that is leading in this way probably has a lot of Pakeha blood. Cause there are no pure-bred Maoris in New Zealand. ... I mean none of the Maoris are pure, and ... have a racial trait, a characteristic that I don't know whether it's going to be dominant or not, but they're basically a lazy people."[111] Mixed Maori-Pakeha writers are negotiating a language of racial hybridity that, although developed in New Zealand in response to the rise of mixed race subjects, has many parallels to the vocabulary of (racial) hybridity that developed in the United States. By including essays on French-Vietnamese writer Kim Lefevre and on the Maori-Pakeha mixed race writing tradition in this collection, a parallel focus on mixed race literary traditions outside the United States, I hope to invite an early dialogue on these heretofore relatively unexplored literatures, a dialogue that will assist in the development of scholarship on American mixed race writing. If, in fact, the essays in this collection serve as a cutting edge exploration of mixed race literatures as a distinct field, the inclusion of essays delving into an evolving international literary tradition not yet illuminated for American readers should only sharpen that edge.

These "international" essays also demonstrate the influences of American literatures on the development of scholarly criticism focused outside the United States (and provide in this collection fertile ground for a continuing global dialogue). Both Pelaud and TePunga Somerville utilize a variety of canonical ethnic and cultural studies critics to explore their texts, including Appiah, Fanon, Lionnet, Said, Anzaldúa, Hulme, and others, as well as integrating these critics' work with new voices whose research has unearthed both parallels to the American and British traditions as well as striking new perspectives on mixed race literatures. Such a merging is epitomized in the TePunga Somerville essay, an essay that I believe presents groundbreaking work in the field of mixed race studies with her development of the traditional Maori *marae* (the symbolic Maori courtyard space, a site of mediation, located in front of the meetinghouse) as a metaphor for the inquiry, mediation, and resolution of opposing and divergent literary traditions. I'm certain that this essay could open the way for American critics to develop similar sites of inquiry and literary resolution. The intersection of these racial formulations and literary texts represents an important field of literary inquiry for Americanists and other literary specialists. Finally, I hope that these essays also nudge readers from the myopia of American models of inventions of race and ethnicity and American literary hybridity, and open new opportunities for an analysis of the relations between parallel mixed race writing traditions.

In the end it is important to read and understand mixed race narratives because they provide an opportunity for us to open our eyes, to gain new perspectives and thus renew ourselves. In *The Signifying Monkey*,

Gates discusses Esu-Elegbara, the Yoruban trickster figure, in a myth entitled "The Two Friends," which has made its way from Africa to the Americas. In this myth, Esu decides to test the friendship of two men who had failed to acknowledge him, and he makes a cap, the left side of which is white, and the right side of which is black:

> Esu came by on a horse, riding between the two men. The one on the right saw the black side of the hat. The friend on the left noticed the sheer whiteness of Esu's cap. The two friends took a break for lunch under the cool shade of the trees. Said one friend, "Did you see the man with a white cap who greeted us as we were working? He was very pleasant, wasn't he?" "Yes he was charming, but it was a man in a black cap that I recall, not a white one."[112]

The two men argue on and on, neither giving way to the other's perspective. Finally, Esu arrives and insists on knowing why the men are fighting:

> Why do you two lifelong friends make a public spectacle of yourselves in this manner? "A man rode through the farm, greeting us as he went by," said the first friend. "He was wearing a black cap but my friend tells me it was a white cap and that I must have been tired or blind or both." The second friend insisted that the man had been wearing a white cap. One of them must be mistaken, but it was not he. "Both of you are right," said Esu.

As Gates argues, "Esu's hat is neither black nor white; it is both black and white. The folly here is to insist, to the point of the rupture of the always fragile bond of a human institution—on one determinate meaning, itself determined by vantage point and the mode one employs to see."[113] Reading mixed race literatures should bring us an awareness of our vantage points, the capacity to hold multiple meanings (as truth), "liberation from imprisonment in unconsciousness," and the acceptance that is essential to the preservation of the fragile bonds between human beings.

Notes

1. Henry Louis Gates, *Figures in Black* (New York: Oxford University Press, 1989), 206.

2. Carol Roh Spaulding, "The Go-Between People: Representations of Mixed Race in Twentieth-Century American Literature," in *American Mixed Race: The Culture of Diversity*, ed. Naomi Zack (Lanham, Md.: Rowman & Littlefield, 1995), 106.

3. F. James Davis, *Who is Black?: One Nation's Definition* (University Park: Pennsylvania State University Press, 1991), 133–34.

4. Gates, *Figures*, 204–5.

5. Rudolph P. Byrd, "Cane," in *The Oxford Companion to African American Literature*, ed. William L. Andrews, Frances Smith Foster, and Trudier Harris (New York: Oxford University Press, 1997), 118.

6. Gates, *Figures*, 200.

7. See Gates's discussion of race as "metaphor" in "Writing 'Race' and the Difference It Makes," in *"Race," Writing, and Difference* (Chicago: University of Chicago Press, 1986), 1–6.

8. Anthony Appiah, "The Uncompleted Argument: Du Bois and the Illusion of Race," in *"Race," Writing, and Difference*, 31.

9. See Anthony Appiah's arguments surrounding race from *In My Father's House: Africa in the Philosophy of Culture* (New York: Oxford University Press, 1992).

10. Naomi Zack, *Race and Mixed Race* (Philadelphia, Pa.: Temple University Press, 1993), 71.

11. Frederick Douglass, *Narrative of the Life of Frederick Douglass* (New York: Signet, 1968), 24.

12. Gerald Vizenor, "Trickster Discourse: Comic Holotropes and Language Games," in *Narrative Chance: Postmodern Discourse on Native American Indian Literatures* (Norman: University of Oklahoma Press, 1993), 188–89.

13. Michael P. Banton and Jonathan Harwood, *The Race Concept* (New York: Praeger, 1975).

14. Vizenor, "Trickster Discourse," 189.

15. Henry Louis Gates, "Talkin' That Talk," in *"Race," Writing, and Difference*, 402.

16. Appiah, "The Uncompleted Argument," 36.

17. Although I frequently use the term mixed race, with the same hesitancy and the same set of restrictions concerning meaning and accuracy, I also utilize terms such as half-breed, half blood, mixed blood, crossblood, and numerous others that have arisen in the dialogue concerning mixed race identity.

18. Jack D. Forbes, *Africans and Native Americans: The Language of Race and the Evolution of Red-Black Peoples* (Urbana: University of Illinois Press, 1993), 100–101.

19. See Forbes, *Africans and Native Americans*, and Davis, *Who Is Black?*

20. William Loren Katz, *Black Indians: A Hidden Heritage* (New York: Atheneum, 1986), 23.

21. See also Herbert Aptheker, *American Negro Slave Revolts* (New York: International Publishers, 1963), 163.

22. Davis, *Who Is Black?*, 33.

23. Terry P. Wilson, "Blood Quantum," in *Racially Mixed People in America*, ed. Maria P. P. Root (Newbury Park, Calif.: Sage, 1992), 109.

24. See Russell Thornton, *American Indian Holocaust and Survival: A Population History* (Norman: University of Oklahoma Press, 1987).

25. Joane Nagel, *American Indian Ethnic Renewal: Red Power and The Resurgence of Identity and Culture* (New York: Oxford University Press, 1996), 245.

26. Wilson, "Blood Quantum," 122.

27. Michael C. Thornton, "The Quiet Immigration," in *Racially Mixed People in America*, 68.

28. Caroline Valverde, "From Dust to Gold," in *Racially Mixed People in America*, 144–47.

29. Teresa Williams, "Prism Lives," in *Racially Mixed People in America*, 283, 296.

30. James W. Loewen, *The Mississippi Chinese: Between black and white* (Prospect Heights, Ill.: Waveland Press, 1988), 136.

31. Ronald Takaki, *A Different Mirror: A History of Multicultural America* (Boston: Little, Brown, 1993), 237.

32. Terry P. Wilson et al., eds., *Peoples of Color in the American West* (Lexington, Mass.: D.C. Heath, 1994), 338–43.

33. See stories on African-Japanese American identity in Teresa Williams, "Prism Lives," in *Racially Mixed People in America*, 296–97.

34. Thornton, "The Quiet Immigration," 74.

35. Amy Iwasaki Mass, "Interracial Japanese Americans," in *Racially Mixed People in America*, 265.

36. Valverde, *Racially Mixed People in America*, 145.

37. John Harre, *Maori and Pakeha* (Wellington: Reed, 1966), 66.

38. Margaret Wetherell and Jonathan Potter, *Mapping the Language of Racism: Discourse and the Legitimation of Exploitation* (New York: Columbia University Press, 1992).

39. Forbes, *Africans and Native Americans*, 5.

40. See Forbes, *Africans and Native Americans*.

41. See Forbes's citations of runaway slave advertisements in *Africans and Native Americans* (p. 226), including:

'A Mustee fellow named Nedd ... short curl'd Hair, but not wooly, thick lip'd, small eyes.'

'Peter, a Mustee ... with black curl'd hair' [listed among 'the following negroes'].

'a Negore woman named Hagar, with her child Fanny, a Mustee.'

Frank, 'of a yellowish or mustee complexion, ... would feign dress, the wool of his head in the macaroni taste, the which being that of a mustee, he has teazed into side locks, and a queue, but when too lazy to comb, ties his head with a handkerchief.'

'Jemmy, a Mustee Fellow ... sharp visaged, not flat nosed, which shews the Indian blood more than the Negro.'

42. Zack, *Race and Mixed Race*, 171.

43. John C. Hawley, ed., *Cross Addressing: Resistance Literature and Cultural Borders* (Albany: State University of New York Press, 1996), 3.

44. It should also be noted, with no little irony, that the Schomburg collection, which includes many mixed race texts, was established by Arturo Schom-

burg, a mixed race Puerto Rican, who although defined by some as black in the United States, most certainly laid claim to an African-Spanish-Taino Indian identity in Puerto Rico.

45. Bernice F. Guillaume, "Introduction," in *The Collected Works of Olivia Ward Bush-Banks* (New York: Oxford University Press, 1991), 7.

46. Henry Louis Gates, "Foreword," Black Women Writers Series, *The Collected Works of Olivia Ward Bush-Banks* (New York: Oxford University Press, 1991), ix.

47. Guillaume, "Introduction," 3.

48. Carol Roh Spaulding, "Go-Between People," 109.

49. Nicolás Guillén, *The Daily Daily*, trans. Vera M. Kutzinski (Berkeley: University of California Press, 1989), vii-ix.

50. See Jonathan Brennan, "Speaking Cross Boundaries: An African/Native American Autobiography," *A/B: Auto/Biography Studies* 7, no. 2 (Fall/Winter 1992), 219–38.

51. Zora Neale Hurston, *Dust Tracks on a Road* (New York: Harper Perennial, 1996), 244.

52. Samira Kawash, *Dislocating the Color Line: Identity, Hybridity, and Singularity in African-American Narrative* (Stanford, Calif.: Stanford University Press, 1997), 172–75.

53. Kawash, *Color Line*, 187.

54. Robert Hemenway, *Zora Neale Hurston: A Literary Biography* (Urbana: University of Illinois Press, 1977), 306.

55. Hurston, *Dust Tracks*, 242–43.

56. Kawash, *Color Line*, 176.

57. Roh Spaulding, "Go Between People," 98.

58. Paul Radin, *The Trickster: A Study in American Indian Mythology* (New York: Schocken Books, 1972), xxiii.

59. Hemenway, *Literary Biography*, 13.

60. See Daniel F. Littlefield Jr., "Introduction," in Okah Tubbee and Laah Ceil, *The Life of Okah Tubbee* (Lincoln: University of Nebraska Press, 1988), xii–xviii.

61. Radin, *The Trickster*, 35.

62. Ibid., 98.

63. Henry Louis Gates, *The Signifying Monkey: A Theory of Afro-American Literary Criticism* (New York: Oxford University Press, 1988), 6.

64. See Hertha Dawn Sweet Wong, *Sending My Heart Back Across the Years: Tradition and Innovation in Native American Autobiography* (New York: Oxford University Press, 1992) for a discussion of successive naming traditions in Native American cultures.

65. William L. Andrews, *To Tell a Free Story: The First Century of Afro-American Autobiography, 1769–1865* (Urbana: University of Illinois Press, 1986), 150.

66. See Donald B. Smith, "Introduction," in *Chief Buffalo Child Long Lance* (Jackson: University Press of Mississippi, 1995), xix.

67. See Daniel F. Littlefield, "Introduction," *The Life of Okah Tubbee.*

68. William L. Andrews, *To Tell a Free Story,* 150.

69. Littlefield, "Introduction," xxxvi.

70. Andrews, *To Tell a Free Story,* 150.

71. Radin, *The Trickster,* 102, 138.

72. Harriet Jacobs, *Incidents in the Life of a Slave Girl,* ed. Jean Fagan Yellin (Cambridge, Mass: Harvard University Press, 1987), 113.

73. Hazel Carby, "Introduction," in *Iola Leroy* (Boston: Beacon Press, 1987), ix.

74. William Craft, *Running a Thousand Miles for Freedom* (London: William Tweedie, 1860), 35.

75. See Brennan, "Speaking Cross Boundaries."

76. See Wong's *Sending My Heart* for discussions of the traditional Crow coup tale form.

77. Joseph Seamon Cotter Jr., *Complete Poems,* ed. James Robert Payne (Athens: University of Georgia Press, 1990).

78. Although Pauline Johnson was a Mohawk Indian (Canadian), as A. La-Vonne Brown Ruoff argues, "because of her popularity here and her importance to the development of literature written by American Indian women, she is included" in a study of American Indian literature. A. LaVonne Brown Ruoff, *American Indian Literatures* (New York: Modern Language Association, 1990), vi.

79. William Wells Brown, *Narrative of William W. Brown, a fugitive slave. Written by himself* (Boston: American Anti-slavery Society, 1847). From Andrews, *To Tell a Free Story,* 27.

80. Douglass, *Narrative of the Life of Frederick Douglass,* 21–22.

81. In the final lines of the Langston Hughes poem "Cross": "Being neither white nor black?" Langston Hughes, *Selected Poems* (New York: Knopf, 1970).

82. See Bernard L. Peterson Jr., "Drama," in *Oxford Companion to African American Literature,* 228.

83. Elaine Kim, *Asian American Literature* (Philadelphia, Pa.: Temple University Press, 1982), 9.

84. Roh Spaulding, "Go-Between People," 101–4.

85. Kim, *Asian American Literature,* 293 n. 14.

86. Hum-ishu-ma, *Cogewea: The Half Blood* (Lincoln: University of Nebraska Press, 1981), 15.

87. Brown Ruoff, *American Indian Literatures,* 66.

88. See Orlando Patterson, *Slavery and Social Death: A Comparative Study* (Cambridge, Mass.: Harvard University Press, 1982).

89. See Wong, *Sending My Heart,* on successive naming traditions.

90. Long Lance, *Chief Buffalo Child Long Lance,* 196.

91. Cynthia Nakashima, "An Invisible Monster: The Creation and Denial of Mixed-Race People in America," in *Racially Mixed People in America,* 167.

92. Kim, *Asian American Literature,* 9.

93. Raymond William Stedman, *Shadows of the Indian: Stereotypes in American Culture* (Norman: University of Oklahoma Press, 1982), 11.

94. *Los Angeles Times*, August 12, 1982.

95. Andrews, *To Tell a Free Story*, 144.

96. Ibid., 92–93.

97. John W. Roberts, *From Trickster to Badman: The Black Folk Hero in Slavery and Freedom* (Philadelphia: University of Pennsylvania Press, 1989), 37.

98. Radin, *The Trickster*, 210–11.

99. Betty Louise Bell, "Almost the Whole Truth," *A/B: Auto/Biography Studies* 7, no. 2 (Fall/Winter 1992), 180–81.

100. Gerald Vizenor, *Crossbloods: Bone Courts, Bingo, and Other Reports* (Minneapolis: University of Minnesota Press, 1990), vii.

101. Bell, "Almost the Whole Truth," 185.

102. Andrews, *To Tell a Free Story*, 211–12.

103. Vizenor, "Trickster Discourse," 88.

104. Radin, *The Trickster*, 211.

105. Stanley Diamond, "Introductory Essay: Job and The Trickster," in Radin, *The Trickster*, xiii.

106. Werner Sollors, *Neither Black Nor White Yet Both: Thematic Explorations of Interracial Literature* (New York: Oxford University Press, 1997), 4.

107. See Mary Louise Pratt, *Imperial Eyes: Travel Writings and Transculturation* (New York: Routledge, 1992).

108. Edward Braithwaite, "Caribbean Culture—Two Paradigms," in *Missile and Capsule*, ed. Jurgen Martini (Bremen, Germany, 1983), 28–54.

109. William J. Scheick, *The Half-Blood: A Cultural Symbol in 19th-Century American Fiction* (Lexington: University Press of Kentucky, 1979), 6.

110. Sollors, *Neither Black Nor White Yet Both*, 29.

111. Margaret Wetherell and Jonathan Potter, *Mapping the Language of Racism: Discourse and the Legitimation of Exploitation* (New York: Columbia University Press, 1992).

112. Gates, *The Signifying Monkey*, 33.

113. Ibid., 35.

The Mixed Blood Writer as Interpreter and Mythmaker

Don't offend
the fullbloods,
don't offend
the whites,
stand there in
the middle
of the god-
damned road
and get hit.[1]

As I sit staring at the face of one of technology's latest gods, my hands on a keyboard that functions as its messenger, I find myself "standin' in the middle of the road" with the rest of my brothers and sisters. Therefore, before leaping headlong into a discussion of the mixed blood writer and the peculiar problematics involved in this occupation that so many of us have found ourselves in, I feel compelled to talk about how mixed bloods came into existence and how they have been perceived by others and by themselves, since I believe this will shed considerable light on the subject at hand.

There was a time in so-called early American history when intermarriage between whites and Indians was advocated as a means of achieving a "bloodless" conquest, one that could be arrived at not by the spilling of blood, but by the mixing of it. Thomas Jefferson expressed these sentiments in 1803: "In truth, the ultimate point of rest and happiness for them is to let our settlement and theirs meet and blend together, to intermix, and to become one people ... and it will be better to promote than retard it."[2]

Missionaries seeking to convert and civilize Indians also held a similar stance, believing the mixed blood was more malleable and would "espouse the interests of civilization and Christianity."[3] A common observation of the time was that mixed bloods were "the first to take on 'white ways': to start farming and acquire an education," as well as serve the quite useful purpose of interpreting (19–20). In the 1830s, Alexis de Tocqueville held that "the half-blood forms the natural link between civilization and barbarism" (20). The idea of the mixed blood as a bridge between cultures may have had its roots in this period.

However, by the middle of the 1800s these beliefs began to deteriorate as reports came in that the mixed blood had failed to live up to white expectations. Mixed bloods quickly became marked as "faulty stock." Since they often chose tribal life over a white one, "Like the Indian, the mixed-blood was viewed as headed for extinction" (27). More than one hundred years later, we continue to disappoint the white man. We continue to live, to acquire education and link our lives to that of our tribes, and we continue to define ourselves in spite of a society that would do that defining for us.

There is no definition for "mixed blood" according to *Webster's Encyclopedic Version of the New Lexicon Dictionary*; however, the definition of the pejorative term "half-breed" reads as follows: "n. someone of mixed breeding, esp. of mixed white and American Indian parentage" (434). While this clinical definition may satisfy the question of the genetic "what," it gives no real insight of any substance.

In the Lakota language, the word used to describe a mixed blood is *iyeska*; however, its meaning does not end there. According to Orval Looking Horse, keeper of the Sacred Pipe of the Lakota people, the term *iyeska* embodies the concept of one who not only interprets between the red and white worlds, but between the world of spirits and of human beings as well.[4] I believe the complete definition places the mixed blood firmly within spiritual and mythic traditions and is the most descriptive of the way the mixed blood writer approaches the writing of literature. It is also a definition that enables one to begin to understand the predicament and complexity of the mixed blood writer as a producer of contemporary Native American literature.

In the introduction to *That's What She Said*, mixed blood Cherokee writer Rayna Green describes the contemporary Native American author as someone who walks "a new Trail of Tears," one that was blazed by the government policy of relocation:

> They go to towns for jobs or to follow their husbands and families. They go to school someplace and they never go home again permanently, or the city

becomes home. Sometimes they get to go back to the Rez. Maybe it's some-place they never were before, and that new experience becomes part of the searching. They can be looking for something Indians call "Indianness"—what sociologists call "identity." ... Because most of them—with few excep-tions—are "breeds," "mixed-bloods," not reserve-raised, they aren't "tradi-tional," whatever that might mean now. Some might say that writing is just their role. ... That's what breeds do. They stand in the middle and interpret for everyone else, and maybe that's so. That's what they are. But "identity" is never simply a matter of genetic make-up or natural birthright. Perhaps once, long ago, it was both. But not now. For people out on the edge, out on the road, identity is a matter of will ... a face to be shaped in a ceremonial act.[5]

While Green focuses on the idea of the mixed blood as interpreter, she also brings up the notion of the quest for identity. Underlying this quest is a sense of alienation that drives the seeker and permeates much of Native American literature today. In *The Sacred Hoop: Recovering the Feminine in American Indian Traditions*, Paula Gunn Allen discusses this preoccupation with alienation in Native American literature and offers insight into the experiences that often shape mixed blood consciousness, while pointing out that acculturated full-bloods can also qualify for a kind of mixed status:

What is the experience that creates this sense of alienation? The breed (whether by parentage or acculturation to non-Indian society) is an Indian who is not an Indian. That is, breeds are a bit of both worlds, and the con-sciousness of this makes them seem alien to traditional Indians while making them feel alien among whites. Breeds commonly feel alien to themselves above all.[6]

Allen also mentions the fact that writers of contemporary Native American literature are predominantly mixed bloods of one description or another and adds that "exactly what this means in terms of writers' rendering of personal experience is necessarily a central concern of American Indian literary criticism" (129). Unfortunately, the import of Allen's observation, as it relates to the complexity and construction of contemporary Native American literature, cannot be fully discussed here. However, a more limited inquiry is possible by examining some of the ways in which Silko's mixed blood status affected the way her novel *Ceremony* was constructed.

If Silko has inherited the mixed blood's historical role of interpreter, she has also inherited a mixed bag full of weighty problems and thorny questions that must of necessity be wrestled with. After a work has been completed, the first problem generally encountered by any writer is getting it published. This can be particularly problematic for a writer of Native American literature.

The American public has not a few preconceived notions about Indians, and they would generally prefer not to have these images disrupted. If the disruption were too severe, would the American public read the books? Most likely not. America knows how it likes its Indians, preferably on film or on the pages of books looking savagely exotic, notably hovering on the brink of extinction or extinct by the last page. The American public dotes on such dramatic endings as the one that non-Indian novelist Marilyn Harris gave to her "Oh, so sympathetic novel" written in 1974, *Hatter Fox*.

Harris's novel is a variation of the "vanishing American" theme that has been repeated over and over in American literature and is a favorite with the reading public. Hatter Fox is a poor, alienated Navajo Indian princess, abused by white and Indian alike. She winds up in an insane asylum and is eventually rescued from the horrors of this snake pit by a good white doctor who works for the Bureau of Indian Affairs and decides it is his sole mission in life to civilize and make a proper American out of her. Of course, he fails because Hatter is too much of a "childlike" Indian to ever learn to be a responsible citizen. She is subsequently killed by not looking where she is going and stepping into the street in front of a tourist bus. The novel ends on these overly dramatic, tragic notes:

> I should have been content to let her be what she was. But there was no room in the world for what she was. And now there is less room for me.
>
> I hear from our bench the chiming of bells for matins coming furiously from the cathedral. The hour before dawn. The last hour of the condemned. How many more are waiting for death? ...
>
> Now is my night upon me. I still wait for her. But she doesn't come. It is the silence that frightens me.
>
> I miss her ... I miss her ...
>
> I miss her ...[7]

Harris's interpretation of Native American experience is the stuff American dreams are made of and, unfortunately, it is what many major publishing houses are generally in the market for. The reader can have a good time feeling bad over the fate of the American Indian, have a good cry, turn over, go to sleep, and forget it. After all, "there [is] no room in the world for what [we are]" (273).

In light of this Western penchant for the "vanishing American," what is the tribal writer to do? How does one present an accurate portrayal of Native American people, one that does not stink of noble savagery on the brink of doom, and still manage to get into print at the same time?

To begin to uncover some of the answers to the dilemma of publishing, we need to look at audience. Who will read these novels? Certainly publishers assume the audience will primarily be a non-Indian one, and that assumption may well be true. However, within the last ten to fifteen years there has been an increase in Native American readers as Indian-written novels and anthologies find their way into classrooms at the secondary and college levels. In spite of this increase in tribal readership, the question of audience remains a valid one, since the number of tribal readers alone is not sufficient incentive for the novels to become published by major publishing houses. Silko's answer to the difficult question of audience is to write for both. However, it is important to note that the audience she writes most directly *to* is a tribal one, while the audience she writes for, in terms of numbers of book sales, is not. The operative word here is "to." The problem that Silko faces lies within this inherited role of interpreter, which requires that she translate tribal realities for a large audience whose culture is distinctly different from that of the tribal audience with whom the author is most concerned.

Situated between worlds, the mixed blood writer faces a difficult task. Clearly, Silko stands in the middle of that road which Carroll Arnett speaks so bluntly about in his poem. If the non-Indian audience is going to read the novel, it must somehow appeal to non-Indian tastes, and that taste has been established, but for the novel to hold up under the scrutiny of Native American readers, it must maintain cultural integrity at the same time. What Silko has done in the face of this perplexity is to take the trickster's path. She wrote a novel that is partly Western and partly tribal and that, as Paula Gunn Allen says, may appear to almost give America what it wants: "As a result of following western literary imperatives, most writers of Indian novels create mixed blood or half-breed protagonists, treating the theme of cultural conflict by incorporating it into the psychological and social being of the characters."[8] However, an important factor to keep in mind is that Silko has created a written work that has been fueled by oral traditions and, like the old stories, this new work is coded or written in layers. Such layered writing works to subvert aspects of the text that may appear at first glance to be stereotypical, while opening it up on another level to a deeper and different understanding by Native American readers. Hence, the appeal to a number of

audiences on a number of different levels. This is certainly the case in
Ceremony.

On the surface, *Ceremony* uses the popular Western themes of alienation and cultural strife, aspects that are, according to Allen, embedded in
the consciousness of the breed as well as the consciousness of the dominant culture.[9] The idea of an alienated hero at odds with the world ap-
peals to the American reading public because it is also such a completely
American theme. American literature abounds with stories about alienation. However, the alienation found in *Ceremony* is alienation with a
twist, and the twist is a distinctly tribal one that works at deflecting the
text from Western stereotypes, while turning it towards a more tribal
mode of perception.

Silko, as mixed blood trickster writer, created a hero who is in opposition to the usual Western protagonist. Euro-American cultural demands for individuality in the extreme dictate that the protagonist must
leave home in order to experience full self-realization. Tayo, Silko's tribal
protagonist, must do the opposite. Haunted by his experiences in World
War II and alienated by his "half-breed" status in a tribal society that
places a great deal of value on "pure" bloodlines, Tayo must find his way
back to his community and his traditions in order to heal. Silko's literary
resolution to Tayo's estrangement accurately reflects the consciousness of
her Laguna people.

In *Recovering the Word*, William Bevis describes this need to return to
community as "homing in":

> In marked contrast, most Native American novels are not "eccentric," cen-
> trifugal, diverging, expanding, but "incentric," centripetal, converging, con-
> tracting. The hero comes home. "Contracting" has negative overtones to us,
> "expanding" a positive ring. These are cultural choices we are considering. In
> Native American novels, coming home, staying put, contracting, even what
> we call "regressing" to a place, a past where one has been before, is not only
> the primary story, it is a primary mode of knowledge and a primary good.[10]

In contemporary Native American novels, the most common way for
the protagonist to "come home" is through a return to spirituality and
the ritual tradition. Certainly the use of the ritual tradition within *Ceremony* represents far more than some idea of accommodating Western
publishing tastes for the exotic Indian. According to Allen, it functions as
an important counterdevice that works against the novelist's acquies-
cence to the theme of alienation:

> But at least since the publication of *Cogewea, the Half-Blood* ... in 1927, this acquiescence to western publishing tastes is offset by a counterdevice. The protagonists are also participants in a ritual tradition, symbolizing the essential unity of a human being's psyche in spite of conflict. This development implies integration in the midst of conflict, fragmentation, and destruction and provides literary shapings of the process of natavistic renewal, a process that characterizes American Indian public life in the last quarter of the twentieth century.[11]

Allen also notes that the focus Native American novelists have chosen is counter to that of the Western protest novel, which concerns itself with the oppressor, rather than the oppressed (82).

Unlike *Hatter Fox*, which portrays a solitary Indian awash in an urban sea of whiteness that ultimately spells her doom, *Ceremony* takes place in a tribal world, peopled with tribal characters. Though the white man's handiwork is seen and discussed, he is largely absent from the novel. The white doctor from the veterans' hospital makes only a brief appearance in *Ceremony*. As she focuses on the oppressed rather than the oppressor, Silko defuses the Western notion of the "vanishing American." Though there are dead Indians at the novel's close, there are still a good number of Indians left alive and kicking.

By limiting the white characters' time in the novel, Silko articulates the reality that Native American people have largely opted to direct their attention to their own traditions and customs and, as Allen points out, "ignore the white man as much as possible" (82).

Lakota historian Vine Deloria Jr. bears this out in *We Talk, You Listen*: "In many areas whites are regarded as a temporary aspect of tribal life and there is unshakable belief that the tribe will survive the domination of the white man and once again rule the continent."[12] This belief is illustrated by Silko's creation of the "witchery" story in *Ceremony*. When Tayo meets the old mixed blood medicine man, Betonie, he is told that the white man is not the "demi-god" he thinks he is, and neither does he possess the power the world has attributed to him. According to Betonie, white people can be managed because Indians created them: "But white people are only tools that the witchery manipulates: and I tell you, we can deal with white people, with their machines and their beliefs. We can because we invented white people; it was Indian witchery that made white people in the first place."[13]

Is Silko's invention of the "witchery" and her use and interpretation of tribal beliefs accommodationist? Has her translation perhaps made the white folks feel more comfortable? I think not. Silko's idea that Indians created white people in no way absolves the white man from historical responsibility in the genocide of Native American people. Throughout the novel, Silko has attached responsibility for what evil has occurred through the white man to the white man, and she has attached what has occurred through the Native American to the Native American, but the blame has been firmly affixed to that force which is truly responsible for man's inhumanity to man. She has moved beyond blaming all white people for what some chose and continue to choose to do, and has opted instead to focus on the greater issue at hand, the resistance of the "witchery" that drives human beings to destroy one another. Silko makes this clear in an interview with Jane B. Katz in *This Song Remembers*:

> In the novel, I've tried to go beyond any specific kind of Laguna witchery or Navajo witchery, and to begin to see witchery as a metaphor for the destroyers, to the counterforce, that force which counters vitality and birth. The counterforce is destruction and death. I tried to get away from talking about good and evil, and to return to an old, old, old way of looking at the world that I think is valid—the idea of balance, that the world was created with these opposing forces.
>
> ...
>
> I try to take it beyond any particular culture or continent, because that's such a bullshit thing—it's all Whitey's fault. That's too simplistic, mindless. In fact Tayo is warned that *they* try to encourage people to focus on certain people or groups to blame them for everything. Another name for the counterforce is "the manipulators," those who create nothing, merely take what is around.[14]

Silko uses the story of the "witchery" to point out that *how* this counterforce came into existence is not the most important thing. What must be acknowledged is the fact that it does exist and that it will manipulate anyone who allows it to do so. The real importance lies in accepting the fact that the "witchery" itself is inextricably a part of our human existence and that it cannot be destroyed. However, one *can* choose not to participate in it, as Tayo did. One can refuse to be manipulated by it and in doing this live a life that is balanced and complete, rather than suffer the fragmentation and chaos experienced by the characters of Harley, Leroy, Pinkie, and Emo.

Lost in the throes of desire for life as they have been told to want it, they exist in a shadowland. Each stumbles through his personal darkness, feeding on beer and twisted memories of wartime mutilations and liaisons with uniform-enamored blondes who do not want them anymore. Tayo, in contrast, recognizes the "witchery" for what it is and moves increasingly away from the material world and into the sacred.

However, could it be said that, even as Silko enabled the character of Tayo to overcome the "witchery," she became tangled in it herself? To more traditional Native Americans, the exposure of the ritual tradition constitutes a violation of the sacred. Silko's novel could possibly be considered the most problematic in this area, because she chose to incorporate a sacred Laguna clan story into the narrative itself, unlike James Welch, who disguises the sacred so thoroughly in his novels that only an "insider" can recognize what is going on mythologically.

In what way should we view Silko's actions? Has she mistaken her role as interpreter for that of ethnographic informer? Since the entire novel rests on and incorporates myth, old and new, I began to explore the possibility of some sort of mythological explanation for her actions. (For clarification, I would like to add that I do not equate explanation with justification in any way.) In order to do this, I turned to my own mythic traditions for insight.

I began to see not only Silko but many mixed blood poets and writers as analogous or metaphorically related to the mythic Cherokee Wild Boy or Orphan, who insisted that he was also the son of First Man and First Woman, and brother to their original offspring, in spite of the fact that he had been produced through the mixing of blood and water and not in the ordinary way. This mythic mixed blood, if you will, spent his life in the pursuit of hidden knowledge and often disclosed secrets.[15]

According to Charles Hudson in *The Southeastern Indians*, the Wild Boy–Orphan is the result of mixing categories and is therefore

> anomalous in two ways: in his strange birth and in his peculiar relationship to his brother. One of the most important features ... is that he came from the water, and water is associated with disorder, innovation, and fertility; thus Wild Boy was always breaking rules and doing new things.[16]

There are several aspects of the Orphan's story and Hudson's analysis that deserve exploration. The relationship between the Orphan and the contemporary fact of the existence of the mixed blood is extremely interesting. Like the Orphan, the "breed" is a product of mixed blood, blood that has been thinned or watered down, so to speak. It is also true that the outside blood that led to the creation of the mixed blood came through or across the water. The association of the mythic mixed blood and the "real world" mixed blood with water is strong. And it is certainly true that many times the mixed blood feels like an orphan and is often treated that way as well. All of the mixed blood characters in *Ceremony* are orphans of one sort or another or in some way associated with abandonment. Silko herself lived on the edges of Laguna society and felt this keenly. It is important to mention that she lived near the river and attached special significance to that fact:

> Look where all the Marmon houses are here by the river, down below the village. I always thought there was something symbolic about that—we're on the fringe of things. The river's just a short walk from here, and I was always attracted to it as a kid. I knew it was a small river, and I didn't make any great demands on it. It was a great place to go and play in the mud and splash around. There are willows and tamarack, and there are always stories. You just hear them. I guess from the beginning there was the idea that the river was kind of a special place where all sorts of things could go on.[17]

Perhaps by taking the clan story Silko was guilty of bad judgment, but she has certainly followed the Wild Boy's lead. Like her mythic predecessor, she created some chaos, broke the rules by exposing what had once been hidden, and gave birth to something new and innovative. She sees herself directly connected to the stories told by the Lagunas about mixed bloods and the "wild, roguish things they did" (189). As a mixed blood, Silko believes she has more latitude, more possibilities for expression, than a full-blood writer like Simon Ortiz, whom she sees as possibly constricted by his family's ties to community religious life (190).

Though Silko constructs the majority of the novel around the bones of Laguna mythology, one may conclude from her remarks that she did not draw on Laguna or Navajo mythology to illustrate the concept of the "witchery" in the novel. The invention of the story of the "witchery" and the casting of Tayo, who, according to Allen, is a traditional Keres mythological character, as a mixed blood in a mixed blood story is not so much an act of accommodation to the exotic tastes of a non-Indian audience as it is an attempt to move toward the creation of a new, mixed blood mythology that demonstrates one way for mixed bloods to become whole within the conflict they are born into.[18]

If one examines the novel carefully with an eye to the mythic dimension, one can see that Silko is doing something very important. At the novel's center is the idea that what is needed is a new ceremony. By calling for this, she is functioning as what comparative mythologist Joseph

Campbell called "the secondary hero," who breathes new life into ancient, sacred traditions so that they continue to function in modern times. Campbell describes this role in an interview with Bill Moyers in *The Power of Myth*: "There is a kind of secondary hero to revitalize the tradition. This hero reinterprets the tradition and makes it valid as a living experience today instead of a lot of outdated clichés. This has to be done with all traditions."[19]

The idea of Silko as "secondary hero" fits well within the Lakota definition of the mixed blood as interpreter between the human world and the spirit world. By placing the mixed blood within the existing Laguna mythic tradition through the characterization of Tayo and thereby creating a new mixed blood mythology, she is showing contemporary Native Americans, mixed bloods and full-bloods, a way to live in modern society. Tayo and the other important mixed blood characters, Betonie and the Night Swan, represent the kind of adaptation that is necessary for survival in the face of contemporary reality. By creating a new ceremony, one that is inclusive rather than exclusive, she has also opened a road upon which the mixed blood can return home to ritual traditions that have fueled the endurance of tribal people for thousands of years and that now have room for him or her as well.

Though Silko cautions all of her readers against acquiescing spiritually to a mechanistic society that erects altars to technology at the expense of humanity, I believe her primary interest is in sending a signal to tribal people everywhere that a resistance path remains. Whether on the land or tied to urban areas for economic reasons, a sacred space must be created that allows one to remain Indian. Through *Ceremony*, Silko demonstrates that there is a way to live in the modern world without giving in to the "witchery." That way is through remembrance, adaptation, and recreation. At the onset of the novel (p. 2) Silko writes:

> I will tell you something about stories,
> [he said]
> They aren't just entertainment.
> Don't be fooled.
> They are all we have, you see,
> all we have to fight off
> illness and death.
>
> You don't have anything
> if you don't have the stories.

For a long time mixed bloods did not have the stories. Now, thanks to Silko, we have new stories and we are part of them as well. Throughout the novel, Silko has successfully translated tribal realities to non-Indians and mixed blood realities to full-bloods. True to form as a mythological descendant of the ancient Orphan–Wild Boy, she has broken some rules along the way, but she has also purchased a contemporary mythic space for mixed bloods everywhere, and through it all she sends a strong message to the camp of the "manipulators." We are being healed. We will return. We have not vanished from this red earth.

Notes

1. Carroll Arnett, "Song of the Breed," *Songs from This Earth on Turtle's Back*, ed. Joseph Bruchac (New York: Greenfield Review Press, 1983), 14.

2. Robert E. Bieder, "Scientific Attitudes Toward Indian Mixed-Bloods in Early Nineteenth Century America," *Journal of Ethnic Studies* 8, no. 2 (1980), 19.

3. Bieder, "Scientific," 19.

4. This definition was conveyed by Mr. Looking Horse during a conversation with a student following his appearance as a guest lecturer at San Francisco State University.

5. Rayna Green, Introduction to *That's What She Said: Contemporary Poetry and Fiction by Native American Women* (Bloomington: Indiana University Press, 1984), 7.

6. Paula Gunn Allen, *The Sacred Hoop: Recovering the Feminine in American Indian Traditions* (Boston: Beacon, 1986), 129.

7. Marilyn Harris, *Hatter Fox* (New York: Bantam, 1974), 273.

8. Allen, *Sacred Hoop*, 81.

9. Ibid., 129.

10. William Bevis, "Native American Novels: Homing In," in *Recovering the Word: Essays on Native American Literature*, ed. Brian Swann and Arnold Krupat (Berkeley: University of California Press, 1987), 582.

11. Allen, *Sacred Hoop*, 82.

12. Vine Deloria Jr., *We Talk, You Listen* (New York: Macmillan, 1970), 13.

13. Leslie Marmon Silko, *Ceremony* (New York: Signet, 1978), 139.

14. Leslie Marmon Silko, "Interview," in *This Song Remembers: Self Portraits of Native Americans in the Arts*, ed. Jane B. Katz (Boston: Houghton, 1980), 193.

15. Many tribes have Wild Boy or Blood Clot Boy myths. There is a Pueblo myth about the Water Jar Boy that is somewhat analogous to this one. The Water Jar Boy came about through the mixture of earth and water. Those interested should see Elsie Clews Parsons, "Tewa Tales," *Memoirs of the American Folklore Society* 19 (1926), 193.

16. Charles Hudson, *The Southeastern Indians* (Knoxville: University of Tennessee Press, 1987), 148–49.

17. Silko, "Interview," 189.

18. Paula Gunn Allen, "Special Problems in Teaching Leslie Marmon Silko's *Ceremony*," *American Indian Quarterly* 14 (1990), 383.

19. Joseph Campbell, *The Power of Myth*, by Bill Moyers, ed. Betty Sue Flowers (New York: Doubleday, 1988), 141.

Was Roxy Black?

Race as Stereotype in Mark Twain, Edward Windsor Kemble, and Paul Laurence Dunbar

Browsing on the world wide web may be the modern equivalent of being a flaneur, for one can find amazing sites. One of them is the University of Virginia library site for Mark Twain's works. There, the complete text of *Pudd'nhead Wilson* is accompanied by Stephen Railton's history of its illustrations.[1] Railton writes about the period of 1893–94, when *Pudd'nhead Wilson* was serialized in *Century* magazine and appeared in book form: "The *Century* used one of its staff artists, Louis Loeb, to illustrate the story for magazine publication; Chatto & Windus used Loeb's drawings when they published the novel ... in England." In the United States, the American Publishing Company used a new technique of "marginal illustrations" by F. M. Senior and C. H. Warren in the hope of generating sales. Railton comments that "although the text treats racial identity as a deep ambiguity, this mode of illustration, because it makes shading impossible, forces the illustrator to depict a character as either as white as the page or as black as the ink." The new technique required certain racial choices. This was most obvious in the case of Roxy, one of the central characters in *Pudd'nhead Wilson*. Her opening word in the novel is "fust-rate," and she tells Jasper a few lines later: "I got somp'n' better to do den 'sociatin' wid niggers as black as you is." Only a little later does Twain's standard-English narrator describe her appearance as follows:

> From Roxy's manner of speech, a stranger would have expected her to be black, but she was not. Only one sixteenth of her was black, and that sixteenth did not show. She was of majestic form and stature, her attitudes were imposing and statuesque, and her gestures and movements distinguished by a noble and stately grace. Her complexion was very fair, with the rosy glow of vigorous health in her cheeks, her face was full of character and expression, her eyes were brown and liquid, and she had a heavy suit of fine

soft hair which was also brown, but the fact was not apparent because her head was bound about with a checkered handkerchief and the hair was concealed under it. Her face was shapely, intelligent, and comely—even beautiful. She had an easy, independent carriage—when she was among her own caste—and a high and "sassy" way, withal; but of course she was meek and humble enough where white people were.

To all intents and purposes Roxy was as white as anybody, but the one sixteenth of her which was black outvoted the other fifteen parts and made her a Negro. She was a slave, and salable as such.[2]

The white outline figure with which the first American edition represented Roxy could not render the complexity of such description. Loeb's Roxy (Ill. 1) had perhaps been closer to the text.

But what are we to make of the 1899 Harper & Brothers edition—one that was reprinted many, many times in the subsequent half-century (see Ill. 2)? The artist was Edward Windsor Kemble, who is known to Twain readers as the illustrator of the first edition of *Huckleberry Finn*, and who had meanwhile acquired national fame as a "delineator" of Negro characters. The illustration, captioned "Roxy harvesting among the kitchens," served as frontispiece; as Railton writes on the University of Virginia web site, Kemble's "representation of [Roxy] is in line with the rest of his 'negro drawings,' and completely at odds with the text's description of Roxy. I cannot find any evidence, however, to suggest that American readers noticed or cared about this d[i]screpancy." Railton also gives a passport picture–style cutout of the cook's face, identified as "Roxy."

Though unfootnoted, this observation has been made by others. One example is Leslie Fiedler, whose pioneering 1955 review made the claim that *Pudd'nhead Wilson* is a

fantastically good book …which deals not only with the public issue of slavery, after all, long resolved—but with the still risky private matter of miscegenation, which most of our writers have chosen to avoid; and it creates in Roxy, the scared mulatto mother sold down the river by the son she has smuggled into white respectability, a creature of passion and despair rare among the wooden images of virtue and bitchery that pass for females in American literature. It is a portrait so complex and unforeseen

—and here Fiedler observed the incongruity of Kemble's frontispiece—

that the baffled illustrator for the authorized standard edition chose to ignore it completely, drawing in the place of a "majestic … rosy …comely" Roxana— a gross and comic Aunt Jemima.[3]

"Was Roxy black?" is thus a question about the representation of "race" and "mixed race" in visual illustrations that accompany literature; and it is a question that opens wider issues concerning the relationship of text and image, the recognizability of illustrative art, and the employment of stereotypes. How can an authorized illustrator represent a character who appears to have been imagined in order to subvert racial thinking—as what Fiedler called "a comic and gross Aunt Jemima"?

Martha Banta followed Fiedler's lead in commenting on Kemble's frontispiece, contrasting it with Loeb's illustration. She found that Louis Loeb "supplied a picture of Roxy the slave woman that follows the description in Twain's written text" (Ill. 1). "Loeb's drawing clearly bears out the irony of the situation which condemns Roxy to be 'seen' as black and a slave by the society in which she lives, notwithstanding the fact that her appearance is that of a white woman." Yet by contrast, when Kemble illustrated Twain's *Pudd'nhead Wilson* (Ill. 2), he followed an entirely different path:

> Kemble did not draw the Roxy Mark Twain portrays. He set down the accepted fictions, "the orthodox opinions," governing turn-of-the-century identification of inferior racial types. A stroke of Kemble's pen wipes out the verbal irony by which Mark Twain set up cross-currents among what Roxy looks like, her bottom-nature, and the racial tag placed upon her by society.[4]

Railton's web page follows this tradition, and it seems plausible to do so. After all, the United States racial system is a binary, dualistic one that rests on the "either:or" quality of black and white. Unlike in Latin America, the mixed race categories were always in danger of being squeezed out of existence in the United States by the pressure of this dualism. In Texas a 1906 law stipulated, "All persons not included in the definition of 'negro' shall be deemed a white person within the meaning of this article."[5] And today, all American readers of this essay are presumed to be either "persons of color" or "white." Thus it was to be expected that Roxy's American illustrators would turn her "mixed race" either into unambiguous whiteness (as in the illustration of the first American edition, which renders the *seen* but not the *heard* dimension of the text) or into unambiguous blackness (which is what Kemble seems to be doing, closely following Twain's mock-electoral racial system according to which "the one sixteenth of her which was black outvoted the other fifteen parts and made her a Negro"—a system that comes pretty close to the old Texas law.) In such a cultural system, can racial ambiguity be

ROXY AND THE CHILDREN.

ILL. 1. Louis Loeb, Roxy (*Pudd'n-head Wilson*, *Century* magazine 1893–94)

ILL. 2. Edward Windsor Kemble, "Roxy harvesting among the kitchens" (*Pudd'nhead Wilson*, Harper & Brothers, 1899)

"WHO DO YOU RECKON IT IS?"

ILL. 3. Edward Windsor Kemble, Huck with Aunt Sally and Uncle Silas, mutilated version (*Huckleberry Finn*, New York: Charles L. Webster, 1885)

ILL. 4. Edward Windsor Kemble, Jim and Huck (*Huckleberry Finn*, New York: Charles L. Webster, 1885)

A FIELD-HAND.

ILL. 5. Edward Windsor Kemble, "The Field-Hand" (for George Washington Cable) ("The Dance in Place Congo," *Century* 9 (1885–86): 517–32.)

ILL. 6. Edward Windsor Kemble, "It's Freedom, Gideon" (for Paul Laurence Dunbar) (Paul Laurence Dunbar, *The Strength of Gideon and Other Stories*, 1900)

"IT'S FREEDOM, GIDEON."

"And ain't ye dhrissed!"

ILL. 7. Edward Windsor Kemble, Katie (for Irwin Russell) (Irwin Russell, "Larry's on the Force," *Christmas Night in the Quarters*, 96–101)

ILL. 8. Edward Windsor Kemble, "Roxy among the field hands" (*Pudd'n-head Wilson and Those Extraordinary Twins*, Hartford, Conn: American Publishing Company, 1899), opp. p. 168. Taken from copy no. 473 of vol. 14 of the De Luxe Edition of the Writings of Mark Twain, in possession of Widener Library, Harvard University.

visualized, can it be imagined at all? The very existence of descendants of interracial unions has often been regarded as a "tabooed topic," and it is easy to come up with examples of how "mixed race" was "themed away" from interracial literature and art.[6] Scholarship on these issues has grown, racial dualism has been subjected to critical scrutiny, and the question has been raised why the U.S. Census as of the year 2000 still finds itself unwilling or unable to provide for the theoretical possibility, in its statistical forecasts, that American children may in fact be born from the unions of "members" of different races.[7]

"Miscegenation" was one of Sidney Kaplan's encyclopedic interests; and his account of the historical moment at which the 1863 pamphlet that coined the word was published as a dirty trick in the Lincoln reelection campaign has remained unsurpassed. As Kaplan reported, the word "took" rapidly, and in 1864 the Republican Party answered a politically slanderous miscegenation cartoon with "the aid of Currier and Ives. In a cartoon on the Chicago convention of the Democrats, the nominees McClellan and Pendleton are portrayed as 'The ... Political Siamese Twins, The Offspring of Chicago Miscegenation,' spurned by two Union soldiers."[8] This image may have been of particular interest to Twain as it anticipated the bringing together of two of the central issues in *The Tragedy of Pudd'nhead Wilson and the Comedy Those Extraordinary Twins* (as the first American edition was entitled): race and twinship. In fact, young Twain was one of the early users of the word "miscegenation" when he was a cub reporter for the *Territorial Enterprise* (in Nevada), a job he left abruptly in May of 1864 as a consequence of a "miscegenation" editorial. A critic has given us this account:

> The money raised at a fancy-dress ball given by the ladies of Carson City, Twain intimated, "was to be sent to aid a Miscegenation Society somewhere in the East." According to Twain's story to his sister-in-law ("I wrote ... that item ... when I was not sober—I shall not get drunk again, Molly"), he showed the editorial to a fellow reporter, agreed that it was a joke, and was dissuaded from publishing it. But the manuscript, left on a table in the *Enterprise* office when the two young men went out on the town ... was found by a press foreman who recognized Twain's handwriting, assumed it was to be printed, and set it up.[9]

After protests by Carson City ladies who wanted a retraction and the name of the author of the piece, Twain apologized for the hoax but kept being drawn to this risky subject. At the time that he was writing *Huckleberry Finn*, he symbolically claimed mixed ancestry in a manner that foreshadows now current claims for "hybridity" and positively recasts the term "mongrel." In "Plymouth Rock and the Pilgrims" (1881) he attacked pure-ancestry-hungry New Englanders and offered the following alternative:

> The first slave brought into New England out of Africa by your progenitors was an ancestor of mine—for I am of a mixed breed, an infinitely shaded and exquisite Mongrel. I'm not one of your sham meerschaums that you can color in a week. No, my complexion is the patient art of eight generations.[10]

In contradistinction to Mark Twain's Roxy, Kemble's illustration can thus be viewed as an allegory for the denied interracial makeup of America, and Kemble's error in representing her may be considered a *systemic* flaw—which is why Railton stresses that American readers did not even notice the misrepresentation.

This would not seem to be Kemble's only systemic flaw.[11] He became famous for such period pieces as *Kemble's Coons*, "humorous" images that were used to support legalized segregation.[12] Kemble's most careful critic, Francis John Martin, viewed the comic black image in part as a modern, lesser equivalent to the Elizabethan court jester—in fact, the very term "minstrel" harkens back to the medieval troubadour and a courtly setting. Martin also listed some of the more popular variants of the image, including that of the "fat handkerchief-head Mammy."[13] In its force as a preexisting, stable mental image that is projected upon a more complicated and changing reality, the artistic "stereotype"—the term derived from a printing process in which a cast mold is used instead of the forme itself, hence designating "something continued or constantly repeated without change" (*Oxford English Dictionary*)—runs against more "realistic" and "individualized" perceptions of the world.

Yet that raises the problem of the recognizability of visual images, especially of images that, like "cartoons," "caricatures," or "illustrations" (the genres in which Kemble predominantly worked) *need* to be recognized in order to serve their function. Derived from Latin *illustrare*, "to light up, illuminate, clear up," an "illustration"—the *Oxford English Dictionary* tells us—is the "pictorial elucidation of any subject; the elucidation or embellishment of a literary or scientific article, book, etc. by pictorial representations." And even a "caricature," from Italian *caricare*, "to load, charge, exaggerate," must bear a likeness of what it represents, though it may be a grotesquely exaggerated likeness.[14] To be recognizable, such images have to comment on a reality that they distort but *still represent recognizably.* In the case of illustrations this means that images have to remain in an intelligible relation to characters from the texts. Only then can illustrations "work." Once they do work, they begin to affect our reading of texts, just as texts (including captions) affect our understanding of images.[15]

In the case of Kemble's Roxy, textual description and visualization do not seem to match. This incongruity is all the more annoying because it seems to be the result of the artist's sloppy reading, a silly error that remained unnoticed for half a century and has now become offensive because of its ideological nature. How could Twain let this happen, furthermore in a novel that has been highly praised not only by critics but also by writers like Langston Hughes and Amiri Baraka for its subversive racial politics?

Pudd'nhead Wilson was not the first occasion for Kemble and Twain to collaborate; it was for *Huckleberry Finn* that Twain first engaged Kemble as an illustrator, and Kemble's frontispiece for the first edition helped to define Huck for contemporaries and later readers.[16] Kemble (1861–1933) was only twenty-three at the time (half the age of Twain, and some years younger even than Twain had been when he perpetrated the "miscegenation" hoax); he was a Californian by birth who had grown up in New York. He was not trained as an artist and was aware of his particular ineptitude at drawing human bodies, especially hands and feet.[17] Yet he published his first drawings in *Harper's Bazaar* in 1880 (at age eighteen), became "staff artist," "cartoonist and character artist" for the *Daily Graphic* (at age twenty-one), and soon worked for *Life* magazine, sketching cartoons on a variety of subjects. One of those subjects was black minstrelsy, and he had close contact with writers who specialized in it. At *Life*, for example, he became friends with the associate editor Henry Guy Carleton, whose "Thompson Street Poker Club" Kemble illustrated for several weeks in *Life* before it was published as a book. The setting of the serial is typically a monthly poker game in which urban black characters like Tooter Williams, Cyanide Whiffles, or Thankful Smith show such surprising hands as "Two Jacks an' a Razzer" or say things like "Whad Yo' Got?" or "Wharjer Git dem Jacks?" Kemble also did political cartoons[18] and humorous drawings, sometimes in pairs or in series, on human foibles. In "Sport," for example, he drew an incompetent hunter from the city who has hit a farmer's cow.[19] In a two-image sequence he made fun of an optimist-turned-pessimist: "'I believe in the horse-shoe theory,' says Boggs, 'everything seems to go better; business seems brighter, you're much happier.' But a sudden lurch of the step-ladder somewhat modified his views on the subject."[20]

As did Twain, Kemble obviously loved the Bergsonian gag (which leads to a release of energy through laughter at the surprising downfall of a character who deserves it), whether the character appears in blackface or not. A two-part Tooter Williams image represents a show-off skater who gets his just deserts. And in a thematically related series of eleven images on "Some Uses of Electricity" in March 1884 (now on the web), Kemble imagined ways in which electricity could help to fend off burglars, punish children, speed up waiters and messengers, or permit a minister literally to shock his congregation.[21] These heretical uses of electricity for a variety of purposes suggested an affinity with Twain's interest in such incongruous clashes of modern inventions and old ways as he would dramatize in *A Connecticut Yankee in King Arthur's Court*. And Kemble and Twain obviously shared a deep anticlericalism.[22] As Earl Briden has shown, it was this work that caught Twain's eye. After seeing this series of drawings, Twain knew whom he wanted for *Huckleberry Finn*: "the man who illustrated the applying of electrical protectors to door-knobs, door-mats, &c & electrical hurriers to messengers, waiters &c."[23]

Twain worked with his own publishing company in which he had set up his nephew-in-law Charles Webster as head so that he was free to choose his illustrator for the first time. Choosing Kemble—who was yet inexperienced as a book illustrator—and agreeing to pay a rather steep honorarium of $1,200 for 174 drawings (all of them now on the web)[24] meant that Twain must have been attracted to the comic style of Kemble's cartoons. Critics have documented how Twain supervised Kemble's work closely, hurrying him on, yet also offering sharp criticism. For example, Twain found the "faces ... generally ugly"[25] and complained specifically that Huck's mouth looked "a trifle more Irishy than necessary," but he never seems to have been dissatisfied with Kemble's Jim. His verdict to Webster, "I *knew* Kemble had it in him," would suggest Twain's satisfaction with Kemble, which led to their further collaboration on *Mark Twain's Library of Humor* (1888), and, for Twain's collected works, *Huckleberry Finn* again, and, as we saw, *Pudd'nhead Wilson*.[26]

The relationship of Twain's and Kemble's Jim has elicited some critical comment. Martin found in Kemble's Jim a "subtle inconsistency in his countenance throughout the novel." Briden believed that Kemble's images form "a pictorial text that holds the black hero fast in the grip of comic typification" and passed the verdict that "Twain might be said to have sold Jim down the river himself." Railton's web page finds Kemble's "racism so deeply held and so naive that it is not even faintly aware of itself."[27] This assessment is also based on Kemble's 1930 memoir, "Illustrating Huckleberry Finn," published in *The Colophon* and available on the web,[28] in which Kemble reports the task of finding models:

> The story called for a variety of characters, old and young, male and female. In the neighborhood I came across a youngster, Cort Morris by name, who tallied with my idea of Huck. ...
>
> From the beginning I never depended upon models but preferred to pick my types out of the ether, training my mind to visualize them. ...
>
> I had a large room in the top of our house which I used as a studio. Here I collected my props for the work. I spent the forenoon completing the drawing, using "Huck" as soon as he was released from school. He was always grinning, and one side of his cheek was usually well padded with a "sour ball" or a huge wad of molasses taffy. Throwing his wool cap and muslin-covered schoolbooks on a lounge, he would ask what was wanted at this session. I would designate the character. "We will do the old woman who spots Huck as he is trying to pass for a girl." Donning an old sunbonnet and slipping awkwardly into a faded skirt, Cort would squat on a low splint-bottomed chair and become the most woebegone female imaginable. ... I used my young model for every character in the story—man, woman and child. Jim the Negro seemed to please him the most. He would jam his little black wool cap over his head, shoot out his lips and mumble coon talk all the while he was posing. Grown to manhood, "Huck" is now a sturdy citizen of Philadelphia, connected with an established business house.

Whereas Shelley Fisher Fishkin traced the possible black oral source ("Sociable Jimmy") for Huck's dialect—which generated the question her book asks in its title *Was Huck Black?*, a question I have chosen to echo— Kemble's Jim was based (as were all illustrations in *Huckleberry Finn*) on the visual model of a white boy.[29] Kemble continues his account in the 1930 *Colophon*: "This Negro Jim, drawn from a white schoolboy, with face unblackened, started something in my artistic career." Was Jim white? we might therefore also be asking.

Kemble's account soon leads to an impressive list of authors he came to illustrate—Thomas Nelson Page, James Lane Allen, Harry Stilwell Edwards, Richard Malcolm Johnson, and George W. Cable—as Kemble became established, in his words, as "a delineator of the South, the Negro being my specialty," before he ever went South at all. "It all seems so strange to me now, that a single subject, a Negro, drawn from a pose given me by a lanky white schoolboy, should have started me on a career that has lasted for forty-five years."

It is hardly surprising that critics nowadays generally regard Kemble's representation of Jim as a racial stereotype that runs against the "subversion" of Twain's "realism" and "growing individualization." Fishkin gave the following account:

> It remains troubling ... that although Twain may have subverted racial stereotypes in the novel, he made no effort to prevent his text from being presented to the public in ways that emphasized its connection to familiar minstrel-show traditions, and indeed, often participated in this process himself. For example, although he complained to illustrator Edward W. Kemble that the first pictures of Huck were not "good-looking" enough, Twain raised no objection to Kemble's drawings of Jim, who (particularly in the early illustrations) looked much like all of Kemble's characteristic "comically represented Negroes."[30]

And Briden goes even further in arguing that Kemble's illustrations make for a "countertext" that runs against Twain's text. Only an anonymous reviewer in *Life* (probably one of Kemble's cronies) found Kemble's illustrations superior to Twain's prose.[31]

The slim literature on Kemble tends to offer the lineup of authors and works he illustrated as self-evident proof of his racism.[32] His Twain illustrations are often placed in the context of his cartoons; yet his career as an illustrator of literature still remains to be examined fully. Among the other works he illustrated is the volume of Irwin Russell's dialect poems *Christmas Night in the Quarters* (1917);[33] for George Washington Cable he contributed many images, among them a rather remarkable illustration entitled "A Field-Hand"[34] (Ill. 5). Though Kemble has been criticized for not taking enough field trips and for imagining rather than observing black life,[35] this image at least appears to be based on observation and is dated "New Orleans, 1885." (Of course, observation is no more a safeguard against racism than invention—or picking types "out of the ether"—is an avenue necessarily paved with stereotypes.)

Kemble's work for *Uncle Tom's Cabin* in 1892 has been commented on by Martin, who argued that Kemble's "depiction of the blacks in the novel," particularly such obvious figures as Topsy, "are excellent recreations of these characters." Yet Martin added that Kemble did not portray blacks "as dark whites," for "this would not have been acceptable in the

1890's to a public concerned about miscegenation." Instead, his figures are "pure Kemble Southern blacks."[36] *Uncle Tom's Cabin,* hardly a typically Southern book by the 1890s, did indeed offer Kemble opportunities to illustrate such characters as Aunt Chloe—an image resembling the one from *Pudd'nhead Wilson* that I mentioned at the beginning and to which I shall return at the end of the essay. Yet the novel also contains the famous scene of Eliza crossing the Ohio with little Harry; and here Kemble's art seems to run against the views of his interpreters. The scene of Eliza fearfully looking into the garden casts her very much in the vein of a Victorian lady. It is striking that Kemble's version of the Quadroon woman Cassy actually resembles his Little Eva; and finally, the image of Cassy's child Elise (the story is one of the prototypes for Toni Morrison's *Beloved*) also runs against the conventional wisdom about Kemble.

The same is true for Kemble's little-known illustrations of Marietta Holley's *Samantha and the Race Problem* (1894—the same year in which *Pudd'nhead Wilson* was first published). The images, not particularly beautiful but effective, include a black slave woman who poisoned her master's child as well as the mixed race Madeline, who is left by her white lover for a white woman.[37]

Kemble also illustrated Paul Laurence Dunbar's volumes *Folks from Dixie* (1898), *The Strength of Gideon* (1900), and *The Heart of Happy Hollow* (1904). Dunbar, the "race poet" par excellence, was known for his position in favor of "humor." When asked by *Century* magazine (in which both *Huckleberry Finn* and *Pudd'nhead Wilson* appeared) whether the magazine had made too much of "the comic character of the Negro," Dunbar assured the questioner that laughter was healthy.[38] Yet Dunbar himself has been enmeshed in the controversy about minstrel stereotypes (as have African American authors from his contemporary Charles Chesnutt to Zora Neale Hurston). Robert Bone made the case against Dunbar, in which Kemble's art provides the decisive evidence. "Dunbar's insensitivity to the implications of the minstrel stereotype is nowhere more apparent than in the illustrations." The "drawings of his white illustrator," Bone wrote, "are at best comic stereotypes and at worst vicious caricatures." He adds:

> It would be damaging enough if, against better judgment, Dunbar had been forced to accept such a collaboration by his publishers. But what are we to say of a black writer who so admired these racist drawings that he asked the artist to let him frame the originals for his den?[39]

Again, the difference between text and image is not very great: Kemble gives us a familiar image for the story "Mammy Peggy's Pride" and a new version of "Dat Jim" (described as "the hardest sinner on the plantation").[40] Yet are all images of "ne'er-do-wells," black aunts, and cooks "gross," "vicious," and inherently "racist"? This would seem a very high price to pay for the fear of falling into familiar "stereotypes." On which ground can the yardstick of "realism" and "individuality" be plausibly established? Do we assume something like an innate bias in any image that an artist like Kemble drew so that, logically, his minstrel cartoons would turn into the touchstones that we hold against all his other productions?

Sidney Kaplan has observed, "The line between condescending sentimentality and objective sensibility is often a tenuous one."[41] And recently Manthia Diawara has argued that all the energy spent in identifying "bad" stereotypes may be misspent—since it is much more interesting to see how they can serve different functions from the ones they were intended to serve. According to him, "positive images are as bad as negative images." "I love stereotypes," Diawara proclaimed, for what matters is "reclaiming them and making them speak another language."[42] This applies directly to the case of Kemble's work for Dunbar, which included the illustration "It's Freedom, Gideon" (Ill. 6) for *The Strength of Gideon* (1900), a work that one can read either as politically conservative (Gideon uses his strength only to remain in slavery) or as downright radical (Martha exhorts Gideon to follow the union troops to liberty). It is noteworthy that Kemble did not choose to illustrate Gideon's punch line, "Yes, Mis' Ellen, I'se a-coming" (which Bone called "the saddest line in Negro literature"), but that Kemble focused on the moment in which the handkerchief-headed female figure reminds Gideon of what he is about to give up.[43] In that sense, Kemble participated in—and in this case, perhaps even radicalized—the ambivalence that has been observed in Dunbar's texts.

A last aside before returning to Roxy. Kemble shared with Dunbar (and with poets like Irwin Russell) an interest in "folk types" that included not only black but also *Irish* types—and that went beyond the question of Huck's mouth. In "Circumstances Alter Cases" Dunbar writes:

> Tim Murphy's gon' walkin' wid Maggie O'Neill
>   O chone!
> If I was her muther, I'd frown on sich foolin',
>   O chone!

> I'm sure it's unmutherlike, darin' an' wrong
> To let a gyrul hear tell the sass an' the song
> Of every young felly that happens along,
>   O chone![44]

In a fifty-word stanza, only fifteen words deviate from standard English, and those include deviations such as "gon'" instead of "gone." (The same ratio applies to Dunbar's "black" poems.) Is there a visual equivalent to these techniques of creating recognizable ethnic types? When Russell tried his hand at Irish brogue, some of the works were illustrated by Kemble. "Larry's on the Force," for example, is about the successful policeman Larry, who is unfaithful—as the woman who is the speaker of the poem has to find out from Katie, with whom she is gossiping (Ill. 7).

> Well, Katie, and this is yersilf? And
>   where was you this whoile?
> And ain't ye dhrissed! You are the wan to
>   illusthrate the stoile;
> But niver moind thim matthers now, there's
>   toime enough for thim;
> And Larry—that's me b'y—I want to sphake to
>   you av him.[45]

The position of the women in front of a black open door frame is reminiscent of "Roxy harvesting among the kitchens," and the maternal "Irish Katie" may resemble the "black mammy" type.

Finally, back to Kemble's image of Roxy herself (Ill. 2).[46] In Kemble's "Roxy harvesting among the kitchens," four figures are depicted in front of the dark rectangle of an open door (a hanging pot suggestive of the kitchen setting). The three adults and the child look startled and worried, as if they had just been surprised (or were afraid of being surprised) in a secret activity. Dressed like a cook, the stately female central figure holds (or is trying to hide?) a basket, looking straight at the viewer; the man (dressed like a butler) at the right edge of the image holds a cup or a bowl and is looking sideways to the right of the viewer—near to where the eyes of the child who is holding what looks like a loaf of bread are also directed. Between the fully shown adults there is another female figure who is, except for her head, obscured by the man; she also casts a meaningful sideways glance at the viewer. It is as if they were worried about an intruder (roughly in the position of the artist as well as the reader and viewer) who has interrupted whatever has been going on so secretly. The fact that the three major figures are holding something, the connecting line of the woman's and the man's arms (from shoulder to elbow to closed hand), and the echo of that angularity in the child's position, all enhance the sense of a secret—guarded against the intrusive gaze of the viewers.

In a book in which the contrast between "kitchen" and "parlor" is analogous to that between black and white; the caption "Roxy harvesting among the kitchens" certainly may evoke the image of the big woman with a basket who is "harvesting" in the way in which minstrel-image figures collect their sustenance. The phrase comes, however, from a passage in the novel that suggests a slightly different context. "As a rule her conversation was made up of racy tattle about the privacies of the chief families of the town (for she went harvesting among their kitchens every time she came to the village), and Tom enjoyed this."[47] Roxy's "harvesting among their kitchens" would seem to refer to the gathering of gossip at least as much as of food. This context would invite us, of course, to think of Roxy not as the black cook, but as *the middle figure* who seems locked in by the arms of the other adults and to whom the diagonal line that begins with the child's elbow leads. Her face is in the half shadow and somewhat lighter than that of the others, thus coming closer to Twain's description of Roxy. Yet the secondary literature tells us fairly unambiguously that Roxy is the cook. Who *is* Roxy?

I believe that the secret is, fortunately, not that well guarded. In the American Publishing Company's numbered "DeLuxe" edition of Twain's works, copyrighted 1899, there are some additional Kemble illustrations, including one for Chapter 18 entitled "Roxy among the field hands" (apparently to illustrate Mark Twain's phrase "mongst de common fiel' han's"). When I opened the book to that page, I found an image that is not yet available on the web (Ill. 8).[48] Recognizable from Kemble's trajectory of representing mixed race characters like Eliza or Cassy, echoing also the title and subject of his 1885 *Century* illustration "A Field-Hand," Kemble's Roxy is not who she is supposed to be—and is, in fact, closer to Twain's description of her in the text than has been assumed, even by such excellent readers as Fiedler, Banta, and Railton. The fact that in the Harper frontispiece she is hidden between minor figures that draw attention away from her would fit her character all the more—as well as Kemble's disposition to be tricky as an illustrator. Did Kemble want to please the viewers who were looking for one of his trademark mammies as well as the readers of the novel who wanted to find the true Roxy? Could Kemble have hidden his Roxy *consciously* in honor of Mark Twain's sentence, "From Roxy's manner of speech, a stranger would have expected her to be black, but she was not"? Could Kemble's drawing be a perfect rendition of "the irony of the situation which condemns Roxy to be 'seen' as black and a slave by the society in which she lives, notwithstanding the fact that her appearance is that of a white woman" (exactly the accomplishment that Banta claimed only for Louis Loeb)?

Whatever Edward Windsor Kemble was, he was not a careless reader. May our own stereotyping lie in expecting and hastily identifying mistakes of the kind Kemble has been accused of making in *Pudd'nhead Wilson?*

Notes

This essay is dedicated to the memory of Sidney Kaplan (1913–93). The text is based on a Sidney Kaplan lecture given at the University of Massachusetts, Amherst, and a Carmel lecture given at the University of Tel Aviv. I am indebted to Jessica Hook for her energetic and resourceful research assistance, to Karen Dalton for helpful suggestions, and to Jules Chametzky, Robert Gooding-Williams, George Hutchinson, and Hana Wirth-Nesher for questions and suggestions. Erica Michelstein proofread the manuscript and double-checked all web sites in October 2000.

1. http://etext.lib.virginia.edu/railton/wilson/pwillshp.html.

2. Sidney E. Berger, ed., Norton Critical Edition of *Pudd'nhead Wilson* (New York: W. W. Norton, 1980), 8–9.

3. Repr. in Berger, ed., 221.

4. Martha Banta, *Imaging American Women: Idea and Ideals in Cultural History* (New York: Columbia University Press, 1987), 182.

5. Willson's *Criminal Statutes of Texas*, 1906, art. 347, cited in Werner Sollors, ed., *Interracialism: Black-White Intermarriage in American History, Literature, and Law* (New York: Oxford University Press, 2000), 6.

6. For examples, see the introduction to my study *Neither Black Nor White Yet Both* (New York: Oxford University Press, 1997; pb. Cambridge, Mass.: Harvard University Press, 1999).

7. Joel Perlmann, "Reflecting the Changing Face of America: Multiracials, Racial Classification, and American Intermarriage," in Sollors, ed., *Interracialism*, 506–33; here 524–25.

8. Sidney Kaplan, "The Miscegenation Issue in the Election of 1864," in Sollors, ed., *Interracialism*, 219–65; here 247n59.

9. J. M. Bloch, *Miscegenation, Melaleukation, and Mr. Lincoln's Dog* (New York: Schaum, 1958), 24–28. Bloch also notes that Twain published two of his earliest sketches in the New York *Sunday Mercury* in February of 1864; and that the *Mercury* "had been the first publication to comment at length on [the pamphlet] *Miscegenation*" on January 17, 1864, so that Twain may have heard the term earlier than has been assumed. When Mark Twain saw a New York performance of *Othello* with Edwin Booth as Iago (around 1869), he commented that it was Shakespeare's play about "the great Miscegenationist." See Justin Kaplan, *Mr.*

Clemens and Mark Twain (London: Cape, 1967), 100. Mark Twain also wrote an obituary in *The Galaxy* for one of the authors of the miscegenation hoax.

10. *The Comic Mark Twain Reader: The Most Humorous Selections from His Stories, Sketches, Novels, Travel Books, and Speeches*, ed. Charles Neider (Garden City, N.Y.: Doubleday, 1977), 66.

11. See Francis John Martin, "The Image of Black People in American Illustration from 1825 to 1925" (Ph.D. diss., UCLA, 1986), who argues: "These images and their clearly derogatory character were simply a reflection of the period, rather than of the attitudes of individual illustrators, who were doing nothing more than satisfying a fashionable prejudice of a period obsessed with racial humor and ethnic idioms" (xxii).

12. Joseph Boskin's nuanced assessment of Kemble's work balances the factors of artistic achievement and ideological blindness: "Clearly, Kemble had a charming style, and his figures evoked considerable sympathy. Yet, despite his often delicate touch, his caricatures conformed to the racial stereotypes of the period. Round-faced and grinning, often in ragged clothing, beset by amusing yet troublesome situations, Kemble's blacks were as stereotypically cast as those of other artists. Indeed, his blacks were so lovingly comical that they appeared to be even more believable." *Sambo: The Rise and the Demise of an American Jester* (New York: Oxford University Press, 1986), 127.

13. Martin, 259, 272.

14. See Karen F. C. Dalton's essay "Caricature in the Service of Racist Stereotypes: Evolution of Nineteenth-Century Caricatures of African-Americans," presented at American Antiquarian Society, Worcester, Mass., February 23, 1993.

15. For a broader examination of the kinds of illustrations that have accompanied African American materials, from turn-of-the-century artwork and Winold Reiss's and Aaron Douglas's designs and images for *The New Negro* to Zora Neale Hurston's use of Miguel Covarrubias as illustrator of *Mules and Men*, see Martha Nadell, "'Nor Can I Reduce This Experience to a Medium': Art, Literature, and Race in America" (Ph.D. diss., Harvard University, 2000).

16. The first edition (New York: Charles L. Webster, 1885) was reprinted, with all illustrations, in Hamlin Hill and Walter Blair, eds., *The Art of Huckleberry Finn* (San Francisco: Chandler, 2d ed., 1969).

17. See Martin, 456n202: "As with many self-taught artists, Kemble frequently had problems drawing the figure. According to his son, Edward B. Kemble, Kemble had great difficulty drawing feet and hands. E. B. Kemble told this writer that even as a mature artist Kemble would try to avoid drawing feet by cutting the figure off at the knees."

18. "The Anguish of a Breaking Heart," *Life* cover (January 24, 1884).

19. *Life* (February 14, 1884), 96.

20. *Life* (January 24, 1884), 68.

21. *Life* (March 13, 1884), 148–49. On the web at http://etext.lib.virginia.edu/railton/huckfinn/kemblea.html. Clockwise from upper left: "Book agent and electric doormat. A wire along the fence isn't bad. The policeman would seldom call to see Hannah if the railing was charged. A BATTERY attached to each res-

taurant waiter might cause him to quicken his pace. A small battery concealed in your umbrella would warn th[ie]ves to keep their hands off. 1:30 AM Hey wifey old gal have yer got that battery turned off the door knob. A gentle shock before going on an errand might throw some life into the messenger. An electric door-knob, heavily charged, would be a great inconvenience to a burglar. When about to begin a sermon the minister would have attentive listeners, could he but spring a shock on his congregation. 'Will you ever play hookey again, sir.' The lady that sells apples. The mat."

22. See, for example, Kemble's "Science," *Life* (January 17, 1884), 36–37.

23. Earl F. Briden, "Kemble's 'Specialty' and the Pictorial Countertext of *Huckleberry Finn*," *Mark Twain Journal* 26, no. 2 (Fall 1988), 2–14. Briden also reproduces an image of a boy stung by a bee that Kemble remembered Twain had seen, but found no such Kemble drawing from before 1888.

24. At http://etext.lib.virginia.edu/railton/huckfinn/twaillus1.html.

25. Among them Martin, 449–60; Briden; and Beverly R. David, "The Pictorial *Huckleberry Finn*: Mark Twain and His Illustrator, E. W. Kemble," *American Quarterly* (October 1979).

26. Twain's loyalty to Kemble is all the more surprising since one of the illustrations caused a crisis in the publication of *Huckleberry Finn*. The exact nature of the problem is not known. However, writing under the apparent pen name "Tak Sioui" one writer offered, and printed privately, an unfootnoted "recreation" of Kemble's prank according to which it was the illustration in Chapter 32 depicting Huck with Aunt Sally and Uncle Silas that had been tampered with (Ill. 3) by Kemble himself so as to look obscene and require resetting. Without giving a source, Sioui claimed that Kemble "said humorously that Aunt Sally's eye was not the defect (one eye may seem crossed at times), 'though the defect might have caused her to look a bit cross-eyed.'" No other critic has adopted this claim. See Tak Sioui, *Huckleberry Finn: More Molecules* (n.p.: privately printed, 1962), 5, 6, 7, and plates I and III. See also http://etext.lib.virginia.edu/twain/twah33s.jpg.

27. Martin, 463; Briden, 12; and Railton at http://etext.lib.virginia.edu/railton/huckfinn/jiminpix.html and at http://etext.lib.virginia.edu/railton/huckfinn/kembl99.html. Briden, 5, writes that "it is difficult to believe that [Twain] was unfamiliar with Kemble's stylistic approach to black subjects."

28. *The Colophon: A Book Collectors' Quarterly* (February 1930), posted at http://etext.lib.virginia.edu/railton/huckfinn/colophon.html.

29. Shelley Fisher Fishkin, *Was Huck Black? Mark Twain and African American Voices* (New York: Oxford University Press, 1993). This situation seems to parallel that of Roxy, who sounds "black" but looks "white."

30. Fishkin, 88. The mentioning of the "early" illustrations would imply the possibility of growth, yet it is the ending of the novel that most invited illustrators to resort to minstrelsy.

31. According to *Life* (March 12, 1885), 146, Kemble's "clever illustrations … enliven many a page of coarse and dreary fun" in *Huckleberry Finn*. See *Mark Twain's Notebooks & Journals*, ed. Frederick Anderson, vol. 3 (1883–91) (Berkeley: University of California Press, 1979), 111n152. Twain's text—in which minstrel

elements also appear in abundance, as does the word "nigger"—would militate against the notion that the illustrator could capture a more serious Jim by the end of the novel.

32. See http://etext.lib.virginia.edu/twain/kemble1.html: "Around the turn of the century, E. W. Kemble produced three new illustrations for the Underwood Edition of Huckleberry Finn, brought out by the American Publishing Co., Hartford, Conn. The edition is copyrighted 1901; the illustrations are dated 1899. Notably, the Underwood Edition contains only three illustrations; the original Huck had 174. Moreover, the three vary greatly from Kemble's 1885 work. By now, Kemble was a well-known illustrator, largely because of his work for Twain."

Eric Lott, *Love and Theft: Blackface Minstrelsy and the American Working Class* (New York: Oxford University Press, 1993), 166, offered a detailed reading of a Kemble drawing of Huck and Jim for the 1899 complete works (Ill. 4, also posted at http://etext.lib.virginia.edu/twain/twahkem2.jpg)—in the now popular context of the sexual dynamic of minstrelsy as transvestitism:

> Huck's brief foray into cross-dressing earns an E. W. Kemble illustration in which Huck flounces around expertly in the foreground ...; the vertical plane of his body intersects that of a horizontal, grinning Jim in the background, Huck's head overlapping and partially obscuring Jim's crotch. The picture brings into contiguity the precise terms of homosexual desire on the one hand, black male sexuality on the other. It also reiterates the spectatorial terms in which blackface transvestitism mapped this desire. ... Figuring a black male heterosexual desire alongside the "wench" offered alternative, and safer, bearers of the audience's look such that more "compromising" desires—for the man under the skirt—might be deflected or remain unacknowledged. ... In the broadest sense, the blackface male's desire for his "wench" acknowledges or represents the relation of the white audience to blacks generally. The blackface male is after all a figure for the audience's looking, however ridiculous he is made to appear; the "wench" encompasses in her person male and female both; and the relationship between the two figures is foregrounded.

Kemble seems to have moved from juvenile prankster to racial stereotyper with a fondness for cross-dressing and minstrelsy for which there may have been a (crypto-homo-) sexual subtext that would implicate both artist and viewer. For other comments on the cross-dressing episode in *Huckleberry Finn*, see Myra Jehlen, "Gender," in *Critical Terms for Literary Study*, ed. Frank Lentricchia and Thomas Mclaughlin, 2d ed. (Chicago: University of Chicago Press, 1995), 263–73, and Marjorie Garber, *Vested Interests: Cross-Dressing & Cultural Anxiety* (New York: Routledge, 1992), 289.

33. *Christmas Night in the Quarters and Other Poems*, introduction by Joel Chandler Harris (New York: Century, 1917).

34. "The Dance in Place Congo," *Century* 9 (1885–86), 517–32. Kemble's field-hand is also in an iconographic tradition of harvesting autumn allegories, and, in

addition, may constitute a comment on contemporary images of "The Man with the Hoe."

35. Martin, xxii, views Kemble as one the illustrators who "used existing stereotypes, but not ... to explore or discover black reality."

36. Martin, 476. Kemble's *Uncle Tom's Cabin* was published in 1892 by Houghton Mifflin Company, Boston.

37. Josiah Allen's Wife (Marietta Holley), *Samantha and the Race Problem* (New York: Dood, Mead, 1894), 104, 110.

38. Martin, 266 and 266n14.

39. Robert Bone, *Down Home: A History of Afro-American Short Fiction from Its Beginning to the End of the Harlem Renaissance* (New York: Putnam's, 1975), 53, referring to Virginia Cunningham, *Paul Laurence Dunbar and His Songs* (New York: Dodd, Mead, 1947), 171.

40. Paul Laurence Dunbar, *The Strength of Gideon and Other Stories* (1900; repr. New York: Arno Press, 1969), opp. 32 and 166.

41. "Notes on the Exhibition: The Portrayal of the Negro in American Painting," in *American Studies in Black and White: Selected Essays 1949–1989,* ed. Allan D. Austin (Amherst: University of Massachusetts Press, 1991), 215.

42. Ethnic Studies symposium, Harvard University, October 24, 1997.

43. Dunbar, *Strength of Gideon,* opp. 22.

44. Linda Keck Wiggins, *The Life and Works of Paul Laurence Dunbar; containing his complete poetical works, his best short stories, numerous anecdotes and a complete biography of the famous poet. With an introduction by William Dean Howells. Profusely illustrated with over half a hundred full page photo and half-tone engravings* (Naperville, Ill. and Memphis, Tenn.: J. L. Nichols & Company, 1907), 327.

45. Russell, "Larry's on the Force," in *Christmas,* 96–101; see also "The Irish Eclipse," 102–4.

46. On the web at http://etext.virginia.edu/railton/wilson/pwkembl1.jpg.

47. Readers may have been thinking of the following passage in Chapter 8 when they assumed that the woman who was "harvesting in the kitchens" would have to be carrying a basket—rather than new and racy information: "She would get along, surely; there were many kitchens where the servants would share their meals with her, and also steal sugar and apples and other dainties for her to carry home—or give her a chance to pilfer them herself, which would answer just as well." Norton edition, ed. Berger, 34.

48. *Pudd'nhead Wilson and Those Extraordinary Twins* (Hartford, Conn.: American Publishing Company, 1899), opp. p. 168. Taken from copy no. 473 of vol. 14 of the DeLuxe Edition of the Writings of Mark Twain, in possession of Widener Library, Harvard University. This volume contains, in addition to a portrait of Mark Twain taken from a painting by Charles Noel Flagg and a Tiffany-designed title page, etched by W. H. W. Bicknell, a total of seven illustrations, six by Kemble, and one by F. M. Senior (one of the illustrators of the first edition).

Out of the Melting Pot and into the *Frontera*

Race, Sex, Nation, and Home in Velina Hasu Houston's 'American Dreams'

Seeking to chart a trajectory, I found myself instead mapping a constellation in this essay. I set out to examine Velina Hasu Houston's *American Dreams*, a play about multiracial marriage, as an end-of-century revision of the ideology that began the century and as a modification of civil rights–era idealisms. Taking my first sighting from Israel Zangwill's 1909 play *The Melting Pot*, with its promise that the love of the younger generation would rejuvenate an America stultified by its ruling generation (and class), I plotted a line to the 1967 Hollywood classic *Guess Who's Coming to Dinner*, whose socially progressive promise again lay in the romantic love of a younger generation, although this time the older generation was to be redeemed and recalled to its own former ideals. But Houston's play didn't fit the curve. Written in 1983, taking place in the early 1950s, *American Dreams* loops back in history, telling the story *of* the previous generation rather than arguing with it in its old age. It refuses to place conflict *between* generations, implying inevitable historical progress, but instead exposes racism, sexism, betrayal, jealousy, and bigotry as the battles of siblings, coinheritors of history. And rather than holding the white patriarchs up for scorn or up to their professed ideals, *American Dreams* leaves them out entirely: they really aren't the important ones here. Love remains as the catalyst and the partial antidote for the conflicts in the play, but there is no promise of "happily ever after." If, as Werner Sollors has argued, *The Melting Pot* offers "loving proof that any parental past, any descent legacy, can be redeemed by consenting youths" (Sollors 72), *American Dreams* explores the problems within such consent and finds that sometimes love "just ain't enough" (*American Dreams*, 59). Where *The Melting Pot* and *Guess Who's Coming to Dinner* argue that personal affection, especially when sanctified by the marriage institution, would bring about national domestic harmony through familial domestic alignments, Houston's play refutes all such neat harmonics. Rather than assuming that the idea of America is splendid, but that we've fallen from it, *American Dreams* calls into question the very foundational ideals themselves. Home is still the figure for the national society, but in *American Dreams* the metaphor operates to reveal discord rather than resolution. The home terrain is heavily policed and highly conflictual. It contains prisons as well as promises. Houston investigates the American dream not only as constantly deferred, but as an act of constant displacement. She uses the familial domestic structure to question the national domestic structure, and then deconstructs the whole thing, leaving America not as homeland but land of homelessness.

Velina Hasu Houston and Her 'American Dreams'

People ain't never liked half-breeds
     —*American Dreams*

Velina Hasu Houston grew up in central Kansas, the daughter of a half African American, half Native American New Yorker and an immigrant from Haro, Japan. Her parents met when her father was stationed in Japan at the end of World War II, her mother's family having just lost their lands to the particular American force of democratization in which Houston's father was an officer.

Houston identifies herself as "Amerasian," a term coined by Pearl S. Buck, and refuses the fragmentation of more recent postmodern labelings. She is remembered by friends at Kansas State, where she went to college, for insisting that her racial identity is its own indivisible entity, not simply a piecing together of her parents' identities. "It's like when you mix blue and yellow. You don't get blue-and-yellow. You get green."[1]

Houston locates her *American Dreams* trilogy resolutely in the overlappings of multiple ethnicity, expressing frustration with audiences and directors who tell her that her plays are "not African American enough" or "not Japanese enough." Either of these categories would elide the specific experience she seeks to chronicle:

> My creative explorations of my family history, though born of artistic and personal passion, are nevertheless historical because they document history— the Japanese "war bride" and the Japanese American experience—that oth-

erwise might have been lost to the mainstream, history that Japan has side-stepped and about which America never knew or cared. (quoted in *Unbroken Thread,* 155)

She presents that history in three plays: *Asa Ga Kimashita (Morning Has Broken)*, *American Dreams*, and *Tea*. All three plays are based on the lives of Houston's parents. The plays move chronologically from the couple's opening romance in Japan to their arrival in the United States to the mother's widowhood in Kansas. They also move thematically. The first tells of the anger and resentment of the maternal, Japanese side of the family; the second depicts the racism the couple encounters when they arrive in the United States; and the final and best known of the three plays disrupts assumed uniformities among the "Asian" community in its creation of five "war brides," each of a different class position, married to men of different ethnicities, and with contrasting feelings about their Japanese heritage and their American existences.

The first and last plays of the trilogy have begun to garner notice, and deservedly so.[2] These two plays not only present characters with depth and interest, but also struggle with the nuances of rebellion and solidarity. Further, they incorporate as well an articulate cultural hybridization: *Asa Ga Kimashita*, while set in Japan, frames its action through a plot that parallels one of the classics of Western drama, *King Lear*, with its portrayal of a patriarch learning to reevaluate his willful daughter's love through the lens of losing his property and authority. *Tea*, set in America's heartland, takes its frame from a traditional Japanese tea ceremony honoring the dead. In addition to blending cultural canons, both plays force these traditional structures to be accountable to race. The generational and possibly feminist rebellion of *Lear* results in the favorite daughter marrying into another nation, a nation that then shifts from allegiance to animosity. In *Asa Ga Kimashita*, the favorite daughter's marriage not only unites her with the already victorious enemy nation, but with a demonized other race. *Tea* uses the traditional ritual for marking the passage over the boundary between life and death to evaluate the crossing of these women into a new nation.

But I want here to consider the neglected of these sister plays, the central (and as yet unpublished) *American Dreams*. This play has not attracted the production and publication attention that the others have, and yet it is precisely in its difficulties that it proves most rich. There are two notable differences between *American Dreams* and the other plays of the trilogy. One is that the ostensible lead roles are dramatically the least in-teresting. The other is that it operates entirely through quotidian realism, with no supernatural, magical, or "exotic" moments. *American Dreams* avoids reveling in fantasy or exoticizing distance. Whereas *Asa Ga Kima-shita* is set in Japan, and *Tea* includes a character who is a ghost, *American Dreams* takes place in New York, amongst characters akin to those of Norman Mailer, August Wilson, Tennessee Williams, or Sam Shepherd. It is tempting to see the play as having languished because it doesn't fit the expected type of Asian ethnicity. There are no myths, mysticisms, or ancient secrets explained here. As Sau-ling Cynthia Wong has argued, playing the native informant works well to garner mainstream American success for Asian American artists. But this drama doesn't play that game.

I would not dismiss the pernicious and continuing power of Orien-talism in American culture. But I think there is also something else going on here. The other two plays of this trilogy have appeared in anthologies edited by Roberta Uno and Houston herself. Houston and Uno may be exploiting the market's fondness for distant places and fantastic charac-ters. But I would also suggest that these two feminist anthologies have emphasized works that fit with feminist issues: the struggle of a daughter to free herself from the patriarchy (as her mother never could) and the conflicts, tensions, victories, and defeats within the lives of strong wom-en.

Of the three plays, *American Dreams* seems the most directly con-cerned with depicting the relationship between Houston's parents (re-named Setsuko and Creed Banks). The couple has more on-stage time to-gether in this play than in any of the others, and their union appears to drive and to resolve the play's action. The central conflict is the disruption and reintegration of the family caused by their interracial marriage. And yet, the interracial couple themselves prove to be dramatic catalysts rather than main protagonists. Setsuko and Creed's relationship is narrated through precisely the same verbal snapshots that appeared already in *Asa Ga Kimashita*, and that are inscribed again in *Tea*. The moment they first meet, when Creed's helmet rolls into the gutter and Setsuko recovers it, and her exclamation that she has never met a man "the color of soy sauce" function as mnemonic devices or relationship epithets (*American Dreams*, 41; *Tea*, 177). We see the importance of scripting a new, international, cross-racial tradition, and we note the ceremonious repetitions. But we don't see deeply into this relationship, or watch it develop. Creed and Setsuko aren't the characters given the most depth, conflict, or complexity in this play of their American immigration. On the contrary, they remain quite idealized. (They have only one fight, about whether it is okay to be completely honest with each other.) Their marriage functions in the same manner as the tag lines that comprise its history. It is the fixed landmark that inspires other narratives and navigations.

The difficulties, tensions, struggles, and reconciliations incurred by blending cultures, histories, languages, and social positions into one family are displaced from the marital union itself to the reaction of the family to that union. The dramatic focal point of the play is Freddie (Fredella) Banks, Creed's sister-in-law, who moves from racist animosity toward Setsuko to sympathetic and somewhat feminist identification with her. With its apparent emphasis on true love as conquering all, and use of sisterhood primarily to bolster troublesome marriages, *American Dreams* can be read as backing away from a radical feminist politics. I would argue, however, that the theoretical tools offered by Chicana theory give us an apparatus for seeing this play not as diffusing racial tension into tepid feminism, but rather as combining feminist, economic, and ethnic deconstructions of the American mythology.

'*American Dreams*' as a Drama of Immigrant Miscegenation

Well, we got rules
  —*American Dreams*

American Dreams continues in a tradition of dramas investigating the forging of a common American culture out of the multiple immigrant, racial, ethnic, and class backgrounds of its residents. I want to turn to two of those dramas that have influenced the way America has conceptualized itself in the popular media, in order to frame the argument that the historical and theoretical moment for *American Dreams* may in fact be now.

At the beginning of this century, America publicly imagined itself as the nation of manifest destiny, helpful bringer of democracy to the rest of the world, which would doubtless welcome it with open arms. The Roosevelt Corollary rationalized our right to police other nations under our sphere of influence; the Panama Canal promised that global efficiency would improve when America regally created new, United States–friendly nations. Simultaneously, America struggled with the clear inequalities of our society. The suffrage movements for women and for African Americans publicly insisted that this nation was still far from being a land of equality, and further, that slow progress toward an assimilationist and conservative parity was insufficient change. The same year that W. E. B. DuBois helped found the NAACP, Israel Zangwill's play *The Melting Pot* appeared in New York, promising a safely assimilationist solution to the challenges of a diverse society. Immigrants, the play demonstrated, were the staunchest upholders of America's founding ideals. Racism, as it operates in the play, is either a vestigial old-world value, or a demonstration of having strayed from the true American principles. Americanness, in *The Melting Pot*, becomes synonymous with fidelity to the dream of liberty for all. By virtue of such belief, immigrants melt into Americans, and America is purged of hypocrisy and hatred by its new, loving arrivals.

The Melting Pot chronicles the love affair of David Quixano, son of orthodox Jews who were killed in pogroms in Russia, and Vera Revendal, daughter of the anti-Semitic aristocracy who arranged the pogroms. Vera is a political reformer who happens to take piano lessons from David's uncle. They meet and fall in love. Despite the competition of millionaire Quincey Davenport, who also wants Vera's hand, and despite the opposition of both the Quixano and Revendal families, they choose to wed. Their union concludes the play with love and willpower conquering all opposition: "Cling to me [David says to Vera] till all these ghosts are exorcised, cling to me till our love triumphs over death" (26).[3]

Two generations later, love again promises to solve social stresses. In 1967, when America was in turmoil over the "Vietnam conflict," when the riots of Watts and the rhetoric of Black Power were inspiring reform and incurring backlash, Columbia Pictures produced *Guess Who's Coming to Dinner*, a movie that took head on the racist refrain of "yes, but would you want your daughter to marry one" by suggesting that, indeed, you would, because your son-in-law would then be Sidney Poitier. When stalwart liberals and legendary lovers Katharine Hepburn and Spencer Tracy come to recognize their own love's reflection in the love between their daughter and her black fiancé, "superficial" differences (skin color) give way before fundamental likeness (overtly, their shared emotional depth; implicitly, their similar educations, values, behaviors, and class mores). Even the future in-laws turn out to be mostly "like us." The movie solves the problem of prejudice by locating it in *pre-emptive* judgment. If we only wouldn't jump to unfounded conclusions about "their" differences, the movie argues, but would instead find out what "they" are really like, all would be well, and safely familiar. Tellingly, the play takes place entirely in the penthouse apartment of Hepburn and Tracy. We never see Poitier's family home. His family is depicted only as it enters, and fits into, the white family setting (not to say the "big house").

Both *The Melting Pot* and *Guess Who's Coming to Dinner* achieve their racial harmonies by downplaying class difference, by privileging personal emotions over social systems, and by posing ethnic conflict as a generational clash. In a manner worthy of Jo Marsh or Dorothea Brooke, Vera Revendal cares naught for wealth, when in poverty she can change the world. Poitier's character and his fiancée may not be equals in wealth (the visual echo between his mother and his in-laws' maid is remarked on during the film), but the two characters met at college, and of course the debonair Poitier is as unmistakably "top drawer" as his mother-in-law, played by Hepburn. In their emphasis on *love*, both plays suggest *choice* as the defining American condition. Zangwill's play, as Sollors has shown, makes American identity itself a matter of choice, not birth: "American ideals are not transmitted by descent, but have to be embraced afresh, even if that requires opposing the actual descendants of America's founding fathers" (Sollors 69). In defining "American" identity through consensual alignment with principles of tolerance and freedom rather than as a fact of birth, legacy, or heritage, *The Melting Pot* reverses the position of privileged Americanness from founding families to young immigrants. *Guess Who's Coming to Dinner* similarly promises that the younger generation will hold to the ideals that have lapsed or proven hypocritical in their predecessors. In doing so, they strip those principles of their historical context. The America thus claimed is the utopia of our national rhetoric, not the messier reality of our country's history.

One mechanism for this decontextualization is the recontainment of the drama within the biological family. The primary opposition in both *The Melting Pot* and *Guess Who's Coming to Dinner* does not in fact come from the "actual descendants of America's founding fathers" so much as it comes from the actual fathers (and mothers and aunts and grandparents) of the protagonists. In both *The Melting Pot* and *Guess Who's Coming to Dinner*, the battle is imagined as between the younger, progressive generation and their ossified elders. In *The Melting Pot*, the couple rejects their biological families (who have proved irredeemably racist), choosing instead the ideological lineage of American ideals. In *Guess Who's Coming to Dinner*, the elders are not rejected but redeemed. Tracy and Hepburn remember their own youthful idealism and bless the interracial couple as the legatees of their own experience.

American Dreams merges the immigrant narrative of Zangwill's play with the racial emphasis of *Guess Who's Coming to Dinner*, but resists their figuration of the enemy as the outdated patriarch. *American Dreams* exposes the less than warm reception that Creed and Setsuko find when they arrive in America. They expect to reunite happily with family and friends, and to settle into the home that Creed's brother Manny bought with money Creed sent stateside while stationed in Korea and Japan. Instead, they arrive to the racial hostility of a community that perceives Setsuko as an enemy "Jap," and to the slow discovery of Manny's betrayal: he spent the house money on a new car for himself and on motel stays with Creed's abandoned first fiancée. Both family and nation reject him: the army he fought for views his marriage with hostility and refuses his request for a New York assignment, stationing him instead in the ethnic homogeneity of Kansas.

Rather than idealizing its protagonists as the midwives of an improved future, nation, or race emerging from the corruptions of an effete past, *American Dreams* focuses on the conflicts within the present, rewriting the conflict from an oedipal battle into sibling rivalry. There are no fathers whatsoever in this play. The death of Creed, Manny, and Blue River Banks's mother is mentioned (a death Manny perceives as abandonment—she "left me" [23]), but the father's absence is so thorough as never to merit description. Setsuko's father committed suicide in the first play of the trilogy, but is given almost no discussion in this play (unlike her mother, whose death is a pivotal memory for Setsuko, and her sister, from whom she is estranged but hopes to reunite). Indeed, Houston alters her biographical history so that the drama stays within one generation. In 1959, when the Houston family arrived to live in the United States, Velina was already two years old.[4] In the play, the Bankses have no children. Setsuko is pregnant, but it doesn't yet show. Previous and next generations of the family remain abstract as memories or possibilities. The actors are generationally synchronic. There is no obvious top of a generational hierarchy to blame or to unite against. Instead, the siblings have to figure it out, make do, and get through their own mistakes.

By containing all the action within one generation, *American Dreams* resists the notion of inevitable historical progress that is implied by patriarchal rebellion narratives, in which the son establishes his right to power by his ability to overthrow his father, whose overthrow simultaneously proves his own obsolescence. When immigrant narratives are told in this structure, the process of Americanization becomes implicitly a narrative of progress, reinforcing the division of the world into "old" and "new" that posits America as a cornucopia of modern plenty, and scripts the rest of the world as doddering under the weight of premodern traditions. Such implicitly imperialist and Orientalizing narratives, however, do little to account for the *ongoingness* of American racism, classism, and xenophobia. Houston's play holds the present generation firmly to account. Hypocritical democracy is not the signal to retire in Houston's play. Instead, it's business as usual.

American Dreams reveals the contemporary xenophobia and racism that drove military/governmental officials to put all the soldiers who married Japanese wives "in the same place" (38) (read *in their place*): Creed's commanding officer tells him that "no harm meant, but if anything you've gone and made yourself twice a nigger. … Keep to yourself. … We warned you. …We had your best interests at heart" (39). Larry, the homeless man who befriends Setsuko, delivers a history lesson that reminds the audience that America's long-standing official policy is one of containment and erasure of the Other:

> Let me break it down for you, baby. It's a white man's country. They stole it from the Indians. … They put people like you—Japanese Americans—in concentration camps. … Just herded 'em up like buffalo … like Indians. White people don't like somebody and they treat 'em like animals. (26–27)

While Houston's drama thus continues in the tradition of *The Melting Pot* and *Guess Who* in that its plot turns on the familial turmoil and social ideals/hypocrisies unearthed by interracial marriage, Houston's story insistently locates this turmoil in the context of historical racism, economic class difference, and factionalization within allegiance. She never lets "the Man" off the hook, but she also investigates prejudice among could-be equals, showing a complex matrix of personal grudges looking for categorical solutions that fit individual agendas shaped by systematically inculcated desires for wealth, beauty, and security.

As Houston draws them, most of Freddie and Manny's actions against Setsuko and Creed stem from their jealousy, and it is primarily the jealousy of those with thwarted desire for those with requited desire. Manny is jealous of Creed for being "everyone's favorite" since they were boys, and Freddie is explicitly jealous of all the women her husband finds more desirable than she and implicitly jealous of the mutual love between Creed and Setsuko, who married despite opposition, in contrast to her own marriage of economic convenience. Both of these jealousies are compounded by economic jealousy, as Creed asks Manny to manage the large sum Creed has saved during a time when Manny's accounts are turning red. Their anger finds an outlet in the racial scapegoat. If Creed has betrayed his race, he is less deserving of fidelity. If he has married the enemy of his nation, he is less deserving of his home(land). If he disregards family loyalty in order to selfishly satisfy his own desires, he cannot condemn Manny for doing the same. None of these is jealousy of the powerful by a usurper, nor is any the conceited territorialism of the haves against ambitious have-nots. They are instead emblematic of the dynamic Houston's characters and her play itself repeatedly enact: displacement.

Race to Gender

Yeah, she's a Sister
—*American Dreams*

Freddie begins the play staunchly allied with her husband, Manny, in their racist resentment of Setsuko, and ends the play aligned with Setsuko, hoping to stop Manny's sexual philanderings. This is a shift not only in the object of allegiance—from husband to sister-in-law—but in the subject at issue—from racism to sexism. In some ways, this is a repressive displacement, in which tension is corralled into a safe and familiar battle between the sexes, thus leaving gender as an unchallenged, fundamental category of difference, to which racial differences are subordinate. But in other ways, as Freddie moves from her belief that Japanese arrivals will mean that for "the first time in years, Negroes ain't ... at the bottom of the heap" to her awareness that she, too, is a prisoner of war in her home, the play enacts a subtle critique of the interweavings of racial and sexual oppression (2).

Throughout the course of the play, Freddie becomes sympathetic to Setsuko in precisely the same measure that she becomes disaffected with her own marriage. Her conversion begins in a moment of bonding over the fact that their husbands have gone out drinking: "Get used to it child: Colored or yellow, we're still women, and they're still men" (16). Setsuko's cousin Fumiko respectfully uses this wedge to pry Freddie's heart open further: "It's hard enough being a woman and a wife, without having to deal with all the culture differences. Surely you know that, Freddie-San" (44). The next scene brings those wifely hardships to the fore, as Blue River bursts into the house with the news that Freddie's husband has been in a drunken car accident with his former mistress. Freddie comes to see her similarity with the other women as more important than their differences.

This realization is helped along by the fact that her husband tends to treat women as interchangeable objects. Throughout the play, Manny's sexual attractions have less to do with the women they are directed toward than with other, indirect motivations. He married Freddie because of her family connections: "He married her, and the business," as Creed tells Setsuko (9). He chases Alexis, Creed's former girlfriend, in order to prove himself to be as desirable as his older brother. When Creed is away in D.C., Manny again tries to usurp his brother's place, this time in sexual liaison with Setsuko: "Give Uncle Manfred a great big kiss. C'mon. Gimme some sugar" (38). Through Manny's repetitive attempts to displace his brother, Houston charts the construction of male desire and fraternal connection through the competition for women who serve as trophies. The objectification emerges from subtlety to directness when Manny chummily bonds with his brother over his plunder: "I can see why you married her. That is one fine fortune cookie" (13). Creed, true to principle as always, immediately chides his brother for failing to "think of her as a human being," but even his annoyance is directed at the racial slur, not the sexual objectification: "Don't think of her as Japanese" (13). (This is an unusual slip for Creed, who is usually quite attentive to the multiple layerings of identity, and resists the efforts of both Freddie and Alexis to make him identify as "Negro" rather than as of mixed heritage.)

Creed apparently doesn't see what the play goes on to make quite clear: that the women's racial position and gender position are inextricable, because so alike. In keeping with the theories of Edward Said and the plays of David Henry Hwang,[5] Houston's drama demonstrates that racial hierarchies are always gendered. But unlike Said and Hwang, Houston does not use this layering to demonstrate that non-whites are rendered effeminate, but to show that women are imprisoned.

In the climactic moment of the play, Manny locks Setsuko and Fumiko in the bedroom, calling them "prisoners of war" (49). Inspired by his conquest, he returns to Freddie in excitement: "Come on, baby. We got a party tonight," he says, as he pulls her close and "puts money between her breasts" (52). His frustrated sexual attraction for Setsuko is vented through demonstration of territorial control; his demonstration of territorial control arouses sexual energy. Having locked Setsuko away "for [her own] good" (50), he turns that sexual energy toward his wife, who is as trapped as her sister-in-law in this domestic arrangement. Freddie, less than turned on by this scenario, links his sexist behavior to racial oppression: "you treat me, your sister, and your in-laws like we supposed to be your slaves" (49). Her reading demotes his victorious rhetoric of national security to the dishonorable status of slave capture.

While she thus links race and gender, Freddie's attack does not mention sexual desire. It is Manny who adds this piece to the puzzle, turning it against Freddie. He picks up the thread of her argument, that he treats women as objects, but uses it only to diminish Freddie's object value: "you're one disgusting specimen of woman-hood. Cow. An elephant. A hippo. Texas" (49). Manny's catalog of insults places Freddie in the categories of domestic property (cow), or lumbering wildness (elephant, hippo). Like the trapped Setsuko, Freddie becomes in these metaphors something to be caged, and something inhuman, Other. The final metaphor, Texas, denies her even consciousness, turning her into territory underfoot.

Their fight is, of course, a variation on the rhetorical language game the "dozens," which is supposed to divert threats into language, thus diffusing and dispersing them. But it doesn't work in this case. Freddie won't play. Manny's insults put him beyond the pale of forgiveness. She rejects the racial bond she shared with Manny at the start. She has moved into another discursive realm—Setsuko's—where language is direct, straightforward, and unfailingly "polite" even when angry. She says nothing. Rather than ritualizing their conflict, shifting it into an even match between two discursive giants (Freddie has already demonstrated her talent at "reading" others), this incident functions in a different ritual: as final, unforgivable exposure of previously repressed conflict. Manny's last insult, "Texas," carries echoes of fierce independence, and inspires a Lone Star revolt in Freddie. Refusing to become downtrodden, domesticated, caged property, or plunder, she becomes instead Ibsen's Nora, and walks out. Door slam and all.

But Houston's play doesn't end where Ibsen's did. The play continues, adding two crucial elements. Freddie finds a community of support in the other women, and she plans to use that support to reform Manny. Although she has moved out of the house at the end of the play, her visits to Blue River and Fumiko will be temporary. She hasn't given up on Manny, but plans to enroll him in AA and bowling programs. This is a very different basis for hope from the familial model offered in either *Guess Who's Coming to Dinner* or *Tea*. Far from David Quixano's "Cling to me till our love triumphs" is Freddie's awareness that "I love that no good brother of yours, but that just ain't enough anymore" (59). No one is here recalled to his best and former self, and no one is completely excluded. The model of the devoted and adoring couple battling all others has been changed.

In her emphasis on tense allegiances, Houston raises questions about solidarity and about activism and about our bases for each. The play seems to refute what it knows—or to reveal that even when we know what we know, we persist in letting it continue, because we don't necessarily want to give it up. Freddie has clearly realized that Manny is not her equal in their partnership, and that she receives much more emotional sustenance from her women relatives than from him. And yet her allegiance with the women is temporary—she may come visit, but the women all return to their husbands and partners, separated from one another geographically by their primary allegiance to their romantic relationships. Freddie, too, plans not to leave her marriage, but to try to reform her husband. The play comes close to saying that Freddie's only option is revolt, but then shifts to reform. At least since Audre Lorde posed the question in 1984, however, feminists have been wondering if reform can in fact occur from within. If "wife" is the label of oppression that united Freddie, Fumiko, and Setsuko, then can Freddie use that identity to reform Manny? When Freddie announces to her friends that she's going to sign Manny up for her bowling league, their telling response is that "if it's a women's league, he'll be there" (59), suggesting inevitable resumption of the cycle rather than the possibility of lasting reform. Displacement of the play's racial tensions into marital discord seems to contain them within a familiar structure. Sexism, the play seems to imply, is a necessary and permanent evil.

One could argue that the play's ending thus returns all characters to the status quo, that the women's solidarity will only solidify their ability to cope with their existing situation, never fundamentally alter it. This is perhaps ominously foreshadowed when, despite her protest against Manny's imprisonment of Setsuko and Fumiko, Freddie is unable to stop it. She can only tell Creed what has happened when he returns home. Setsuko's closing solution, to "live Japanese" in her own home, to draw her own national border at the threshold of her home, parallels this accommodationist solution. Both women end by trying to create some space of their own, within the given structures of their lives.

But such a reading would fix in place relationships and struggles that this play shows to be elusive and ever-moving. The play displaces miscegenation anxiety about Creed's marriage onto fidelity anxiety about Manny's marriage. It displaces Freddie's rejection of Setsuko with her temporary rejection of Manny. And it displaces identification by race with identification by position, and then with identification by affection. In doing so, it may never resolve power inequities, but in emphasizing their very shiftiness, Houston reveals a strategy for resistance.

Home Sweet Homelessness

> Waiting in the streets for ... the American Dream
> —*American Dreams*

American Dreams opens on the scene of Freddie ripping to shreds the Japanese flag Setsuko has sent as a gift. This beginning emphasizes immediately the violence with which contests over nation, identity, and territory will be fought. It also immediately draws audience attention to Freddie as the central figure through whom these tensions will be explored. With this move, Houston's play could be seen as repeating the all too common exploitation of the black woman to ground and explore racial issues.[6] It has often been noted, recently by Jamaica Kincaid, that "everyone in every place needs a boundary; in America the boundary is the phrase 'I am not black'" (73). Within the family conflict, it is Freddie, self-proclaimedly "Negro," who holds the racial lines firm, while Blue River, whose name linguistically recalls the family's Native American maternity, is much more tolerant of racial blurrings. Certainly, whether it is through the blackface of Al Jolson in *Jazz Singer* or the walls covered with posters of black jazz and blues singers in Frank Chin's *Chickencoop Chinaman,* immigrant dramas have long figured their encounter with American culture through the popularized images of black America, defining their own Americanization through and against these images.

But I would argue that Houston is in fact revising rather than perpetuating this use of "black" culture to mark off racial boundaries. In the play, it is Setsuko who appears as the Other that provokes emphatic boundary drawing and resistance to strict definitions. Freddie welcomes the chance to relinquish her position "at the bottom of the heap": "Let them Japs slide on over to the US of A" (2). Houston's treatment of this issue is complex. Freddie uses her disdain for "Japs" to elevate herself in the social hierarchy. Creed's commanding officer tells him that to align himself *with* a Japanese is to make himself "twice a nigger" (39). In neither case is blackness the defining boundary of Americanness. Freddie finds an Other enemy to document her American loyalty, and the officer turns the label "nigger" into a name for the lowest position in the American hierarchy, simultaneously separating it from race, since what makes Creed *more* "nigger" is his marriage to someone not black at all, and also racializing the caste system in this choice of label.

Setsuko's presence repeatedly provokes all kinds of identity specification and explanation. It provides the opportunity for Creed to expound his "crayon box" philosophies, as Freddie calls them (5), about multiplicity rather than simple dichotomies, and it allows Alexis to refute the idealism of such rainbow rhetoric in a "world [that] is colored and white, and ain't no room for nobody else" (35). Setsuko is the disruptive third term. As symbol, she provokes declarations in others. Freddie's flag ripping is thus as much about putting Setsuko at the heart of the battle as it is about making Freddie the battleground.

As the opening setting, the flag-tearing scene also revises another trope of immigrant drama, the "ethnic room" in which such dramas are set.[7] Rather than defining the immigrant space as having one wall devoted to artifacts of the "homeland" and the other to symbols of the United States, Houston makes her immigrants literally homeless. The symbol of Setsuko's homeland is in tatters, as is her nation, and her ostensibly purchased new home in America is only a dream. Home isn't here created as the space between two boundary cultures, with the characters traversing back and forth. Neither a buffer, a welcome haven, nor a space of manifest destiny, the domestic space Houston creates is one of historical conquest, layered construction, and heavy policing. Home is *la frontera*, the place that doesn't exist except in the moment of definitional struggle. It is only in the moments of delineating the boundary that the identity of the home comes into existence. Theories of *la frontera* provide a critical context that make feminism, ethnicity, and identity inextricable from one another.

Resignification of the mythically central "American frontier" as *"la frontera,"* a contested borderland, seeks primarily to do three things: 1) To "make history present," particularly the "legacy of conquest," as José David Saldívar and Raphael Perez-Torres suggest, spotlighting the linguistic, cultural, and nationalistic struggle that America has ignored on our continent. 2) To show that "foreign relations do not take place outside the boundaries of America, but instead constitute American nationality," as Amy Kaplan puts it, resisting American isolationism and self-defined uniqueness (16). And 3) To destabilize our sense of national security. Gloria Anzaldúa promises that to survive the borderlands is to become a dangerous crossroads, inspiring Chela Sandoval's answer to postmodern cynicism: the oppositional consciousness formed in the "guerrilla training of daily life for women of color"(15).

That Houston's play makes history present is readily apparent. As Setsuko learns what America is, she learns it as a history of radical erasures of the native population, and incarcerations of arbitrarily perceived enemies (Larry tells her about the "concentration camps" for Americans of Japanese ancestry and the "herdings of Native Americans"). She learns America as a nation in which those with power (policemen and commanding officers) use that power to "wash the streets" of populations they dislike (Larry is constantly "moved along" and Setsuko and Creed themselves are banished reservation-like to the prairie). And she learns to see America as a place where those without power often try to gain some by further oppressing any who might have less (Freddie's hope to move up a rung by stepping on "Japs" is echoed by the refusal of neighborhood Latino and African American storekeepers to serve Setsuko). Both the legacy and the ongoing project of conquest are everywhere apparent.

In regard to the second goal, Setsuko herself personifies American nationality being constituted through foreign relations. Defeated national enemy, displaced person, or willing immigrant, Setsuko struggles to define herself and her new nation. Not sojourning, seeking amnesty, or disenfranchised, Setsuko enters America apparently doubly endorsed by institutions: she is a *military wife*. Foreign relations here constitute not only nationality but family. The official structures of nation and family, however, do not accommodate her position. Setsuko's delegitimation as "war bride" linguistically keeps the marriage permanently unconsummated ("bride," not "wife") and frames it with conflict, chaos, and plunder rather than the apparatus of state ("war," not "military").

Setsuko, deciding that despite reconciliation with Freddie she doesn't much care for America, resolves to recreate her former country within this new nation: "I must hold on to my culture. I must be able to live Japanese, even in the middle of this Kansas where we are going," she tells Creed (58). He responds with the promise that their new home can become her displaced homeland: "As soon as we move into a home, I'll start taking off my shoes for you." Setsuko hopes to recreate her homeland in the midst of Kansas, drawing a replacement boundary to resist her displacement. Yet the need to draw this boundary emphasizes the severity of her lostness more than the security of her oasis. Her need to protect her

identity by policing its physical borderland is a fantasy the play deconstructs by pairing Setsuko's military-enforced move to her new home with
the policeman's invitation to Larry, the homeless man, to come to his
"home": "I tell you Larry, why don't you come on over to my house for
awhile ... a warm, safe cell" (61). As the structures of the state crack down
inflexibly on deviance, *American Dreams* offers its most pointed critique.
The final line of the play leaves Setsuko, still confined within her in-law's
house, looking out for Larry. When Creed asks her who she seeks, she answers, resonantly, "An American" (61). Not the inheritor of American
ideals, not the safe neighbor, this quintessential American is the sign of
permanent displacement.

By sustaining conflict as a permanent element of the domestic configuration, by demonstrating the constant policing necessary to maintain
boundaries, and by pairing vagrancy and institutionalization as the quintessential American alternatives, Houston's play leaves the American
dream "waiting in the streets." Home is not safe. And it is not where the
heart is. Homes are POW camps, prison cells, and reminders of displacement. Policed, bounded, lost. This constant displacement has the
effect of deconstructing any idea of a recoverable center.

Like *The Melting Pot* and *Guess Who's Coming to Dinner*, *American
Dreams* synecdochally figures national tensions and conflicts through the
domestic family. Like *Asa Ga Kimashita* and *Tea*, *American Dreams* uses
the family and community structure to expose bigotry and sexism, and to
emphasize the particular animosities and support between women.
Unique among them, *American Dreams* refuses to resolve its struggles or
to redeem its characters. It leaves them, and us, finally, and provocatively,
unsettled.

While Houston's play reveals that the American dream is eternally un-
reachable, I wish to argue that the time for *American Dreams* is now. The
play has been shadowed by its sisters, against whom its feminism can appear to fall short. Rather than enacting the successful rebellion of the
daughter, or the complex strengths of independent women, *American
Dreams* seems to fall back on the "behind the throne" role for women as
the reformers of men. But the insights and tools that Chicana theory has
brought to prominence insistently unite feminist issues with questions of
nation and ethnicity formation. With these tools, we can more clearly
read *American Dreams* as both a feminist drama and a drama of immigration and miscegenation. Thus seen, *American Dreams* updates the visions
of *The Melting Pot* and *Guess Who's Coming to Dinner*. No longer promis-

ing that a younger generation will redeem the errors of its predecessors, and in so doing reinforce the predecessors' original values, *American Dreams* poses a more threatening critique. The creation of home and nation are shown in this play to be inseparable from prison making, fantasy, and betrayal. The redemptive promise Houston offers lies not in the reclamation of traditional domestic values, but in refusing to draw bounded identities. The community of women who support and challenge one another in this play does not fix a new and strict identity group. These women perceive momentary patterns. They see significance in their arrangement, drawing lines of connection rather than boundaries. American identity in this play is not only a matter of consent, but of perception. It is in the interpretive connections—seeing the lines of the design—that individuals become communities. The constellation thus produced is ephemeral. Its lines are at once affectionate ties, imprisoning bars, exclusive boundaries, and opportunities for intersection. And they are constantly being redrawn.

Notes

My deepest thanks to Gregory Eiselein, Linda Brigham, Melinda Gough, Larry Rodgers, and Rachel Rubin for their advice and encouragement in writing this article. And to Josephine Lee and Norman Fedder for directing me to Houston's work.

1. This anecdote was related in an introduction to "A Native American Tale at the Racial Harmony Walk with Oral Storytelling," Manhattan, KS, Oct. 5, 1997.

2. See Yasuko Kawarazaki, "Women's Struggles in Velina Hasu Houston's *Tea*," *AALA* 2 (1995): 47–55; Masami Usui, "Japan's Post-War Democratization: Agrarian Reform and Women's Liberation in Velina Hasu Houston's *Asa Ga Kimashita* (Morning Has Broken)," *AALA* 5 (1998): 11–25; and Masami Usui, "Voices from the 'Netherworld': Japanese International Brides in Velina Hasu Houston's *Tea*," *Chu Shikoku Studies in American Literature* 34 (June 1998): 45–64.

3. See Werner Sollors's detailed discussion of the way this play moves identity from a matter of lineage to a matter of will in *Beyond Ethnicity*. Sollors further examines the revisions and transformations of Zangwill's "melting pot" metaphor in subsequent dramas, pageants, and other cultural rhetorics.

4. See introduction to "Tea" in *Unbroken Thread*, 156.

5. See especially Hwang's *M. Butterfly* (1988; New York: Plume, 1989) and Said's *Orientalism* (New York: Vintage, 1978).

6. My thanks to Valerie Hernandez-Bell for helping me to see this connection.

7. See Werner Sollors's description and tracing of the prevalence of the "ethnic room" in *Beyond Ethnicity*.

Works Cited

Anzaldúa, Gloria. *Borderlands/La Frontera: The New Mestiza*. New York: Consortium Books, [1987] 1999.

Guess Who's Coming to Dinner. 1967. Directed by Stanley Kramer. Columbia Pictures.

Houston, Velina Hasu. *American Dreams*. Unpublished manuscript. Copies can be obtained through the author's agent: Ms. Merrily Kane, The Artists Agency, Los Angeles, Calif. Quoted by permission of the author.

———. *Asa Ga Kamashita: The Politics of Life—Four Plays by Asian American Women*, ed. Velina Hasu Houston. Philadelphia: Temple University Press, 1993.

Kaplan, Amy. "Left Alone with America." In *Cultures of US Imperialism*, ed. Amy Kaplan and Donald E. Pease. Durham: Duke University Press, 1993.

Kincaid, Jamaica. "The Little Revenge from the Periphery." *Transition* 7, no. 1 (1998): 73.

Lorde, Audre. "Can the Master's Tools Dismantle the Master's House?" In *Sister Outsider*. Freedom, Calif.: Crossing Press, 1984.

Perez-Torres, Raphael. *Movements in Chicano Poetry: Against Margins, Against Myths*. New York: Cambridge University Press, 1995.

Saldívar, José David. *Border Matters: Remapping American Cultural Studies*. Berkeley: University of California Press, 1997.

Sandoval, Chela. "U.S. Third World Feminism: The Theory and Method of Oppositional Consciousness in the Postmodern World." *Genders* 10 (1991): 1–24.

Sollors, Werner. *Beyond Ethnicity: Consent and Descent in American Culture*. Cambridge: Oxford University Press, 1989.

Uno, Roberta. Introduction to *Tea*. In *Unbroken Thread: An Anthology of Plays by Asian American Women*, ed. Roberta Uno. Amherst: University of Massachusetts Press, 1993.

Wong, Sau-ling Cynthia. "'Sugar Sisterhood' Situating the Amy Tan Phenomenon." In *The Ethnic Canon,* ed. David Palumbo-Liu.. Minneapolis: University of Minnesota Press, 1995.

Zangwill, Israel. *The Melting Pot*. New York: Macmillan, [1909] 1924.

"The Hybrids and the Cosmopolitans"
Race, Gender, and Masochism in Diana Chang's 'The Frontiers of Love'

In 1956, Diana Chang's novel *The Frontiers of Love* became the first novel published in the United States by a Chinese American (the next two were Louis Chu's *Eat a Bowl of Tea* [1961] and Shawn Wong's *Homebase* [1979]). Chang, the daughter of a Chinese father and a Chinese American mother, was born in New York but spent much of her childhood in China, leaving at the end of World War II and later attending Barnard College. Her first novel is a protofeminist bildungsroman centered primarily on three young Eurasian residents of Shanghai under Japanese occupation.

Chang's protagonist, Sylvia Chen, and her sophisticate friends live in Shanghai during the closing months of World War II. Like Chang, Sylvia grew up in China, the daughter of an American mother and a Chinese father. Her friend, Mimi Lambert, and eventual lover, Feng Huang, are also Anglo-Chinese. Even her white friends (Swiss and Irish) occupy a marginal "neutral" status that serves to justify their presence in Japanese-occupied Shanghai. The specific political and temporal setting of the novel in an international city under eight years of military occupation evokes a "dilatory yet tense, superficially pleasure-loving yet paranoid intensity."[1]

This novel provides an interesting counterpoint to much of the recent critical theory regarding the cultural production of mixed blood writers in that much of such theory is grounded in a Spivakian assumption that such writers adopt the voice of the dominant culture in an attempt to speak from the subject position of a subaltern.[2] This model cannot easily be applied to Chang's novel because the Chinese were never as "colonized" by Western forces as, for example, India under British rule. Furthermore, insofar as the trope of the search for an (absent) mother has come to be associated with a recovery of a subject's subaltern homeland, this model likewise is turned on its head in Chang's novel to the extent that two of the three significant mother figures are American or English, and fully present rather than absent.[3] There is indeed an element of a thwarted nostalgia for an America the protagonist can hardly remember and did not love, but the driving force of a search for "home" is mapped entirely onto Chinese terrain.

The Frontiers of Love fully appropriates a Western mode of discourse— specifically, American romantic fiction—to a quest for selfhood. As Mimi's cynical Aunt Julia remarks, "most people in love are just … trying to rid themselves of themselves, to acquire a new self" (173).[4] Sylvia in particular valiantly attempts to wrest the components of selfhood from her environment and construct one for herself. In one sense the narrator's preoccupation with selfhood seems very Western; the entire group of characters privileged by both wealth and class seem to measure themselves against a notion of self as "a web of privileged characteristics [in which] all 'I's' are rational, agentive, unitary … effectually what Spivak has termed the 'straight white Christian man of property.'"[5] Thus Feng sees everyone as "acutely imprisoned" in his own self (102). Larry (Irish) says of Robert (Swiss) that "Lushes have an urge toward transcendence. They desire a release from self-hood" (113). Robert, however, seems "unreal to himself," saying, in a singularly apt self-description of the postcolonial dilemma of the white man of property, "I'm a window standing in the middle of a ruin." To Robert, it seems that Mimi is the one who is "real, legitimate, certified, branded with a hallmark" (129). But Sylvia, "marked" with the same ethnicity as Mimi, is "haunted by doubt of her own existence. She felt a fraud, an illusion, where *she* should have been" (127). None of the characters seem, at least initially, to have any notion of self as having any potential other than rational and unitary. Sylvia eventually makes some progress toward accepting a heterogeneous concept of selfhood.

The problem of masochism stems from the problem of selfhood for the mixed race characters. Often expressed in terms of a recurring motif of blindness and insight, the masochism issue is explored within an ambience of impending doom that seems to pervade the novel. This overall threat must be read in terms of the novel's specific political and temporal setting in cosmopolitan Shanghai, crossroads of East and West, at one of the most significant political moments of the twentieth century.

Consider first of all the determinative force of racial identification in the context of the end of the Second World War. Spatially situated a world apart from Auschwitz, Chang's characters nevertheless experience more than mere existential anxiety as to their racial and national identities. Sylvia's mother, an American free from internment only because she is married to a Chinese, is required to wear a numbered red arm band. Racial identities are inscribed on bodies to varying extents, and their implications are situational; they change with the setting. The potential danger of such racial or national ambiguity is highlighted in the scene at the midpoint of the novel during which the occupying Japanese soldiers have arrested Sylvia, Feng, Mimi, and Larry Casement, who, having heard the rumor of Japanese defeat, are out after curfew on August 4, 1945; readers of the 1950s would recognize this date as two days prior to the dropping of the bombs on Hiroshima and Nagasaki. .

Larry Casement is Irish and the only one of the main characters who is not wealthy, a white colonial subject entitled to neutral status under the terms of the Geneva convention. When the guard vindictively tears up his identification, Larry is left with the physical demeanor (the appearance and accent) of a British enemy national and is thus subject to incarceration in one of the internment camps for the duration of the war. The entire scene with the Japanese officer evokes the darkly comic caricature of the German commandant of the prisoner of war camp in *Stalag 17*, the 1953 film later used as the basis for the television series *Hogan's Heroes*. The subtle ridicule of the Japanese soldiers throughout this scene evokes a whistling-though-the-graveyard tone that makes sense only in terms of the reader's foreknowledge that the Japanese are about to lose the war.

"'You are Chinese!' the Japanese asked wonderingly, glancing back at Feng's photograph on the certificate" (118), and sends Feng off to one side. Feng, though he has Asian features, has earlier been described as large and muscular, with brown hair and freckles. Next, the officer interrogates Mimi, whose father is Australian and mother Chinese, both dead.

> "You are English?" he barked. "Yes or no?"
> "Yes—no, I'm Australian."
> "Why not in internment camp?" he asked, sucking in his breath.
> "I—my aunt, she happens to be Chinese. She is my guardian."
> "Ah-so. You are foreigner, but too young. You are Chinese, however not exactly so."
> "But my father was Australian," she said firmly.

He waved her to the corner where the foreigners stood. "The Chinese look like white devils tonight," he said to everyone at large, but only his simpering adjutant tittered. (118–119)

When Sylvia lies to the officer that she had been riding with Feng, he tells her to "go with the other white Chinese" (119). So the Japanese officer has classified Mimi as a foreigner and Sylvia as Chinese, though the narrator has described them both as physically unmarked: "[Sylvia] could no more look Chinese than Mimi. Their eyes were brown; their hair, too, and turned reddish in the sunlight. And their exoticness lay in the truth that they seemed to have no racial identity at all" (12). "At their best," the narrator says, "half-breeds who had Chinese blood in them had fine features, thin skins and eyes that caught the light in a blaze" (144).

As "exotics" with seemingly "no racial identity at all," Sylvia and Mimi have some wherewithal to construct their racial identity as they please. They are limited, however, by the historical contingency of this significant moment in the history of Shanghai and of Asia. They are also marked by their individual histories and even more so by their gender. Mimi performs the discourse of a prefeminist Americanized passive aggression to a perfection that founders on the shoals of her racial identity: her Swiss lover finds her ultimately unmarriageable due to her Chinese ancestry. The figure of Mimi serves to articulate the masochistic position of the raced woman vis-à-vis Western civilization: we last see her being ravished up against the wall of a church. Sylvia, on the other hand, overcomes this somewhat stereotypical role.

In her introduction to the new edition of *The Frontiers of Love* (1994), Shirley Geok-lin Lim focuses on the postcolonial ramifications of the novel and argues that it advocates "the operation of feeling in the politics of identity ... a displacement of the policed identities of nationalities and races that produce the horrors of the Second World War" (xxi), policed identities, in Lim's view, replicated in the nationalist "strategic essentialism" (xix) that Feng pursues in joining the communists. In Lim's interpretation Sylvia achieves a greater, though incomplete, "resolution" of identity than Feng, whose essentialism costs him "a loss of feeling for others, an impotency of the self" (xx). But how is it that Sylvia successfully negotiates such a construction of subjectivity and Mimi does not? Lim attributes Sylvia's success in resisting Mimi's "replication of patriarchally inscribed sexuality" to "the grace of intelligence" (xviii), which Mimi lacks, being the "least fully drawn" of the main characters (xiv);

Lim sees in this character a repetition of the "stereotyping of the Eurasian as the subject of conflicting race identities, resulting in self-hatred and sexual confusion and laxity" (xiii).

It is true that Mimi replicates the literary convention of the raced female martyr to the progress of Western civilization. In the context of American literary depictions of Asian women she is recognizable as a sort of fallen Madame Butterfly, a trope with a long history in Anglo-American literature, dating back to John Smith's story of Pocahontas offering her life for his and the "tragic mulatto" figure of eighteenth- and nineteenth-century drama. But in drawing out the counterpoint between the fate of Mimi and the fate of Sylvia, Chang does more than merely state and refute the stereotype. She explores the dynamics of masochism in the context of both gender and mixed racial identity (though the male character Feng also has masochistic thoughts) and maps the terrain of selfhood in terms of space and vision: seeing and being seen.

One of the important ways in which Sylvia and Mimi construct their identity is through their clothing. Mimi "would not have dreamed of wearing a Chinese dress. 'There are enough people in this country who *have* to wear them,' she'd say" (12). Sylvia's clothing is described in the novel's opening passage, a sensual scene describing Sylvia emerging from a bath and lying down wet on a straw mat in her room before carefully dressing for a party:

> The trouble with Chinese dresses [was that] they expressed a kind of aristocratic demureness. But foreign clothes didn't suit her entirely either. Their full skirts seemed to stand out from her, making her slighter than she was, orphaned in them. I shall have to design my own kind of clothes, a modified Chinese dress, she thought. I shall do that when the war is over. (4)

This discourse of the body and its appearance permeates the novel. The use of clothing to define subjectivity has been one of the more significant forms of agency for women in patriarchal cultures, though, as in the "demureness" Sylvia dislikes, the patriarchal authority is often replicated in the apparel.[6]

In their choice of clothing described in the first pages of the novel, Mimi's blindness is already being set in contrast to Sylvia's insight in imagining new possibilities. But there is more involved here than mere superior intelligence on Sylvia's part.

Mimi positions herself in terms of the male gaze to negotiate status and her own desire. Whereas Sylvia imagines a new dress design more in terms of her own image of herself, Mimi's self-expression, verbal and nonverbal, her perceptions and desires, are feminized in a way to make her most desirable to men: "Long ago, when she was twelve, she had studied herself in the mirror and decided how to toss her hair back, how to cross her impeccable legs, how to look into a boy's eyes for the maximum results" (33). In the Freudian theory casually discussed at parties by the characters in the novel, such manipulations of the male gaze began even earlier in childhood: "the active aims—to look, know, and master— are reversed for the girl so that their predominant expression becomes passive. At an early age, she is encouraged to prefer being looked *at*, not knowing, and being mastered."[7] Mimi is attempting "self-conscious subversion that mimes cultural expectations of femininity to achieve the protagonist's freedom."[8] She situates her stance as "different from" men to achieve her own desires, or what she perceives as her own desires: to negotiate status in a man's world through her sexuality: "Until him, she had not known she was essentially homeless. Now she knew that by loving him and being loved by him, she was assured of status for herself and a 'society' to which to belong" (74). In her sexual relationship with Robert Bruno, Mimi is not invariably passive. Sometimes

> she felt maddened as though with hate. Since he was so elusive most of the time, she was satisfied only then, deeply appeased, almost as though she had killed him, and so had him forever. ...
>
> Other times, she dared him, provoked him to a male chauvinism, so that he would conquer her, so that she would 'die' beneath his arrogance. 'Do what you will with me!' she had cried one afternoon. ... He had taken her violently—as she had so intensely willed and yet so passively received. Her utter capitulation had felt like her greatest triumph, and she knew that it was Robert, the victor, who had been lovingly used. (73–74)

Mimi is more than the mere stereotypical fallen woman of women's sentimental literature in terms of her refinement of the manipulative strategies of passive aggression. The plot itself also resists the stereotype in that Sylvia becomes sexually active without befalling a similar fate. The author utilizes both characters to explore the masochistic theme, moving from Mimi's conscious adoption of the role of the passive exhibitionist to Sylvia's self-conscious surrender to the role of the ravished:

> "Kiss me!" she ordered.
> He pulled her abruptly against his hard body. Predatory and fierce, he kissed her, holding her arms pinned to her sides. She felt blinded, sucked

away into a simple universe. His hands dug into her arms, made her a victim at her own crucifixion. ...

She wanted to die, to die under the calvary of his body, to pass away, out of herself. (147)

Later, after Sylvia ends their relationship, she "did not want to kill" her desire for him: "She wondered how masochistic she was being, enjoying her own pain. It seemed to her that perhaps people created their own pain because only when in pain were they truly sure that they were alive. 'I hurt, therefore I am'" (235).

For Freud, female masochism arose from guilt over the young girl's fantasies of incest with her father.[9] But Michelle Masse's critique of masochism in the gothic novel acknowledges an understanding that "the intertwining of love and pain is not natural and does not originate in the self: women are taught masochism through fiction and culture, and masochism's causes are external and real." She argues that masochism "can further individual psychic survival when pressed into the service of a besieged ego."[10] Mimi and Sylvia, though members of a privileged class, are "besieged" by their own uncertainties about their identities. This is where, in this text, the "double consciousness," that is, racial ambivalence and internal conflict, intersects with the problem of gender. Pain, for both women, comes to signify penance for their guilt. For whose sins does Sylvia desire to be crucified?

Sylvia's articulation of her perception of her besieged ego can be traced throughout the text. At the end of the first chapter, "She was guilty—she was guilty of not knowing who she was," that is, American or Chinese. "And her own existence seemed to mean nothing to herself or the world. She felt forsaken" (19). Later, with Feng,

she couldn't be sure of anything, not even of herself. She knew suddenly that she had always been haunted by doubt of her own existence. She felt a fraud, an illusion, where *she* should have been. And if she wasn't there, how could he make love to her?

But ... [s]upposing she looked in the mirror and discovered her own face there? She was also afraid to be real—it would demand too much new courage of her. (127)

Sylvia's American mother, though still in a functioning marriage with Sylvia's father Liyi, has a racist attitude toward un-Westernized Chinese, a problem that comes to the fore when a country cousin, Peiyuan, comes to live with the family. Sylvia has to some extent internalized her mother's attitudes: Sylvia has never visited the Chinese sector of Shanghai, though she had lived in Beijing and seen the "squalor" there. She respects the "past" of China as represented by ruins of stone altars around which the overcrowded peasants maintain a respectful space, but sees the hordes of displaced Chinese as "too many ... it was so easy to claim distinction, to be ennobled—as though one had somehow achieved it through conscious effort—just by speaking English and looking, not even Aryan, but just non-Chinese" (85–86).

At the same time, though, she cannot accept her mother's irrational racism and paranoia. Sylvia interjects herself into her mother's screaming rage against Peiyuan, guilty of speaking in Chinese to Sylvia's brother behind a closed door: "'I am Chinese, too!' Sylvia shouted. 'I—I—I! Chinese, do you understand!' 'I hate everything you stand for!' Helen screamed" (140). Sylvia leaves the house, running by her mother's church: "Reverend Ssu-tu ... save me from my trinity: my father, my mother and myself. ... save me from my duality: my flesh, which believes in life; my spirit which belongs nowhere" (142).

Mimi, whose parents are no longer living, does not have to contend with the same sort of family-imposed self-hatred. But her racial "contamination" thwarts her seemingly successful negotiation of her "cosmopolitan" identity when she becomes pregnant with Robert Bruno's child. Robert will not marry her because his father, an international financier from Switzerland, would object because she is not white. Inflicting the consequences of her conflicted subjectivity upon her body, she spontaneously miscarries the child: "In trying to mutilate (Robert and Aunt Juliet) with her hatred, she had hurt herself" (204). Though in a sense she "hurts" herself by introjection of her own hostile feelings, Mimi's ability to expel the abject fetus from her body is obviously best for all concerned in the long run and constitutes a more powerful form of agency than Sylvia ever develops. This feat is not inconsistent with other aspects of Mimi's personality. Though she situates herself wholly within a patriarchal construct of femininity, she "lives large"—with an ambition and self-confidence that Sylvia and Feng can only wish for, having already internalized the guilt that only comes upon Mimi after Robert's rejection. Psychologists of the 1950s might have called Mimi manic-depressive. As a child she leaped off a rooftop in an ecstasy of simulated flight and broke her leg.

Her adventures and downfall in Shanghai society echo her romantic childhood recklessness. Relieved of the burden of the unborn child, Mimi ultimately "would seek promiscuity as a mortification ... a willing victim as she leaned against the column, making her body pliant, asking any man to punish her and to find her beautiful." This scene, Mimi's last appearance in the novel, is outdoors, "cold and public" (232) in front of the Russian church. It is foreshadowed in the account of her first tryst with Robert, when "to her the house seemed to expand into an infinite place" (41). Mimi fails in her attempt to "place" herself in Robert's truly "paternal" world and instead ends up deadened to the world.

Whereas Mimi seems unaware that her ego is besieged until her pregnancy, Sylvia is aware from the beginning. In both cases, mixed racial identity is the force pressing on the sense of self. Mimi has been so preoccupied with using the master's tools to construct a gender identity that she has overlooked the implications of her raced body. The text thus critiques the model of femininity, represented by Mimi, that was accepted fairly unproblematically by American women at the time this novel was published. Mimi's mixed racial identity problematizes the critique, but Mimi becomes the tragic mulatto not merely because she is of mixed blood, nor because she lacks Christian standards of morality (the masochistic crucifixion motifs notwithstanding), but because she has wholeheartedly adopted a Westernized construction of femininity that Sylvia resists. Sylvia may rise above this "replication of patriarchally inscribed sexuality" through "the grace of intelligence" (Lim xviii), but she is aided by Feng, whose aggressive masculinity is more generally focused on Chinese sovereignty than on the ravishing of women.

It is consistent with the masochistic theme that all three main characters are being exploited in some fashion. Mimi is exploited by Robert because he knows he cannot marry her; Feng initially pursues a relationship with Sylvia to gain access to her father on behalf of the communist resistance; the communists use Feng for this purpose without trusting or accepting him. Feng meets a "tragic" end in leaving Shanghai in the service of the resistance, after unwittingly causing the death of Sylvia's cousin Peiyuan at the hands of the same communists. His almost impossibly courageous political stance, considering his class background, is a material element of Sylvia's attraction to him. She wants him "to inflict upon her his aggressiveness" because he "made the truth seem brutal," as opposed to her father, whose "gentleness ... kept her and Paul [her brother] from the simplest truths" (182).

"Don't you darling me," Feng shouts at her. "I know I'm right. What makes you think you know anything about it? Why, you aren't even interested" (181). Feng has no interest in the type of femininity played to perfection by Mimi. Sylvia is attracted to his idealism and willingness to act. She wants to have, or at least understand, the kind of agency he seems to have. He has called her a "goddam Taoist" for talking about "what [people] are" instead of "the things they get done" (105). Yet despite his seeming functionality, Feng, too, is still struggling in a masochistic trap: "Part of him denied ... even the sprout of pain that reminded himself that he, too, was alive" (219).

The motif of blindness resonates back and forth between Sylvia and Feng. After Peiyuan's death, Sylvia says she was "blind" to trust Feng (223). "Only in blind work and in idealism" can Feng, he thinks, "expend this distaste for himself" (226). Later, Sylvia thinks "she had been blind, and she would be blind again" (236). The narrative voice shifts throughout the novel among the point of view of the main characters, and in this particular passage the unreliability of Sylvia's point of view is underscored by the initial lack of clarity in her thoughts. "His idealism, she now saw, led him to commit outrages against the human spirit"—yet Feng has done nothing intentional to harm anyone. "His social conscience ... would violate society"; Feng is now a synecdochic representation of the Maoist revolution to come. As Sylvia narrates herself into a position of autonomy—"she had learned from her dependency the necessity for being separate"—she psychically inflicts her conflict on her own body: "her body doubled up in a scissorslike contraction. She felt something snap, leaving a white scar across her consciousness. Like a twig, she had been broken in two, the strong nerve of her attachment of dependency giving way at last." And then she castigates herself for her "egocentricity" and "pretentiousness," confessing to herself that "despair was a sin." She seizes upon a new respect for life and her own autonomy due to the Christ-like martyrdom (to her way of thinking) of her Chinese cousin: "because of his absence, she had realized what life was. ... The body must be holy!" (236–37).[11]

Masse says that "the masochist's transition from blindness to insight can lead to purposive action through aggression or subversion."[12] Feng is pursuing "blind work," feeling "impotence" and "distaste for himself" (226), and Sylvia will be "blind again" (236), but as they go their separate ways there is a recuperation of agency for Feng, at least, whose subversive revolutionary activities carry him off the page. In an American novel published at the height of the cold war, we cannot expect this trajectory to go any further. The morning of the incipient discovery of Peiyuan's death and Sylvia's ensuing rejection, the narrator says, "he did not know that he had awakened that morning with a foretaste of damnation" (218). But after Sylvia's rejection, any further tragedy in his fate is left to the imagination.

Sylvia's insight in the search for her selfhood leads toward a proto-feminist "subversion" of the romantic plot. Sylvia challenges the terms of gender identification by pursuing an autonomy that echoes the rugged individualist paradigm of American individualist heroes. Her search for identity does not, however, achieve a totally satisfactory resolution in terms of establishing a transgendered, cross-racial, cross-cultural subjectivity that possesses a clear sense of agency. At the end of Sylvia's narrative, she is "alone but not lonely. She expected a new and sudden vision" (240). She is still behaving passively, waiting to be acted upon by something unknown. There is a mysticism in her point of view—it is mentioned early in the novel that she sometimes has prescient dreams (42)—that is a marker of her hybrid cultural identity and perhaps connected to a fatalism in her point of view that Feng resists. She conflates notions of Emersonian transcendentalism, Christianity, and Taoism. Feng is correct in saying that she cares more about what people "are" than what they "get done."

Nostalgia and spatial constructs of home play a prominent role in the narrative, as does a tension between closed space and infinite expansion. Sylvia and Feng prefer living in China to living in America; in this regard, their mothers represent a problematic aspect of their identities. But their nostalgia is for a father- rather than a motherland. Sylvia's father is a positive figure in the text, a "gentle" yet strong person who is significant in Sylvia's reconstruction of gender identity as well as in her concept of a fatherland. Sylvia reminisces about Beijing (formerly called Peking or Peiping), her childhood home: "So went Peiping into spring, breaking fearfully like girlhood into love, so went hamlet, village, town, city, all the explored and seminal land, peopled for so long by so many dark heads" (60). Enclosed spaces like Peiping make the characters feel secure—even Mimi's Australian father, "an adventurer who had wandered into an exotic garden and found its walls not too restricting" (91). There is a fence around Shanghai, due to the Japanese occupation, but immediately after describing this fence, the narrator describes "Sylvia's world" as being "bounded by" the university and the plain home of a former Chinese consul (86).

Like Mimi, Sylvia associates sex with infinite space. In Sylvia's out-of-body crucifixion fantasy with Feng, "the sweet, specific joy and torment swept her out into a vast, shining Pacific. They floated near the rims of a young world. They came back from far away," down to earth and the inevitable cigarette (147–48). Later, "the world was her home, because Feng and she loved each other" (214). These transcendental moments, crossing the frontiers of love, so to speak, are placed in opposition to the way in which the narrative is constantly constructing space in order to position the characters' sense of place and home. Sylvia, though securely placed and enclosed in her bedroom in the opening passage, nevertheless feels more at home at the Jastrows' home: "'*My* living room!' Sylvia wanted to exclaim, unreasonably. 'I am going to *my* living room!'" (6). She is "always lurking in other people's doorways, trying to overhear their lives" (9). "In other people's houses, Sylvia felt more real, her face was given back to herself. Other people's homes did not seem like jails to her, the way her own sometimes seemed." Yet then she realizes "every individual was an eye, an eye as large and limitless as everything it could take in. Yes, after all, everyone's home was a prison" (87).

Thus Sylvia is constantly positioning and repositioning herself in a "seeing" relation to others. The narcissism implied by this process is echoed in the scene where Sylvia's mother, Helen, appearing in this passage as a somewhat stereotypically obsessive American housewife, charges around the house seeking the appropriate place to set some narcissus bulbs. Cousin Peiyuan is, of course, occupying the place she wants to put them (52–54). The narcissus bulbs are, in fact, roots. Helen cannot find a place to put them, and what she really wants is to go back to America. Helen and the rest of her enclave community, "the hybrids and the cosmopolitans, all that were left in China," represent a colonialism that never had more than a precarious foothold, and now will no longer have a place in China. They are

> survivors of a colonialism that was fast becoming as antique as peace. ... [They] still moved, she knew, with the subtle authority of foreigners. Colonialism was still a perfume behind their ears. ... they ... felt superimposed on [the Chinese] like a montage, as though they displaced another dimension in the city, as though the Chinese were somehow invisible. (86)

This is one of the few passages in the novel where the description of the Chinese hails into being (but only "as though," the narrator describing, and distancing, the colonizer's gaze) the "anonymous, opaque collectivity of undifferentiated bodies" of colonizing discourse.[13] But if the collective Chinese are invisible or opaque to the Western presence, nevertheless, "everyone wants us to make ourselves over in their image," as Feng says (179). Feng resists such appropriation of change; of all the characters he is the most aware of the problem of how to effect change while maintaining autonomy.

Thus, though nostalgia plays a role in the dynamics of the subjectivity Sylvia and Feng are trying to construct, it is not an uncritical nostalgia. Even Sylvia's "half-relic, half-contemporary" father Liyi (43), the most nostalgic of the characters, acknowledges the influences of Westernization:

> The dead hand of the scholar was being repudiated, the modern spoken language was advocated. ... the roots of the language were struck a blow— systems were being evolved to make the learning of Chinese itself easier, in order to combat illiteracy. ...
>
> Confucius was being supplanted by Christ and John Dewey; free love was taking the place of family-arranged marriages; emulation of the West was replacing ancestor worship; birth control, Imagism, proletarian literature, co-education, divorce, the doing away with the subtleties of a double standard for men and women—Liyi was in the midst of all these changes. (163)

Liyi, having reconstructed his own space by renting a vacation villa, has the last word in the novel. "His children, free from any narrow chauvinism, were the new citizens for an expanding century. ... He felt that he could sleep at last, and wake up ready for clarity" (245–46).

There is a bittersweet quality to the vision sought and achieved in this novel. The rich, descriptive passages that impressed critics in the 1950s are poignant reminiscences of a China that no longer exists. The visual depth of the narration and the recurring motif of vision and clarity confound the paradigm of the master's colonizing gaze to situate the focus of seeing where it belongs: in the seeing subject. But the position of spectator is not necessarily a position of dominance. It can also reflect the position of the oppressed in the classical Freudian beating scenario: the spectator is relieved that the "child is being beaten" and not the spectator. As Masse puts it, "the role of spectator seems to promise protection. Minimally, you are safe for the duration of the spectacle."[14]

Early on, Liyi tells Feng, "We liberals have too many eyes and no hands. That's the tragedy" (69). Liyi, the journalism professor whose university was closed by the Japanese, has indeed been observing a spectacle—the eight-year Japanese occupation of Shanghai, the rape of Nanking, all the horrors of the war—and though the Japanese have left, the spectacle is not over. For Sylvia, perhaps, to see clearly—the "new and sudden vision" she is awaiting (240)—is all she hopes to attain. What will she do as the novel ends? We don't know whether she will leave or stay to see the new China, though we last see her looking toward the ocean (240). Ultimately, we know as little about her fate as about Feng's. She does not feel compelled to pursue a career; she is privileged by wealth and does not need to. This will be the most problematic aspect of the novel for many readers. Chang's subversion of the marriage plot would destabilize 1950s readers' expectations regarding gender roles, but her protagonist's negotiation of her racial identity is incomplete. She cannot yet, as Feng does, engage with the reality of "so many dark heads."

Notes

1. Shirley Geok-lin Lim, Introduction to *The Frontiers of Love* (Seattle: University of Washington Press, 1994), v–xxiii, vi.

2. Gayatri Spivak, "Can the Subaltern Speak?" in *The Post-Colonial Studies Reader*, ed. Bill Ashcroft, Gareth Griffiths, and Helen Tiffin (London: Routledge, 1995), 24–28.

3. Mimi's mother is Chinese and very absent, having been killed in a bombing raid along with Mimi's father. Mimi has, however, a surrogate mother in her Westernized Chinese Aunt Juliet.

4. Diana Chang, *The Frontiers of Love* (Seattle: University of Washington Press, 1994; first published 1956), 46. All subsequent page number references to this publication will be cited parenthetically.

5. Sidonie Smith and Julia Watson, eds., *De/Colonizing the Subject: The Politics of Gender in Women's Autobiography* (Minneapolis: University of Minnesota Press, 1992), xvii.

6. Sylvia's thoughts here call to mind the course taken by Shawnee Ray Toose in Louise Erdrich's 1994 novel *The Bingo Palace* (New York: Harper Collins, 1994). Shawnee Ray embarks on an off-reservation career, escaping the overbearing presence of her son's father with six books of designs of "fashion with a Chippewa flair" (67, 73).

7. Michelle A. Masse, *In the Name of Love: Women, Masochism, and the Gothic* (Ithaca: Cornell University Press, 1992), 84. In this particular passage Masse is discussing Freud's essay "Instincts and Their Vicissitudes" (1915).

8. Ibid., 240.

9. The essays most pertinent to this discussion are "'A Child Is Being Beaten': A Contribution to the Study of the Origin of Sexual Perversions" (1919) 17: 175–204, and "Instincts and Their Vicissitudes" (1915) 14: 117–40, in *The Standard Edition of the Complete Psychological Works of Sigmund Freud*, trans. and ed. James Strachey et al. (London: Hogarth Press, 1953–74).

10. Masse, *In the Name of Love*, 3, 41.

11. Peiyuan had no intention of being a martyr, despite the suggestive language of the cited passage: he dies, in the inimitable phrase of the Mexican revolution, by "ley de fue" (killed while attempting to escape).

12. Masse, *In the Name of Love*, 264.

13. Smith and Watson, *De/Colonizing the Subject*, xvii.

14. Masse, *In the Name of Love*, 40.

'Mettise Blanche'

Kim Lefevre and Transnational Space

> It is thrilling to think—to know that for any act of mine, I
> shall get twice as much praise or twice as much blame. It is
> quite exciting to hold the center of the national stage, with
> the spectators not knowing whether to laugh or to weep.
> —Zora Neale Hurston, "How It Feels to Be Coloured Me"

In the movie *Indochine*, Catherine Deneuve becomes a potent symbol of
France during its withdrawal from Viet Nam. In the movie, although
Deneuve loses "her" land to the Vietnamese, she wins the heart of her
adoptive Vietnamese son, embodying a French reconceptualization of a
Viet Nam whose independence was won at the cost of its soul. By making
France the mother, and by adopting Eurasians as "her" children, France's
movie industry—like Hollywood—is reimagining their nation's military
loss as a French "victory."

Such a reimagining is contested by French-Vietnamese writer Kim
Lefevre in her "autobiography" entitled *Metisse Blanche*. The novel/auto-
biography was a best-seller in France in 1989. The only American critiquing the book was Jack Yeager, yet both Yeager and the writer of the
preface to *Metisse Blanche*, Michele Sarde, are perhaps subsumed by
popular academic notions of difference, seduced by romanticized notions
of ethnic "others," or misled by their readings of the ethnic (particularly
the mixed race) autobiographer as a translator of culture. Sarde reads Lefevre's text as a story of the mixed race narrator's turn to her paternal
France for salvation, while Yeager focuses his reading of the text on the
protagonist's mixed race ancestry so as to explicate her various states of
ambivalence. Although the theme of ambivalence is central to the text,
the textual state of ambivalence experienced by the protagonist should
not be framed solely in terms of a crisis (or resolution) in mixed race iden-

tity. To do so overlooks questions of colonialism, power, class structure, and patriarchy while perpetuating the essentialization of mixed race people as a group marked by tragic flaws. Alienation is not necessarily the fate of the mixed race subject but the result of the nation's readings of political affiliation, the grappling with linguistic dominance, and the expatriate status of its narrator, whose textual interventions ultimately allow her to define a transnational space, a recovered community, and finally a resurrected memory of Viet Nam that serves as a metaphorical hyphen bridging multiple identities.

If spaces situated in between systems of representation are increasingly regarded by theorists as capable of decentering hegemony, it is necessary to insist that these are not the only spaces from which a mixed race subject can speak.[1] My calling for a careful reading of *Metisse Blanche* is inspired by Chandra Mohanty's warning that a dehistoricized reading of texts written by women of color can lead to the treatment of their protagonists as truth-tellers of "their own oppression." Just as in third world women's narratives, mixed race women's narratives in themselves cannot serve as evidence of decentering official histories and subjectivities simply because of their mixed race status. Agreeing with Mohanty, I echo the idea that "it is the way in which they are read, understood, and located institutionally which is of paramount importance" (Mohanty et al. 34).

Metisse Blanche became one of France's best-sellers at a time when a nostalgia for the former colonies was rife among the French populace, when "exotic" Indochinese cultural production was in vogue, and when businesses and government officials were searching for ways to control, once again, Viet Nam's economy through imperialist means.[2] In *Metisse Blanche*, Lefevre tells the story of a Eurasian girl, Kim—or Eliane (or Thérèse) for the French—growing up in Viet Nam in the 1940s and 1950s. Because of her French paternity, the protagonist lives as an outcast; her mother loses her social standing for what is perceived as her unforgivable "mistake," producing a mixed race offspring with a French soldier. Abandoned by the soldier, the mother marries a man she does not love and who treats her with indifference. Kim is never fully integrated into Vietnamese society and, with her mother's support, fights against all odds to gain an education. The story ends with the narrator's departure from Viet Nam to France, where she is able to pursue her education. Lefevre's second book, *Retour à la saison des pluies*, breaks with the conventions of chronological narrative and follows protagonist Kim as she returns to

Viet Nam after thirty years of absence. By returning "home," Kim comes face to face with a past she thought was closed to her.

In his reading of *Metisse Blanche*, Yeager focuses on Kim's mixed racial identity. His thesis rests on the assumption that "the interplay between reality and illusion, between remembering and forgetting, and finally between being Vietnamese or being French, emblematizes the dualism at the heart of a 'metisse blanche'" (Yeager, "Kim Lefevre's *Retour*," 49). For Yeager, "this duality motivates the creation of the text, itself mixed, bringing together the strands of two cultures, two parents, two ancestral lines, two educational formations, two languages, and two literary traditions" (ibid. 50). Yeager concludes that this mixing is as unstable as autobiography itself, the "problematic hybrid, forever unstable [is] ... an enabling metaphor of transculturation with revolutionary potential" (ibid. 56). Such revolutionary potential, he argues, springs from the fact that the narrator speaks for all Eurasian women (ibid.).

Although Yeager raises important issues of tranculturation and Vietnamese/French cultural tension, when he addresses Lefevre's work as an example of the ambiguity existing between autobiography and fiction, he accompanies his reading with an imposition on *Metisse Blanche* of a desire for representationality of the mixed race woman (ibid. 48). In spite of his "awareness" about genre, Yeager regards the protagonist's life as providing anthropological information about Eurasians, and the autobiography is treated as an authoritative account of the "exotic" other. Written almost thirty years after Lefevre's departure from Viet Nam, however, the story emanates from Lefevre's memory and imagination. When asked to describe her text at the Nha Viet-Nam in Paris on May 28, 1989, Lefevre referred to *Metisse Blanche* as a "novel," not as an autobiography, and further said:

> My life was carried outside of Viet Nam, floating so far away from where my roots took place. It is like a river from which the spring is so far away that it seems to be enveloped with mist. And when my memory turns to it, I have at times doubted of its reality. (Lefevre, *Retour*, 13)

The category of mixed race is, like race, a social construction whose role shifts with time and political climate. By focusing on what he argues to be Lefevre's duality, Yeager's analysis leads to the essentializing of the "metisse" and the proposition of tragic ambivalence, thus giving to the narrative the task of representationality that ultimately can lead to ethnic ghettoization (Spivak 61). In Maria Root's classic work on mixed race identity, *Racially Mixed People in America*, Cindy Nakashima notes a standard set of misperceptions of racially mixed people that echo Yeager's assumptions. According to Nakashima, people of mixed race descent are consistently represented as marginal and tragically flawed:

> (a) in relation to biological reasoning (that it is unnatural to mix the races, that multiracial people are physically, morally, and mentally weak; that multiracial people are tormented by their genetically divided selves; and that intermarriage lowers the biologically superior White race), and (b) in relation to sociocultural reasoning (that people of mixed race are socially and culturally marginal, doomed to a life of conflicting cultures and the unfulfilled desire to be one or the other, neither fitting in nor gaining acceptance in any group, thus leading lives of confused loneliness and despair). (Nakashima 165)

By emphasizing the split nature of the Eurasian in conjunction with the mixed nature of the text itself, Yeager accepts the sociocultural reasoning projected onto people of mixed race descent whereby they are seen as doomed to suffer because of their duality, a strategy traditionally used to critique intermarriages and multiraciality (ibid.). To read the text as an authoritative account of people of mixed race descent (inherently tormented and torn) can replicate a logic of domination using fixed ethnic identities as a form of oppression in order to overshadow categories of political and social structures that contribute substantially to such textual ambivalences. As Michael Omi and Howard Winant argue in *Racial Formation in the United States*, the category of mixed race, just like the larger category of race, is not fixed. Amerasians have been mistreated (for instance, in Viet Nam in the early 1990s) for many different reasons: "they were abandoned and endured Communist persecution because their mothers' involvement with Americans was viewed as a symbol of national treason, they suffered prejudice because they were born in a racially homogeneous society, and they were victims of classism because they were fatherless in a patriarchal society that ostracizes alternative family structures" (Valverde 146). Class and the influences of patriarchal structures are crucial in understanding their stigmatization. If Kim in *Metisse Blanche* was ill treated in Viet Nam at the outset of decolonization, she is welcomed upon her return some thirty years later. It was the turn of the Amerasians to suffer ostracism, the alienation through political affiliation that resulted from the French having passed on the imperial baton to the United States. Lefevre's body no longer incarnated the French enemy but instead was romanticized, as France and its culture had by then become a source of nostalgia for a certain segment of the Vietnamese population.

In addition, the socioeconomic aura of the Viet-Kieu (the Vietnamese from overseas), in conjunction with Lefevre's success as a writer, wrapped her body with a desirable aura in a place that suffered immense social and economic devastation due to colonialism and the American war. Reading *Metisse Blanche*, it is crucial to keep in mind that Kim's position as a stigmatized subject of Vietnamese society in the 1940s and 1950s is not only due to her mixed race ancestry, but is also directly connected to the country's mobilization against French colonialism.

Succinctly summarized, Viet Nam was a French colony for eighty years. With colonization came not only the exploitation of natural resources and human labor, but also the imposition of an ideology based on "nineteenth-century European faith in progress and the moral superiority of the white man" (Bousquet 29). Colonialism was presented by the French as a humanitarian act, the so-called *mission civilizatrice*. Also present was the strong belief in the ultimate value of assimilating the Vietnamese into French culture and the use of such assumptions to rationalize force and coercion to carry out their civilizing mission. In the context of colonization, a French education was said to be generously provided in order to assimilate the colonized. But the ultimate function of the colonizer's presence was "to discover the wealth of a country, to extract it and to send it off to the mother countries" (Fanon 102). A French education, in conjunction with the colonizer's military and administrative presence, was part of these exploitative tools. According to historian David Marr, the French education also served as a mode to erase the previous Chinese colonizer's influences, as an efficient tool to obtain the loyalties of the small bourgeoisie, and to create a faithful native managerial class that could govern and administrate their colonies on their behalf. Vietnamese writers such as Nguyen Tien Lang have consistently been acutely aware of the tensions caused by such impositions:

> And now that the Occident has come to us, transforming the deepest side of our soul ... we no longer can continue to rejoice from the same joys, to be saddened by the same sadness, love, hate, to become angry in the same ways as we did before. (Nguyen in Yeager, *Vietnamese Novel*, 35, my translation)

According to Nguyen, colonization was a Manichean struggle that violated the Vietnamese people's minds and hearts. The colonized have been transformed in spite of themselves. The realization of such transformation was a source of great fear and nostalgia to him. If this education did, as Nguyen suggests, deeply affect aspects of the Vietnamese soul and culture (and I believe that it did, particularly among the elite and the bourgeoi-sie), does this mean that the Vietnamese people molded themselves to be exact copies of the French?

Frantz Fanon has fervently condemned the traumatic effects of colo-nization on the mind, with its resulting painful dualities for the colo-nized. For Fanon, it is through language that the various "teachings" of the colonizer are fully internalized. Following a similar approach, Albert Memmi writes in *Portrait du colonisé* of the damaging effects on an indi-vidual when they are stripped of history. Deprived of an institutional and cultural role to control their destiny, the colonized, he argues, have been led to forgo participation in history. Without a sense of responsibility, colonial subjects became through time mere "masks" under which they suffocated and slowly agonized (Memmi 119). Even in the active stance of revolt, the colonized is said to "think, feel and live against and therefore in relation to the colonized and to colonization" (ibid. 153). In this sense, Memmi explains, the colonized can almost never succeed in "coinciding" with him or herself (ibid. 154).

While recognizing the same destructive effects of colonization, Homi Bhabha, in *The Location of Culture*, has conceived of colonized subjects differently, focusing on the gaps within the process of colonization. Bhabha describes a colonial space that emphasizes the agency of the co-lonial subject. Introducing terms like colonial "mimicry," Bhabha ad-dresses "the desire for a reformed, recognizable Other, as a subject of a difference that is almost the same, but not quite" (Bhabha 86). In suc-cinct terms, Bhabha presents the colonized as mimicking, or "acting up," his or her assigned role as colonized subject. This subversive act, because it is partly staged and because it does not escape the colonizer's gaze, Bhabha argues, brings the colonizers "off balance" in the face of such un-disciplinable questioning of their authority. "The menace of mimicry," Bhabha asserts, "is its double vision" (ibid.).

Metisse Blanche, however, is a postcolonial text in which mimicry, if it does take place, does not serve the function advanced by Bhabha. The colonial space as introduced in the book seems instead to correspond to Fanon and Memmi's portraiture of such a system, and suggest that the more marginalized a colonized subject is, the less likely she will be a source of "anxiety" for the colonizer. How can a young girl, ostracized by the Vietnamese community in which she lives, and deprived of all mate-rial resources and social status, be a threatening source for the colonizer?

Kim's emphasis on the degree of agency held by the colonized shadows the powerful effect of colonization on the colonized's mind, an experience thoroughly described by the protagonist:

> I still see kindergarten classes when every morning little Vietnamese kids used to line up behind the others, singing at the top of their lungs 'Marshal, here we come' ... , in front of the French flag. They were teaching us the superiority of the intellect above brutal force. (Lefevre, *Metisse Blanche*, 16)

Marshal Pétain, whom all children under colonial rule had to honor, was the man in charge of the Vichy regime, the same regime that collaborated with Nazi Germany. In the text, the "superiority of the intellect" represents the French colonial cultural supremacy, and the "brutal force" the French perception of the "natives," the Vietnamese culture that had to be degraded in order to be ruled. The education provided was in this context not aimed at inculcating "knowledge" for the benefit of the colonized, but as a tool for discipline and surveillance. The flag, an imaginary symbol of nationhood in front of which they stood, was not Vietnamese but French, a symbol in front of which the everyday practice of salute was aimed at colonizing the minds: "We were taught that France was our nurturing mother, our nation. It was toward her that our heart had to be turned" (ibid. 71). As a "mother," France was the one to provide unconditional support to the children and, metaphorically speaking, serve as substitute for their own mother. Such a process of the disavowal of national history is a source of inner tension when experienced by the colonized who, like Kim, were French educated.

Yet the protagonist's relation to the material she studied was, like her behavior, strictly monitored: "I think that the most difficult thing is that we were supposed to learn this literature not as foreign literature but as if it were ours. ... We were under the obligation to act as if we were familiar with things that in reality we were only discovering" (ibid. 343). The mimicking acts—although here differently acted upon than in Bhabha's sense of the term—are presented in *Metisse Blanche* as a colonizer's command. In this context lessons are impositions and acts of violence. By learning lessons by heart as if they were "theirs," the colonized could either, according to Bhabha, forge a critical space leading to resistance or, according to Fanon, develop collaborationist attitudes. But for Kim, marginal to her society because of mixed race heritage, class, politics, and patriarchy, the colonial experience does not clearly and directly lead to either of these theoretical paths. For her, these lessons were simply learned as a form of accommodation driven by the desire for survival. Such forms of acceptance are described in the text as very costly. Kim describes openly the ambivalence she had acquired vis-à-vis her family and their ways of living after having studied a few months at a convent. She recalls, "I accused [my mother] of superstition and obscurantism" (ibid. 308, my translation). This ambivalence is not rooted in her mixed race ancestry as suggested by Yeager, but stems directly from her French education; in other words, it is a by-product of her colonization (and even a gesture toward Fanon's colonial collaboration).

Lefevre's description of this process is complicated by her retrospective intervention throughout the text. In other words, for Kim, the critical space, or space of "resistance," for which Bhabha searches can only be opened thirty years later, when she is no longer marginalized from both the Vietnamese society and the colonial system, now a middle-class educated "French-Vietnamese" woman living in France and writing for a French audience. "Knowledge," she writes, "was a poisoned fruit" (ibid. 89). Kim recalls beginning her career as a French teacher, spending her first day teaching French to Vietnamese students next to a zoo: "I expressed myself in French naturally, as all respected professors do. ... I was still trying to find the method of teaching to use when strident monkey screams brutally broke the silence" (ibid. 398).

Reminiscent of the monkey, an animal commonly perceived as lacking in awareness and noted for its mimicking qualities, Kim "naturally" acts as a French teacher and then remains unconscious of her condition as a caged, colonized subject. Poor and a woman, periodically stigmatized by the response to her mixed race appearance, Kim can hint at the resemblance of her past actions with those of monkey only through the distance created through time, immigration, and political changes. Kim's action was not mirrored by the colonizer's gaze in this scene, but by other Vietnamese who saw in her body the presence of the colonizer.

The French language is frequently a site for struggle, and the inherent tension between the French and Vietnamese languages is a classic "Manichean" struggle as defined by Abdul R. JanMohamed, who argues that Homi Bhabha ignores Fanon's definition of the conqueror/native relation. This is powerfully illustrated during a childhood scene in which the protagonist learns French from her mother's employers at the Oceanographic Institute of Nha-Trang:

> He decided to initiate me to the French language and, to meet his goal, forced me to circulate in the large room, touching and naming common objects: the

cup, the spoon, the cap. ... My lessons followed dinner after dinner. We
formed a strange group: from one side the Vietnamese—my mother and my
sisters—small, reserved, as if erased against the wall; from the other side the
director, giant, blazing, milky complexion, eyes translucent like sticky barley
sugar, large mouth, thundering laugh; and me inside the empty space in between the two, little bee landing sometimes on one object, sometimes on another, chanting my litany of nouns. But at the moment, the spectacle seemed
all natural to us. (ibid. 165)

In this scene, the moment, once perceived as "natural," is through reflection described in a way that highlights the dualistic relationship that is
inherent to colonialism. The relationship between the colonizer and the
colonized is described as one regimented by fear. The acquisition of the
French language, at other times described as a desirable asset, is presented
in this scene as a master's fantasy imposed by "force," a fantasy driven by
the contact between the colonizer and the Eurasian girl. The "master" and
the "natives" are described with opposites: "small" versus "giant," "reserved" versus "blazing," to show the inequality of power relations separating them. The perspective of the child serves to emphasize what she
describes as grotesque differences. The space she enters is one that is situated "in between" the two, bridged by her mixed race heritage and the
master's perception of her ability to acquire his language, regardless of
her will. This bridge is described as fluid. Like an innocent "bee" she
moves, chanting her litany of nouns as if she were "free," but, like a bee,
she is governed by rigid rules. These lessons are learned by heart like the
songs sung in front of a French flag; like them, the chant is described as
an imposition free from meaning. Although each signified corresponds to
a signifier, such as a "cup," a "spoon," a "cap," they are yet isolated from
the reality of her family's life, for at the time they are homeless, with few
material possessions. But because the contrast presented between her
mother and sister and the French employers is extreme, it defies theoretical works that insist, sometimes too rapidly, upon the elimination of binary oppositions such as dominated versus dominant. In this scenario the
little girl's performance provides a spectacle for the employer. It is a moment designed for her family to witness his total domination, a way also
to construct Kim's differential status. Set as spectacle, the situation does
not lead to anxiety for the colonizer nor to mimicry and resistance for the
colonized. They are simply too afraid.

I would argue that Sarde's writing in the preface of *Metisse Blanche*
and, to a lesser degree, Yeager's readings of Lefevre's autobiography illus-

trate Chandra Mohanty's concern that the autobiographies of women of color can be easily co-opted, even by those who want to celebrate their subversive qualities.[3] Mohanty warns her readers about the danger of de-historicization and of constructing a monolithic category of women of color:

> In spite of the fact that the growing demand among publishers for culturally diverse life (hi)stories indicates a recognition of plural realities and experiences as well as a diversification of inherited Eurocentric canons, often this demand takes the form of the search for more "exotic and different" stories in which individual women write as truth-tellers, and authenticate "their own oppression," in the tradition of Euro-American women's autobiography. ... Thus, the existence of third world women's narratives in itself is not evidence of de-centering hegemonic histories and subjectivities. It is the way in which they are read, understood, and located institutionally which is of paramount importance. (Mohanty et al. 34)

Inherent in these ideas is a vehement critique of colonialism, a system that, in order to maintain its structures, requires a sexist and racist ideology. This system, Mohanty suggests, did not dissolve in the era of decolonialism. Mohanty applauds the recent proliferation of autobiographies by women of color because they demonstrate a growing openness toward diversity on the part of the dominant society. She celebrates these publications because the very act of writing can be a source of identity and political awareness for women of color, but she also expresses cautious concern about the co-optive power of the capitalist system. For these narratives to potentially decenter "hegemonic histories and subjectivities," she suggests, a radical reading is necessary.

Such a reading cannot be found in the preface of *Metisse Blanche*, in which Michele Sarde reads Lefevre as a translator of culture, whose task is to reveal the "private" and therefore the "real" Vietnamese culture: "In this endogamous community intolerant of differences, where every day someone marries someone he does not love, and someone loves whom he does not marry, women are reduced to passivity and submission to the father, to the husband, to the elder son, to the mother-in-law" (Sarde in Lefevre, *Metisse Blanche*, 7). Through this lens, the protagonist and her mother are seen as exceptional examples of women who have transgressed these rules. By focusing on the patriarchal and oppressive society of Viet Nam, Sarde ignores the fact that, although various forms of domination and injustices against women in Viet Nam undeniably exist, Vietnamese women from both recent and more distant history were/are "independent agents in the public economy" (Haines 64). Sarde's reading contributes to the notion that Vietnamese women immigrating to the first world are "unmistakably striving for the Western, modern and, of course, emancipatory values" (Morokvasic 20) of the West, and such a reading thus ignores the multiple oppressive conditions set against these women in the context of resettlement. According to Sarde, what saves Kim is her "Confucian" thirst for knowledge. Sarde explains to the reader that it is Kim's ability to use her "White part in spite of the stigmas associated with it in Viet Nam, a source of stigmatization, rejection, humiliation and pain" that actually helped her, and asserts that what saves Kim from eternal stigmatization is her departure from Viet Nam to France (Sarde in Lefevre, *Metisse Blanche*, 11). Sarde's reading of "the metisse" implies that only France can be generous and open enough to accept her difference, thus positioning France and its citizens as naturally holding ethnic values superior to those upheld by native Vietnamese, an assumption reminiscent of colonial discourse.

My reading does not imply, however, that Lefevre fails to open a space in between systems of representation. The fact that *Metisse Blanche* and *Retour à la saison des pluies* were written is significant. Mohanty has argued that the process of writing itself can be significant for creating social change for many third world women writers. She finds that "the very practice of remembering and rewriting leads to the formation of politicized consciousness and self-identity" (Mohanty et al. 34). It is through Lefevre's perceived role as a cultural guide that she acquired the critics' recognition and her book became a best-seller in France; it is also through this role that Lefevre was invited to speak on *Apostrophe*, the popular literary television show on which successful authors are invited to discuss their works. It is in this context that Lefevre's retrospection and distancing with respect to Kim's colonization are consequential, for they signify the failure of colonization upon its subject. The author has, despite all odds, and despite the assumptions of the French media and publishing world, never fully assimilated to the colonizer's viewpoint and therefore to Sarde's assumption of French moral superiority, a failure that may have been triggered, as Mohanty suggests, through the very process of remembering and writing.

We can indeed follow throughout the text a critical shift in the author's attitude toward Viet Nam. In the beginning of the book, she writes, "I knew that there would not be a return for me" (Lefevre, *Metisse Blanche*, 32). Two hundred pages later she writes, "I did consider myself fully as a child of Viet-Nam. This country was mine, it was my land and my nation. I did desire to live there to the very end" (ibid. 238). Finally, one hundred pages later she observes, "I realize now my attachment to Viet Nam, to its culture which I now understand, as time goes by, has had a deep imprint on my being" (ibid. 321). Shortly after the publication of her book, after thirty years of avoiding all opportunities to return, after rupturing all communication with Vietnamese people, she decides to visit her family in Viet Nam. Unlike the son of Catherine Deneuve in *Indochine*, France has lost Lefevre and Kim's heart, for she did not assimilate: "In this return to the upstream from which almost nothing from what once was subsists any longer, my family is my point of reference, the cord that is linking me to this country where I was born" (ibid. 221). In this sense I do agree with Yeager. Lefevre's memory of Viet Nam is the metaphorical hyphen between two identities. If mimicry takes place, it is only thirty years later, between the author and her audience. Through the process of writing, Lefevre has formed a politicized consciousness and self-identity. Vietnamese by birth, Eurasian by sociopolitical conditions, French through colonization and assimilation, Lefevre has become transnational, developing and maintaining multiple relations that span borders (Glick Schiller et al. ix). After her trip to Viet Nam, Lefevre began to write letters to her family there, to speak to them on the telephone, to plan more trips there. In Paris, she began to shop in the ethnic community and converse with her friends from her past who reappeared in her life after the publication of the book, and she notes a fundamental transformation:

> Everything changed after the publication of the book. Through writing I turned on, without being conscious of it, a time machine. And the light years that I wanted to throw between Viet-Nam and me, between my childhood and me, like a big space of forgetting, suddenly found themselves abolished. (Lefevre, *Retour*, 6)

For Lefevre, France is no longer the center, and neither is Viet Nam.

While refraining from Yeager's enthusiasm in attributing decentering qualities to the Eurasian discourse, I do agree that *Metisse Blanche* disrupts the French and Vietnamese official national narrative. It is Kim's mixed race heritage, but also her French education, her class, and her ability to move to France and escape the American war that allow for a subversive space to emerge. I have argued that, if generalizations must be made, it is a narrative of "hybrid ethnically conscious elements of the population" (Wong 6) rather than a dual narrative emblematic of the mixed race person. Kim occupies, like a bee floating in between various discursive spaces, a role that, conducted as a child, was unthreatening and entertaining to the employer, but that as a narrator can affect a vast audience. Lefevre's "community" is not composed solely, as mixed race theorists at times have called for, of other mixed race people living all around the world (see, for example, Kish 263–76), but extends to Vietnamese people living in Paris and in Viet Nam trying to free themselves from the colonizer's teachings of self-hatred. And yet the literary space opened by Lefevre has been reappropriated and incorporated into French society. As such it does serve, in spite of, and to a certain extent because of, its celebrated decentering qualities, to nurture France's colonial "phantasmatic construct" of "the idea of Indochina" (Norindr 15), serving to pave a road for a more politically savvy but no less imperial return to Viet Nam. The nuances of representationalities in such a social context are crucial when reading texts written by racially mixed women. These identities and experiences have traditionally and historically been fixed in such a way that their writings have been, and still are, read as a work of authentication, even though such an authentication is being dismantled in front of the critics' own blindfolded eyes. To face and read these complexities and contradictions present and provoked by such narratives is a step forward in displacing such tendencies.

Notes

1. I use the term hegemony in a way comparable to Lisa Lowe in *Immigrant Acts*:

> The reality of any specific hegemony is that although it may be for the moment dominant, it is never absolute or conclusive. Hegemony, in Gramsci's thought, is a concept that describes both the social processes through which a particular dominance is maintained, as well as the processes through which that dominance is challenged and new forces are articulated. When a hegemony representing the interests of a dominant group exists, it is always within the context or resistances from emerging groups. (Lowe 69)

2. In the preface of *Metisse Blanche* (p. 5), Michele Sarde reads the text as an autobiographical account providing readers with "true" insights into the Vietnamese culture. Sarde claims that Lefevre "has found intact in her memory, precise as a mechanism of a clock, the reality of her childhood." Through Lefevre's text, Sarde posits an "authentic" Viet Nam, rarely offered to Francophone readers.

3. By "women of color," Mohanty means a movement whose "members" identify themselves through their allegiance to a common philosophy and political outlook, mainly one of resistance.

Works Cited

Bhabha, Homi K. *The Location of Culture*. London: Routledge, 1994.

Bousquet, Gisele. *Behind the Bamboo Hedge: The Impact of Homeland Politics in the Parisian Vietnamese Community*. Ann Arbor: University of Michigan Press, 1991.

Fanon, Frantz. *Peau Noire, Masques Blancs*. Paris: Editions du Seuil, 1952.

Glick Schiller, Nina, Linda Basch, and Cristina Blanc-Szanton. *Towards A Transnational Perspective on Migration: Race, Class, Ethnicity, and Nationalism Reconsidered*. New York: New York Academy of Sciences, 1992.

Grewal, Inderpal, and Caren Kaplan, eds. *Scattered Hegemonies: Postmodernity and Transnational Feminist Practices*. Minneapolis: University of Minnesota Press, 1994.

Haines, David. "Vietnamese Refugee Women in the U.S. Labor Force: Continuity or Change?" In *Postcolonial Subject: Francophone Women Writers*, ed. Mary Jean Green et al. Minneapolis: University of Minnesota Press, 1996.

JanMohamed, Abdul. "The Economy of Manichean Allegory: The Function of Racial Difference in Colonialist Literature." *Critical Inquiry* 12 (Autumn 1985): 59–87.

Kish, George Kitahara. "In the Margins of Sex and Race: Difference, Marginality, and Flexibility." In *The Multiracial Experience: Racial Borders as the New Frontier*, ed. Maria P. P. Root, 263–76. London: Sage Publications, 1996.

Lefevre, Kim. *Metisse Blanche*. Paris: Editions Barrault, 1989.

———. *Retour à la saison des pluies*. Paris: Editions Barrault, 1990.

Lionnet, Francoise. "Logique Metissesi: Cultural Appropriation and Postcolonial Representations." In *Postcolonial Subject: Francophone Women Writers*. Minneapolis: University of Minnesota Press, 1996.

Lowe, Lisa. *Immigrant Acts*. Durham: Duke University Press, 1996.

Memmi, Albert. *Portrait du colonisé*. Paris: Gallimard, 1985.

Mohanty, Chandra, et al., eds. *Third World Women and the Politics of Feminism*. Bloomington: Indiana University Press, 1991.

Morokvasic, Miriana. "Women in Migration: Beyond the Reductionist Outlook." In *One Way Ticket: Migration and Female Labour*, ed. Annie Phizacklea, 13–31. London: Routledge, 1983.

Nakashima, Cynthia. "An Invisible Monster: The Creation and Denial of Mixed-Race People in America." In *Racially Mixed People in America*, ed. Maria P. P. Root, 162–78. Newbury Park, Calif.: Sage Publications, 1992.

Norindr, Panivong. *Phantasmatic Indochina: French Colonial Ideology and Architecture, Film, and Literature*. Durham, N.C.: Duke University Press, 1996.

Omi, Michael, and Howard Winant. *Racial Formation in the United States*. New York: Routledge, 1986.

Payne, James, ed. *Multicultural Autobiography: American Lives*. Knoxville: University of Tennessee Press, 1992.

Root, Maria, ed. *Racially Mixed People in America*. Newbury Park, Calif.: Sage Publications, 1992.

Rosaldo, Renato. *Culture and Truth: The Remaking of Social Analysis*. Boston: Beacon Press, 1989.

Said, Edward. *Orientalism*. New York: Vintage Books, 1978.

Spivak, Ghayatri Chakrovorty. *The Post-Colonial Critic: Interviews, Strategies, Dialogues*. Ed. Sarah Harasym. New York: Routledge, 1990.

Trinh T. Minh-ha. *Women Native Other*. Bloomington: Indiana University Press, 1989.

Valverde, Kieu Linh. "From Dust to Gold: The Vietnamese American Experience." In *Racially Mixed People in America*, ed. Maria P. P. Root, 144–61. Newbury Park, Calif.: Sage Publications, 1992.

Wong, Sau-Ling. *Reading Asian American Literature: From Necessity to Extravagance*. Princeton, N.J.: Princeton University Press, 1993.

Yeager, Jack. "Kim Lefevre's *Retour à la saison des pluies*: Rediscovering the Landscapes of Childhood." *L'Esprit Createur* 23, no. 2 (Summer 1993).

———. *The Vietnamese Novel in French: A Literary Response to Colonialism*. Hanover, N.H.: University Press of New England, 1987.

Smuggling Across the Borders of Race, Gender, and Sexuality

Sui Sin Far's 'Mrs. Spring Fragrance'

Sui Sin Far's collection *Mrs. Spring Fragrance* (1912) is fundamentally concerned with the process of naming. However, names are important in this text not as absolute descriptors of racial, gendered, or sexual identity, but rather as the space for a certain smuggling across the borders of dominant categories of identity that finally undermines them. As critics have already noted, Sui Sin Far's own name may be a comment on her identity as an "Eurasian"—as a mixed race individual—and characters in her stories are often named in such a way as to encourage readers to cross and recross racial borders. Yet Sui Sin Far also destabilizes identificatory norms of gender and sexuality, and this topic has received little critical attention.[1] In stories such as "A Chinese Boy-Girl" (1904) and "Tian Shan's Kindred Spirit" (1912) characters cross-dress, and names function as a site where not only racial, but also gendered, identities are crossed and recrossed; finally, names install a space where the complicity of discourses of race and gender are thrown into relief and (sometimes) remade. Even more radically, cross-dressing and cross-gendering stories such as "The Smuggling of Tie Co" (1900), "The Story of Tin-A" (1899), and "The Chinese Lily" (1912) attempt to undo the binary structures of not only gendered and racial difference, but of heterosexuality itself, and once again names function as key sites for the interrogation of dominant identificatory practices.[2]

Yet in undermining the identificatory norms of heterosexuality, Sui Sin Far may seek to replace them with something more transgressive, something she could only sign at through fissures in the discursive fabric that opened up once the binary categories of gender and sexuality had been destabilized. Is this not quite sightable/citeable subject what Amy Ling has called "a lesbian sensibility"? And what would it mean to say that Sui Sin Far portrays homosexuality in her writing through coded signs and metaphors, through silences and gaps—through what we might be tempted to call an epistemology of the closet?[3] Most provocatively, what is the significance of the fact that she structures her own name and body into texts about such not quite sightable/citeable subjects: is she encouraging us to read identificatory practices at work not only in her texts, but in her life? I will finally suggest that Sui Sin Far's five gender-crossing stories ask us to interrogate the name as a site of identificatory practices that construct the racial, gendered, and sexual subject, but that also construct the creator of this subject—not only the author, but also (and most importantly) the reader herself.

Names That Matter

In *Bodies That Matter*, Judith Butler argues that a persistent feature of some texts is a destabilization of gender and sexuality through the name. At issue in such works is "how to read the name as a site of identification, a site where the dynamic of identification is at play, and to read the name as an occasion for the retheorization of cross-identification or, rather, the crossing that is, it seems, at work in every identificatory practice."[4] Later in this study, Butler examines Nella Larsen's *Passing*, arguing that its destabilization of gender and sexuality is tied to a destabilization of race and that, once again, the name functions as a site to examine the crossings that are at work in every identificatory practice, a textual marker that allows the interrogation of racial, sexual, and gender norms (172). Sui Sin Far employs naming practices, in general and in her cross-gendering fiction in particular, to contest the construction of both racial and gendered identificatory practices, as well as to demonstrate their complicity. Names of individuals (either proper names, or descriptive ones) appear in the titles of the majority of her stories, and they explicitly function as markers of class, race, ethnic identity, and gender. Sui Sin Far does not, then, see female (or male) characters as constructed through a simple practice of opposition (such as <man> equals <not woman>), but rather her names point to the ways identity is formulated through multiple social, cultural, linguistic, and discursive matrices.

This concept of naming is, to some degree, congruent with a psychoanalytic theory of identity formation. Lacan, for example, argues that names stabilize a series of transient imaginary identifications; thus the "permanent appearance over time [of the human subject is] ... strictly only recognizable through the intermediary of the name."[5] For Lacan, to be named is to be positioned within a Symbolic order structured by the Law of the Father. However, Sui Sin Far demonstrates that this law functions through a set of racializing and sexualizing, as well as gendering, norms that operate simultaneously. Titles such as "The Chinese Lily" or "A Chinese Boy-Girl" explicitly demonstrate that the construction of sexual difference does not precede the construction of racial difference, and that the Symbolic is also a racializing set of norms. Furthermore, Sui Sin Far also uses names as sites for the de-scription (or the un-writing) of categories of identity. Many of Sui Sin Far's names undermine the workings of the racializing and gendering set of norms that is the Symbolic through a certain opacity: they can be read as male and female, and Chinese and white. For example, many of them have items that seem explicitly "masculine" or "feminine" in them—Fin *Fan* (of "Tian Shan's Kindred Spirit") or *Tie* Co. For English readers, fans would have a feminine connotation, ties a masculine one, but in both cases this construction is undermined: Tie Co turns out to be a woman (dressed as a man), while Fin Fan eventually adopts male clothing in order to be reunited with her lover. Moreover, although names like "Tin-A" or "Tie Co" or "Fin Fan" may sound Chinese, if we look closely we see they are composed almost entirely of English words (tin, tie, fin, fan). So are such names Chinese or English, male or female? All of the above, we might be tempted to respond.

Indeed, we can see in Sui Sin Far's writing a complicated critique of racial, gendered, and sexual categories of identity that works through the name. Categories of race and gender are crossed and recrossed; this does not mean that these categories disappear, but that their boundaries become more permeable. This crossing sometimes works linguistically— through language itself—as well as on the level of race and gender. Sui Sin Far herself was not fluent in Chinese, but there is evidence in her fiction that she knew some of the connotations of her Chinese characters' names and was aware of the gender these names would reveal to Chinese-speaking readers. At times she created complex linguistic crossings or tropes revolving around these names. For example, for her main audience (Anglo-American readers unfamiliar with Chinese), a name such as "Ku Yum" (the title character in "A Chinese Boy-Girl") would seem ungendered. A Chinese-speaking reader, however, would likely know that Ku Yum is a stereotypically female descriptor, roughly translatable as "miserable person" or "daughter," a name Annette White-Parks claims is the most frequent one for female characters in Sui Sin Far's fiction as a whole (*Sui Sin Far* 88). Therefore, a Chinese-speaking reader would appear to have "inside" knowledge—a certainty that Ku Yum is a girl. What does it mean, then, when the character named "Ku Yum" actually turns out to be a boy dressed as a girl? An English-speaking reader would be disconcerted by the gender crossing, but even a Chinese-speaking reader might be surprised by the "name crossing"—by the fact that this stereotypically "feminine" name turns out to be attached to a masculine subject, a masculine body. In the end, the name "Ku Yum" does not so much instantiate a fixed racial and gendered identity as become the space for linguistic, sexual, and racial crossings that undermine an ability to "know" identity.[6]

Furthermore, Sui Sin Far's naming practices recognize that names produce a domain of bodies enfranchised by the dominant discourse, but also a domain of bodies *outside* this order. Butler argues that "the exclusionary matrix by which subjects are formed ... requires the simultaneous production of a domain of abject beings, those who are not yet 'subjects,' but who form the constitutive outside to the domain of the subject" (3). The subject is therefore created through forces of exclusion and abjection that produce an abject outside which is, still, inside the subject as its own founding repudiation (3). In this context, Butler asks a provocative question: "How, then, might one alter the very terms that constitute the 'necessary' domain of bodies through rendering unthinkable and unlivable another domain of bodies, those that do not matter in the same way?" (xi). Sui Sin Far's stories that involve both gender crossing and racial crossing use names to render an "unthinkable" and perhaps "unspeakable" domain of bodies that "matter" in an unstable, and also "different," way.

Perhaps Sui Sin Far's own life encouraged her to conceptualize categories of race, gender, and sexuality as more fluid than fixed, and to consider what might lie outside "traditional" conceptions of identity. Viet Thanh Nguyen argues that Sui Sin Far's "mixed-race heritage, which granted her the possibility of passing, revealed to her the performativity behind race" (39). But having realized the performativity behind race, having realized that there was no such thing as an "authentic" or "essential" Chinese identity separate from her "white" identity, it is possible that Sui Sin Far began to see that other "traditional" categories of identity—such as male versus female or heterosexual versus homosexual—could be unwritten, destabilized. Her fiction represents an awareness that categories of racial, sexual, and gendered identities are not separate matrices but rather work through each other to formulate the "subject." And the most subversive way of unhinging these categories was through simultaneity—the deconstruction of *multiple* matrices of identity formulation at one time.

Of course, characters who attempt to cross racial categories, but not gendered ones, are present in Sui Sin Far's writing. For example, in "'Its Wavering Image,'" Pan, a "half white, half-Chinese" (61) woman, initially believes that she can be white but finally chooses to be Chinese, saying, "A white woman! ... I would not be a white woman for all the world" (66). In "The Sing-Song Woman," on the other hand, Mag-gee sees herself as American in both race and culture, despite her Chinese heritage. "I was born in America, and I'm not Chinese in looks nor in any other way. See! My eyes are blue, and there is gold in my hair; and I love potatoes and beef, and every time I eat rice it makes me sick, and so does chopped up food" (127), exclaims Mag-gee. Such stories seem to reflect a final positioning within one racial category or another, rather than a de-scription of these categories; race is crossed, but then it is contained.[7] Sui Sin Far's stories that concern *both* gender and racial crossing, however, move toward a permanent destabilization of binary categories such as "male" versus "female," "Chinese" versus "Anglo-American," and "heterosexual" versus "homosexual." Examining the construction of identity through a matrix that sees the simultaneity of racial and gendered identificatory practices allows Sui Sin Far to create a more complex and ultimately more open politics of race, gender, and sexuality.

Racial and Gendered Identificatory Practices in "A Chinese Boy-Girl"

How do names "matter" in "A Chinese Boy-Girl"? This text concerns a young child who is almost removed from parental custody when the white, missionary teacher who runs a girls' school thinks the "girl" is being brought up improperly. Miss Mason, a young American teacher new to the Chinatown district where she teaches in Southern California, believes that the child, Ku Yum, is not being raised to be a good, properly "demure little" maiden (156).[8] Miss Mason interests the Society for the Prevention of Cruelty to Children in the case, and they order Ku Yum's removal to a home for Chinese girls. But this action is averted when Ku Yum's father, Ten Suie, reveals that his "daughter" is not in fact a daugh-

ter but a son whom he has been protecting from an evil spirit he believes
has killed his four other sons.[9]

The most obvious theme of this story is the distance between white
and Asian perspectives—the way the Western mind (exemplified by Miss
Mason and the Society for the Prevention of Cruelty to Children) tries to
force its doctrine onto that of the Eastern world (exemplified by Ten Suie
and the Chinese community), as well as the way the East resists this colonization. But the story's gendered themes also mark the distance between
perspectives on male and female roles in the world—the way the Symbolic is structured through an abject realm of racialized, sexualized, and
othered bodies that seem to reside outside its logic. It is clear that in both
cultures (Chinese American and Anglo-American) girls are expected to
play inferior (secondary) roles. Miss Mason believes that girls should be
docile, demure maidens, confined in physical spaces such as schoolrooms
and homes for girls, while Ten Suie believes they are worthless things not
wanted by the spirits. Furthermore, Ten Suie mourns the loss of his four
sons but not the wife who produced these sons, who is also now dead.
The story thus suggests the gap between not only Chinese and American
expectations of the world, but also between the male "subject" and the
(female, racial, abject, or other) "object."

Yet names function in this story to begin to undo those practices that
create subject and object. "A Chinese Boy-Girl" clearly demonstrates that
identificatory practices create gender and race. Because Ku Yum is dressed like
a Chinese girl, "in blue cotton garments [with] her long, shining hair in a
braid interwoven with silks of many colors" (155), and called "a little Chinese
Girl" (155), the teacher assumes she is a Chinese girl. Here recognition of the
signs (the ribbons, the hair, the name), not the body, produces the gendered
and racial subject. Sui Sin Far writes about the process of gender and racial
ascription, which she locates firmly in the realm of discourse and language.
For example, the naming of the girl as girl ("'Come in, little girl, and tell me
what they call you.' ... 'Ku Yum be my name,' was the unhesitating reply"
[155]) initiates a process by which the girl is brought into the domain of
language and kinship through the interpellation of gender. So the "girling of
the girl" (to borrow a phrase from Butler) is shown to be a product of the
ritualized repetition of gender norms; dressed as "one girl," called "one girl"
(159), Ku Yum in fact becomes "one girl." Furthermore, the "racing of the
girl" also occurs in this exchange; as Ku Yum's name and dress do not seem to
be American or male, she is read by the teacher as both feminine and racial, "a
little Chinese girl" (155).

Naming the "Chinese Boy-Girl" at first seems to stabilize the inter-pellative process, but later is shown to overturn it, to spawn unexpected possibilities. "Your father, by passing you off as a girl thought to keep an evil spirit away from you; but just by that means he brought another" (160), comments the teacher. Ku Yum's name does not reflect his/her gender, then, but rather becomes the site for a certain crossing of gender that explicitly questions the suturing over of the subject in, and by, a name. The crossing of the "boy-girl" first from male to female, and then, at the end of the story, from female back to male, therefore stages a transfer of gender that undermines the process whereby gender and race are substantialized, codified, and rigidified through the name. Ku Yum claims s/he will "*never* be a good girl" (159), but at times "her expression is so subdued that the teacher could hardly believe that the moment before she had defiantly stated that she would never be a good girl" (159). Ku Yum's final admission in the story—"I never be good girl, but *perhaps* I be good boy" (160, my emphasis)—leaves open the question of what s/he will finally "be." The story, then, while explicitly seeming to enforce gen-der and racial difference, implicitly deconstructs the identificatory prac-tices that constitute and construct gender and racial norms.

I want to pause for a moment to consider the hyphenated figure of the "boy-girl," of the boy who is "passed ... off as a girl" (160), of the child who passes back and forth between gender identities on the slim beam of a hyphen, and to ponder how this gender passing connects to racial crossing. In her autobiography, "Leaves from the Mental Portfolio of an Eurasian," Sui Sin Far describes herself as a "crosser": "So I roam back-ward and forward *across* the continent. When I am East, my heart is West. When I am West, my heart is East" (230, my emphasis). The descendant of a Chinese mother and an Anglo father, Sui Sin Far becomes the hy-phen in <Chinese-American>, the fragile bridge that allows a crossing between different worlds: "I give my right hand to the Occidentals and my left to the Orientals, hoping that between them they will not utterly destroy the insignificant 'connecting link'" ("Leaves" 230). Sui Sin Far's construction of her identity encourages a movement back and forth be-tween categories that are supposed to remain separate, an inhabiting of several categories simultaneously that is meant to undo these categories. Gloria Anzaldúa comments that the "juncture where the mestiza stands is where phenomena tend to collide."[10] We can read the figure of the Eura-sian, and of the Boy-Girl, as functioning like the mestiza—as becoming a site where phenomena collide, and are also remade. And the language of the text is complicit with, and in fact creates, these collisions, these collusions, by continually using names that foil and baffle those reading practices with which we mark, and in fact create, categories of race and gender.

Unlike "A Chinese Boy-Girl," the other cross-gender and cross-racial texts I will discuss most frequently depict women who pass for men, but the process of naming continues to play a definitive role. In these stories, women pass for men to gain freedom of movement, license to choose whom they will marry, and economic empowerment. To borrow a phrase from Yuko Matsukawa's essay on Sui Sin Far's sister, Onoto Watanna, then, many of these women "cross-dress for success."[11] But Sui Sin Far cross-dresses her characters to show that gender and race are linguistic and identificatory performances. Her female characters smuggle across the borders of race and gender to show the boundaries of these borders, as well as how these borders can be reconstructed to create another kind of body that counts, another kind of body that "matters."

Becoming the Name of the Father: "Tian Shan's Kindred Spirit"

Like "A Chinese Boy-Girl," "Tian Shan's Kindred Spirit" demonstrates the complicity of discourses of race and gender. The male protagonist of the story, Tian Shan, is described as "a wily Oriental" (119)—a description explicating the process of racialization, the construction of derogatory racial categories—because of his racial status, Tian Shan is not seen as fully human. Yet after announcing this, Sui Sin Far undercuts it, saying, "had Tian Shan been an American … he would certainly have far outshone Dewey, Peary, or Cook" (119). Tian Shan's name gets translated by a racist white public as "wily Oriental," yet if he were "American" his name would overshadow the names of more famous heroes. Sui Sin Far also undermines the stereotype of the Asian as insensitive, unfeeling, or unfathomable by telling her readers that Tian Shan "loved Fin Fan, even as the American man loves the girl he would make his wife" (121). Furthermore, she resists what Sau-ling Cynthia Wong has called the "ethnicizing of gender" (the process whereby certain races are hypersexualized or feminized as "essential" components of their racial makeup). Nineteenth-century racist discourse often configured Chinese men as not only "wily" or "insensitive," but also asexual and/or effeminate.[12] By insisting

Tian Shan is not a "wily Oriental" and that he also loves even as an "American man" would, Sui Sin Far seeks to interlink and overturn racialized and sexualized discourses that create abject, feminized, disempowered Asian subject-positions.

It is no coincidence, then, that the story's actual plot focuses on the ferrying of various "abject" bodies across borders, for Tian Shan makes his living smuggling Chinese from Canada to the United States. Tian Shan, then, is a border-crosser, but when he falls in love with his "kindred spirit" Fin Fan, he decides to give up this dangerous activity for a less precarious way of earning a living. However, on a last smuggling mission he is caught and the authorities plan to deport him to China. Here cross-dressing enters the story: Fin Fan dresses as a man so she can smuggle herself into the United States, get caught by the authorities, and then be deported with her lover back to China.

What are we to make of these characters' multiple border crossings: from China to Canada, from Canada to the United States, from the United States to Canada, and from Canada back to China? What seems to be at stake for Sui Sin Far is the connection between smuggling over physical borders and smuggling over gendered and sexual ones. For Tian Shan, smuggling itself may be an act of phallic sexuality; for example, he speaks of his "canoe" "rising on the swells and cutting through the white-caps, until at last he reached the shore for which he had risked so much" (121). Given that in Sui Sin Far's fiction smuggling usually involves only men, we must also wonder whether it has a homoerotic element. Crossing or smuggling may represent a refusal to take one's place within a stable, heterosexual identity, a desire to live beyond, or outside, the laws governing sexual identity.

Fin Fan herself encourages Tian Shan to give up border crossing, to take his place within the law, which at first might seem to mean she adheres to a system that configures her as the female object allowing the construction of the male, heterosexual subject. Fin Fan is also defined through a male; as the title states and the story reiterates several times (119, 120), she is "Tian Shan's Kindred Spirit." Fin Fan's name is a blank in the title; she seems to function as an inverted mirror of the male. Yet from the story's start, we are told explicitly that Fin Fan is not a "proper Chinese female" (120); she refuses to accept Christianity (120) or obey her father's orders that she marry a Chinese merchant described as a "proper man" (122). Fin Fan therefore lives in "an atmosphere of outlawry" (120). Like many of Sui Sin Far's cross-dressing women and men, Fin Fan is described as improper, deviant, resistant, outside the law. Indeed, as Annette White-Parks argues, both Tian Shan and Fin Fan are trickster figures who slip over racial and geographic borders (*Sui Sin Far* 216–17). So while Fin Fan initially encourages Tian Shan to take his place within the Symbolic law, there is also an unruly element in her personality that believes in the possibility of bodies and sexualities that exist outside this law, or rather, of bodies and sexualities that can manifest themselves before the law has instituted its closure. Fin Fan cross-dresses, then, to express this possibility of a sexualized body that refuses to be caught up in the matrix of gendered and racial norms. When she cross-dresses, "fresh air and light ... come into her soul" (124)—clearly, gender bending frees her, allowing her to move spatially and psychologically.

Gender bending may also help Fin Fan avoid (at least temporarily) the processes of identity that construct her as a feminized and racialized object—as a Chinese woman defined only through her relationship with a masculine subject. In fact, Fin Fan actually becomes her father, adopting "a suit of her father's clothes" (124) to cross-dress. Fin Fan may, then, become a subject through assumption of the patronym; dressed as her father, looking like her father, she would be called by her father's name. But does this becoming the Law of the Father, this miming of the functioning of the patronym, allow her to escape her positioning within the Symbolic order? When Tian Shan first sees the Chinese girl dressed as her father, he does not recognize her and asks, "What do you want?" (125), a potentially subversive question. What does the cross-gendered, cross-dressed subject who has left her traditional racial positioning *want*? But Fin Fan's answer is highly conventional: "'To go to China with you and to be your wife,' was the softly surprising reply" (125). In this moment, the misrecognition is crossed out: "'Fin Fan!' exclaimed Tian Shan. 'Fin Fan!'" (125). Fin Fan is installed under her name, situated within the Law of the Symbolic by having been called a name that secures her identity as the not-subject, as the Chinese female object, as the dutiful wife defined through the male. Oddly enough, though, Fin Fan's crossing remains a destabilizing textual and discursive presence, as the last lines of the story indicate:

> "Fin Fan!" exclaimed Tian Shan. "Fin Fan!"
> *The boy* pulled off *his* cap.
> "Aye," said *he*. "'Tis Fin Fan!" (125, my emphasis)

By using the pronoun "he" and calling Fin Fan a "boy," the discourse of the text forces us to question to what extent the exchange of gender it has staged can be crossed out, undone. Pronominal confusion or dysphoria, as Marjorie Garber has argued in another context, functions as "an indicator of the boundary crossing that makes gendered subjectivity so problematic," implying that the lines demarcating sexual identity are not absolute.[13] What identificatory practice can encompass this puzzling pronominal "he" who refuses to disappear into the "she" pronoun at the end of "Tian Shan's Kindred Spirit"? Only one that sees the way categories normally kept separate by these practices (such as male and female, he and she) actually overlap. Overall, Fin Fan's miming of the male gender finally reinforces those norms it would seek to undo, but the text does create a site for the contestation of gender and racial norms.

Like "Tian Shan's Kindred Spirit," "The Smuggling of Tie Co" also employs cross-dressing, but in this text gender identity is never rigidified. Furthermore, "The Smuggling of Tie Co," like the next two stories discussed, questions the stability of heterosexual subjectivity through the presentation of an almost unsightable/unciteable homosexual desire. In these stories, the paternal law, the Law of the Symbolic, is cited through the name, but it is cited differently, in such a way that heterosexuality is exposed and its power displaced by the assertion of a desire and a body that refuses to be caught up in its closure.

Destabilizing Sexual Identity Through Homosexual Desire: "The Smuggling of Tie Co"

As demonstrated, Sui Sin Far's texts about gender crossing often involve smuggling: the illicit crossing of a body into a forbidden space (a "boy" smuggles into a classroom for Chinese girls, a "girl" smuggles out of the country in her Chinese father's clothes, a man smuggles "Chinese" bodies across "American" borders). Smuggling represents a process whereby a hidden, forbidden knowledge insinuates its way into a binary opposition, and in so doing begins to dismantle it. Trinh Minh-ha comments that "the body, the most visible difference between men and women, the only one to offer a secure ground for those who seek the permanent, the feminine 'nature' and 'essence,' remains thereby the safest basis for racist and sexist ideologies."[14] But as a trope in Sui Sin Far's fiction, smuggling involves the traversal of the identificatory practices that create a domain of racialized and feminized abject bodies, as well as a crossing, and perhaps a crossing out, of the borders that govern these bodies.

"The Smuggling of Tie Co" explicitly makes the connection between border crossing and body crossing, for Tie Co is, quite literally, a body smuggled across the border from Canada to the United States by Jack Fabian, a white man who earns his living ferrying such "cargo." Fabian is another heroic smuggler, but when laws are passed that allow Chinese to enter the United States legally, provided they have the right documentation, Fabian loses all his business. It is at this point that Tie Co, a young Chinese boy with a good job in Canada, offers Fabian fifty dollars to smuggle him into the United States. On the voyage, Fabian realizes that Tie Co was only allowing himself to be smuggled because of love for Fabian, and he resolves to take the boy back to Canada. But the two are caught, and in order to protect Fabian from prosecution, Tie Co commits suicide, jumping into a raging river. In death it is discovered that Tie Co is a woman, cross-dressed as a male.

Like "A Chinese Boy-Girl" this story demonstrates that interpellation, not the body, actually creates identity; gender and race are discursive and performative. The body found is said to be "Tie Co's body, and yet not Tie Co, for Tie Co was a youth, and the body found with Tie Co's face and dressed in Tie Co's clothes was the body of a girl—a woman" (108). Tie Co has been cross-dressing for a number of years, and only death reveals the "real" gender of the body. The gender performed seems to be that of a male, while the body (the "real" body?) seems to be that of a female. Yet, to use Eve Sedgwick's terms, rather than clarifying this riddle the text produces "merely a series of intensification of it" (94)—the language itself is equivocal ("Tie Co's body, and yet not Tie Co"). As Min Song explains, "although the discovery of a female body putatively dispels the homosexual meaning of Tie Co's romantic statement, the narrator refuses to concede epistemological clarity about his or her identity" (304).[15] Furthermore, the language of the text refuses to confirm Tie Co's "real" gender, for it continually describes Tie Co as male, even after insisting that a "female" body has been discovered: "Tie Co had come out to Canada with a number of other *youths*. Though not very strong *he* had always been a good worker and 'very smart.' *He* had been quiet and reserved ... and a great favorite with Mission ladies" (109, my emphasis). This passage harps on Tie Co's male gender, using discourse to recover, reclothe, the "female" body in the garb of "masculinity." "The Smuggling of Tie Co," insists, then, that gender is performed (or constructed) through a language that may have little to do with the riddle of the "real" body.

Language also creates a racial identity that is often at variance with the "real" race, while simultaneously suturing race and gender. As often as Tie Co is referred to as a "boy," a "lad," or a "he" (twelve times in this four-page story), he is also insistently referred to as a "Chinaman" (eight times). Border crossing itself is initially shown to be connected to masculinity and to race, to an identity as a "Chinaman." In the early twentieth century, laws were passed that permitted Chinese to come to the United States if they could prove they already had a father living there; this led to the phenomenon of "paper sons"—of individuals who claimed to have a Chinese father in the United States but were in fact unrelated to the person they listed as their relative. For Sui Sin Far, the "paper son" phenomenon offers an explicit mechanism for portraying the connection between paternity, masculinity, and being "American." Jack Fabian learns that "any young *Chinaman* on payment of a couple of hundred dollars could procure a *father* which *father* would swear the young *Chinaman* was born in *America*—thus proving him to be an *American* citizen" (105, my emphasis). The significance of gender in this exchange is highlighted: a "China*man*" (which Sui Sin Far repeats twice) achieves a paternity, a *father* (which Sui Sin Far repeats twice), and becomes an *American* (variants on which Sui Sin Far repeats twice). The male individual (the "Chinaman") is allowed to cross from "Chinese" to "American," then, not by virtue of his race, but by virtue of his gender identification, by virtue of his maleness.

In and of itself, this is an interesting conjunction that links the crossing of racial borders (from Chinese to "American") with a particular name indicating a masculine identity (the "Chinaman"). Here, "American" is figured as a racial identity rather than a purely geographic one, but one can only cross to this racial identity if one already inhabits the category of "male." This conjunction also silently renders a domain of bodies that cannot cross these borders (that is, become "American") because of their female and racial status. Yet Sui Sin Far complicates this configuration by revealing that Tie Co, the "Chinaman" smuggled across geographic borders, was himself (herself?) a woman. And while it may seem that Sui Sin Far's use of the derogatory term "Chinaman" panders to the prejudices of her (mostly white) audience, in fact she reappropriates this term. Tie Co is a "Chinaman"—yet s/he is neither from China, nor a man. The "logic" of the prejudicial term "Chinaman" is undone. Further, it is resignified to describe an individual who exercises agency, an individual who chooses where s/he will go, and when, and why. Sui Sin Far uses the language of the "Chinaman" to create bodies that *do* matter, that are invested with significance, despite (or perhaps because of) their status as "Chinamen." She undermines the discourse that would repudiate her race, but she also makes her claim for another kind of body that matters precisely *through* this discourse.

The body of Tie Co, then, is clearly meant to be a "Chinaman's" body that matters. But it is also supposed to be a body that matters differently, first by resisting labeling, and second by undermining the compulsory heterosexuality of patriarchal society. According to Xiao-Huang Yin, Tie Co is "the image of a self-sacrificing Chinese girl" (69), but the story seems to deliberately confuse such a reading.[16] By continually repeating the fact that Tie Co is male, a "he," a "Chinaman," even after the body has been read as female and not from China, Sui Sin Far suggests ways to subvert the logic of ritualized repetitions of gender and race. As the text reiterates that Tie Co is a "Chinaman" we begin to question whether this reiteration actually fixes the status of the subject in some irrevocable sense. Tie Co's name and his gender/racial status diverge, perhaps producing a crisis in the construction of the subject that works through names but finally refuses to stabilize either race or gender. The body matters differently in this text because it cannot be contained within a stable racial or gendered matrix of discourse.

Furthermore, the body matters differently in this text because of its violation of prohibitions against both homosexuality and miscegenation. The male narrator describes Jack Fabian as the epitome of (white) masculinity: "Uncommonly strong in person, tall and well built, with fine features and a pair of keen, steady blue eyes, gifted with a sort of rough eloquence and of much personal fascination" (104). If the narrator's description of Fabian exhibits a certain homoeroticism associated with Fabian's ability to "smuggle," then what does it mean that when Fabian cannot "smuggle" he becomes "restless" and "glowering" (105)? Is Fabian, the epitome of white, heterosexual masculinity, not really as "heterosexual" as he appears to be? Consider the following statements about Fabian's trip with Tie Co: "They had a merry drive, for Fabian's liking for Tie Co was very real"; "It was a pleasant night on which the two men set out"; "Fabian had a rig waiting at the corner of the street; Tie Co, dressed in citizen's clothes, stepped into it unobserved" (106). This language seems associated less with an illegal operation of ferrying human "cargo" and more with an elopement, a honeymoon. The following exchange between Tie Co and Fabian also illustrates that something more than literal smuggling is occurring:

> "Haven't you got a nice little wife at home?" [Fabian asked]. "I hear you people marry very young."
>
> "No, I no wife," asserted his companion with a choky little laugh. "I never have no wife."
>
> "Nonsense," joked Fabian. "Why, Tie Co, think how nice it would be to have a little woman cook your rice and to love you."
>
> "I not have wife," repeated Tie Co seriously, "I not like woman, I like man."
>
> "You confirmed old bachelor!" ejaculated Fabian. (107)

A reader is certainly not prepared for Fabian's "ejaculation," nor is she prepared for the final admission that Tie Co actually likes not men in general, but a particular man—Jack Fabian (107). Up to this point, we have not suspected that Tie Co is a woman (in fact, readers may not suspect this until the story's very end), so Tie Co's admission that he "likes men," or a man, is surprising, as is Jack Fabian's easy acceptance of this statement. Upon hearing this, Fabian does not abandon Tie Co, but rather plans to take him back to Toronto. Fabian seems to accept (or at least not reject) the love of the individual he fully believes to be a boy, Tie Co.

We must recall here that Fabian is a smuggler, a border crosser, and that Sui Sin Far often associates such geographical activities with crossings of other kinds. I want to suggest that her text opens up a space for the possibility of a homosexual desire that cannot be contained within the norms of heterosexual logic. Why does Tie Co seem "so different from the others" (107)? Is it because Fabian somehow "knows" that Tie Co is "female"? Yet the text does not enforce this reading: Fabian never refers to Tie Co as a "she" or a woman, even though he is said to ponder, "long and earnestly over the mystery of Tie Co's life—and death" (109). Fabian sees Tie Co as "different" not because s/he is female, but because s/he seems to initiate Fabian into the possibility of homosexual desire. After Tie Co's death, we are told that "Fabian is now very busy; there are lots of boys taking his helping hand over the border, but none of them are like Tie Co" (109). Fabian is helped by other boys "over the border" he may have negotiated with Tie Co—the border between heterosexual and homosexual desire. And finally, no one can explain the "mystery" of Tie Co, the fissure in the system of sexual signification that is this boy/girl, this male/female, this Asian/American, this heterosexual/homosexual subject.

"The Smuggling of Tie Co" therefore suggests the radical possibility of a desire that is both homosexual and miscegenating. This almost unsightable/unciteable desire exists beyond the compulsory heterosexuality of patriarchal culture. Homosexuality and miscegenation are shown to be the "outside" of a normative heterosexuality, but they are also brought inside the heterosexual norm through a phallic character like Jack Fabian, who seems to accept (at least partially) his desire for an individual who is both "male" and racialized. I would like to think that this desire is able to exist precisely because of the way this story's discourse creates bodies that can vacillate between racial and gendered identities. The discourse demonstrates that what is excluded from the body for the body's boundary to form is an unnamable, improper, miscegenating desire, but that this desire reasserts itself at crucial moments, such as in Jack Fabian's "ejaculation." When the discursive boundaries of the body disintegrate, and what is excluded from the body makes its way back into the hegemonic domain and language, racist and sexist ideologies begin to be undone.[17]

In this context, it is interesting to note that in "The Smuggling of Tie Co," as in several other stories discussed, characters who "pass" for the opposite gender die at story's end. Yet these deaths do not "cross out" the crossings that have occurred. Tie Co's suicide, for example, does not shut down the radical possibilities that this transgressive, transracial, transgendered body has rendered. Tie Co becomes a query in Fabian's mind that perhaps causes him to question his own identity, and perhaps causes readers to wonder about this s/he body that somehow matters differently, but does matter. Garber has argued that the boundary lines of gender and subjectivity, never clear or precise, are constantly being drawn and redrawn in an anxious effort to define, to delimit, to *know* them (333). Yet in death, Tie Co's body escapes this anxious process of definition, of delimitation, remaining unknown. Therefore, although some of Sui Sin Far's passing characters suffer a literal death, the challenge their "abject" bodies posit to the Symbolic order continues to operate.[18]

The next text discussed is also concerned with a homosexual desire that challenges the compulsory heterosexuality structuring the Law of the Father. Yet in "The Story of Tin-A," this desire can be read through covert narrative strategies that at times seem to place the author's own body into the text. This story demonstrates the necessity of escaping the heterosexual system of language and logic that reduces women's racialized bodies to objects of barter, but finally implies that heterosexism can be escaped only at the price of sexuality, of the exclusion of the body's desires.

"The Story of Tin-A": Placing the Body in the Text

"The Story of Tin-A" is narrated by a traveler who asks a "tiny Chinese woman" tending a luxurious garden of flowers to relate the history of her life. As a young girl, Tin-A lived on the island of Formosa and played with a childhood friend called A-Ho, with whom she spent many happy days collecting flowers. When A-Ho marries a man who lives on the other side of the island, Tin-A is bereft. Ironically, Tin-A is eventually pledged as a second wife to her friend's husband, Ah Kim. At first Tin-A is exhilarated by the possibility of reunion with her friend. However, when her friend writes begging her not to come, Tin-A resolves to escape the marriage. But her father only tells her that if she does not marry Ah Kim, Ah Kim will choose another woman, and her stepmother, as Tin-A says, only "thought that my mind was sick" (102); the attempt to avoid the marriage is read by the parents as futile or insane. Desperate, Tin-A asks a group of Chinese actors to smuggle her to the United States, dressed as a male, so that she too can become an actor. They refuse, only agreeing to take her there to find a husband. Once in San Francisco, however, Tin-A refuses to marry, spending her time tending her garden.

As the scene in which Tin-A watches the actors perform makes clear, this story is centrally concerned with the performance of gender and race, and with their radical alterability. Since only Chinese males are allowed to become actors, the men must play the parts of Chinese females. Gender and race are shown, once again, to adhere in clothing and display, in "performances" and "tinsel and fancy dress" (102). As Tin-A watches the actors, she "longs to be a man and an actor" (102). In this subversive scene, a woman, watching men play women, longs to be a man herself (so that she can play a man *playing* a woman). Tin-A realizes that she does not have to be "Tin-A," the tiny Chinese woman without agency, but could, rather, perform the role of the Chinese male actor (or acter, or agent). The play therefore stages an exchange of gender that suggests the possibility of an escape from heterosexual norms that configure Chinese women as objects in a cycle of barter between Chinese men.

In this cycle of exchange, Tin-A and A-Ho are interchangeable others, Chinese wives dependent on their husbands for social identity. Indeed, because A-Ho has not produced a male son for her husband, she is even judged to be an inferior object. Therefore, if Tin-A marries Ah Kim she will actually supersede her friend, becoming the "first wife." Chinese wives are ordered in a hierarchy of exchange according to how well they perpetuate the male patriarchy—governed by the Law of the Father, the Law of the Husband, and finally the Law of the Son. This law is extremely destructive to the female body, for A-Ho dies less than four years after her marriage, and perhaps she dies in childbirth, desperately attempting to produce a male progeny. Clearly, she is reduced to a body that she cannot escape, a body that has only one function: replication of a patriarchal system that denies her own subjectivity. Unlike her friend, Tin-A attempts to avoid this system by crossing the ocean to the United States, where she cannot be forced to marry. But what exactly is "outside" this system? Is there an "outside," or only a way of being positioned "inside" that is somehow "different," defiant, improper?

"Remembering A-Ho, I fear to wed" (103), Tin-A tells her interlocutor, the nosy narrator. This statement can be read as having a double meaning—as expressing not only Tin-A's fear of marriage to Ah Kim, but also her love for A-Ho. Something glimmers vaguely between the lines of this text, something neither Tin-A, nor the narrator, nor the discourse of the text will admit—the idea of a potential desire between women. Without A-Ho in Tin-A's life, "the very sun seemed to have ceased to shine" (103), and when Tin-A tries to slip out of the marriage noose she is called "sick" (102). This "sickness," this dis-ease, this unhappiness, could well have to do with a desire for A-Ho that gets configured as illness. Imagery surrounding the relationship between A-Ho and Tin-A strongly suggests that there is something like love between them. The two are said to be "very intimate" (103). Together, they pick flowers (a traditional symbol of feminine sexuality and eroticism) and explore nature, spending "many a happy day … together" (102). In this natural world, Tin-A and A-Ho exist not as opposites of each other, but as mirrors, as the linguistic similarities of their names suggest (Tin-*A*, *A*-Ho). Tin-A and A-Ho are also the same age and they look similar, further implying this is a world of doubling, of mirroring and similarity, rather than social and sexual division.

In San Francisco Tin-A assiduously tends a garden, and when the narrator sees her she is picking flowers. The garden that Tin-A grows in San Francisco may reproduce the "garden" of her childhood, then, and its flowers may symbolize an outlawed sexuality. Yet without A-Ho, the garden as symbol becomes a realm where only flowers "bloom" and are "pluck[ed]" (101)—flowers, not the bodies of women, become receptacles for desire. Tin-A herself feels great sadness and regret over her "unfilial conduct"—over her refusal to follow her father's dictates and be a dutiful Chinese daughter. She also experiences pain because of A-Ho's death, with which the story ends. This melancholia may, perhaps, reflect a refusal to acknowledge (and grieve for) the loss of her own desire, her desire for a body that was like her own. Finally, the text does not create a space for this desire in the body of its characters.

Or does it? Something is coded into the discourse that we might call the fictive body of the author, and this fictive body opens up the possibility not of an "outside" to the system of heterosexual exchange, but a way of positioning oneself differently within this "inside." In her descriptions of Tin-A, Sui Sin Far seems to be placing her own body into the text. Sui Sin Far herself, like Tin-A, was described as "tiny."[19] Tin-A's name sounds like the word "tiny," perhaps doubling us back to the author, to the body of the author. Furthermore, Sui Sin Far may place herself into the text through the figure of the narrator, who Annette White-Parks reads as representing Sui Sin Far's own autobiographical experiences of traveling through California in search of stories (*Sui Sin Far* 134–35). Perhaps this story is also autobiographical in being about Sui Sin Far's meeting of Tin-A, a "tiny" woman who is like herself, but who is also, actually, in some sense herself (her double, her mirror, her fictional representation). The story's use of flower imagery suggests more doubling between character and author, for Sui Sin Far's name has been translated as "water fragrant flower," "Chinese lily," "water lily," or "narcissus."[20] Tin-A crosses water to get to her garden in America, and in America she tends flowers and is in fact tending one when the narrator sees her. In Tin-A, does Sui Sin Far see a mirrored image of herself, of her body? Narcissus, of course, falls in love with a reflection. Does Sui Sin Far love this reflection of herself, of the self that she creates in the space of her fiction, of a woman who desires another woman? Does she desire this self, or to *be* this self?

"The Story of Tin-A" raises these troubling questions, but it then refuses to answer them. For example, if the narrator saw a woman tending a flower that could definitely be allied with the identity of Sui Sin Far (such as a narcissus or a water lily or a Chinese lily), it might be easier to read this story as reflecting a lesbian sexuality. But when the narrator sees Tin-A, she is tending a geranium. Sui Sin Far begins to write her own body into texts about cross-dressing and cross-gendering characters who attempt to escape racialized norms for Chinese women, but then the body goes unnamed. The marker of what could be a lesbian sexuality, as Adrienne Rich would say, "is mute."[21] Yet this muteness signifies—it must be read. Eve Sedgwick has argued that "'closetness' itself is a performance initiated as such by the speech act of a silence—not a particular silence, but a silence that accrues particularity by fits and starts, in relation to the discourse that surround and differentially constitutes it" (3). In the next story to be discussed, "The Chinese Lily," Sui Sin Far's name actually enters the text and becomes attached to a body that is both fictive and "real." But again, we must read the particularity of the silences to see the discourses that constitute and construct the meaning and identity of this cross-gendered, cross-racial, and cross-desiring body.

"The Chinese Lily": Representing the Self as Fictive, the Fictive as Self

In discussing the possibilities of a lesbian sexuality, Butler comments that it would need to be read as a specific textual practice of dissimulation produced through the very historical vocabularies that seek its erasure. Lesbian sexuality may exist within a text through "a perpetual challenge to legibility" (145)—through what goes unsaid, what goes unnamed, what exists as subversion of a nameable, heterosexual desire. Sedgwick has made a similar argument that "the *homosexual body*" exists within discourse not as an unalterable representation but as "a *gap* in the discursive fabric" (43). These concepts of representation are helpful in understanding "The Chinese Lily." As we have already seen, Sui Sin Far often investigates the intersection of gendered and racial identities, and the name in this story's title seems to install racialized ("Chinese") and feminized ("Lily") identificatory categories. And yet, it is unclear just exactly what this name refers to, so the name itself may exist as a "challenge to legibility," a "gap in the discursive fabric." Does the name refer to a person—one or the other woman in the text? Or does it refer to the object exchanged by the two women—an actual Chinese lily? Or, since Sui Sin Far was sometimes called "the Chinese lily," does the title refer to the author?[22] The title is certainly meant to refer to all these things (and more), and to install a space for the crossings at work in identificatory practices, crossings that Sui Sin Far shows to be both multiple and unstable. And what produces these unstable crossings is an almost illegible lesbian sexuality.

"The Chinese Lily" is the only text discussed in this essay that does not involve cross-dressing, although it does concern cross-gender identification. In this story, another "little Chinese" (101) woman finds—and loses—a double. Because the protagonist, Mermei, has been crippled by a fall, she is supported by her brother Lin John, who is also her only source of companionship. One night when Lin John does not come for his usual visit, Mermei's lonely weeping is overheard by another young Chinese woman called (significantly) Sin Far. Sin Far and Mermei become friends, but when a fire breaks out in Mermei's building, Lin John can save only his sister, or her visiting friend (Sin Far, with whom he has fallen in love). Sin Far silently commands Lin John to save his sister, and he does. Mermei is saved, while Sin Far dies, but Lin John has done his "duty" (104).

On the face of it, this story seems to concern the value of masculine and feminine duty; Lin John fulfills his obligation to his sister, while Sin Far, as Lorraine Dong and Marlon Hom argue, seems to be "a traditional selfless woman who lives and dies not for herself but for others."[23] Like many Chinese women in these stories, both Sin Far and Mermei seem to accept a feminized and racialized status that leads to disempowerment, passivity, and even death. But another story is written below the dominant text, one that must be read through cryptic symbols and clues. In the first few lines we are told that Mermei is different, that she "never went amongst" the other "little Chinese" women, that she is "not as they were" (101). What is the accident that has "scarred her face" and "twisted her legs" (101), the "accident" that makes her not as "other Chinese women"? Recalling that a discourse of illness was present in "The Story of Tin-A" when the heroine did not wish to marry, and that Fin Fan, who cross-dressed, was described as "improper," we must wonder if Mermei's physical deformity is a trope for another kind of "illness," a sexual "deformity" or "impropriety" that might constitute a kind of lesbian identification. In *The Ego and the Id*, Freud suggests that self-love (or narcissism) must be replaced by love for an object—that one must finally love another person in order not to become sick.[24] Commenting on this idea, Butler argues that "perhaps the sexuality that appears as illness is the insidious effect of ... a censoring of love" (65). In giving characters like Mermei, Fin Fan, and Tin-A mysterious diseases and improprieties (especially ones that "twist" their "legs,") Sui Sin Far may be suggesting the censoring of a lesbian desire that results in insidious illness.

There are, then, two ways (at least) of reading the scene where Mermei and Sin Far (the character) meet. Looking out her window, Mermei sees "six young girls of about her own age, dressed gaily as if to attend a wedding" and she begins crying softly (102). Mermei could be crying because she wants to be like those young Chinese girls—marriageable, mobile, attractive. Or, she could be crying because she wants not to be *like* those young girls, but *liked* by them—desired by them. The text leaves open the possibility that Mermei's grief is the result of a heterosexual melancholy created when gender identity is formed precisely through an exclusion of the feminine as a possible object of love. Yet her weeping, her perhaps unconscious desire for these girls, seems to conjure an object she can desire—"the most beautiful young girl that Mermei had ever seen" (102), who stands on Mermei's threshold extending to her a blossom from a Chinese lily plant. In this ambiguous threshold moment a crossing of gender identification is produced: "Mermei understood the meaning of the offered flower, and accepting it, beckoned for her visitor to follow her into her room" (102). Within the code that Sui Sin Far has been developing, the "meaning of the offered flower" may have a just-barely-legible connotation. Given that the woman (Sin Far) whose name is translated within the text as "Pure Flower" or "Chinese Lily" (103) presents a blossom from a Chinese lily plant to Mermei, and that flowers are associated with eroticism and the body of women in Sui Sin Far's fiction, one way of reading this exchange is that Sin Far offers herself, her body, her flower, as an object of desire, as a replacement for the bodies of the gaily dressed women that Mermei desires, the bodies of the Chinese women who are entering the heterosexual marriage plot.[25]

Other patterns of imagery underscore the possibility of a reading of desire between these characters. Mermei and Sin Far are described as "chatter[ing] out their little hearts to one another" because "one can't talk to a man … as one can to one the same as oneself" (102–3). The two women, then, in some sense are talking to themselves, to a "one" that is not like a man, a self that exists before the heterosexual division between male and female has taken place, a self that can be female and desiring of other females. Again, we have imagery of doubling and mirroring that echoes back to the author's name (sometimes translated as "narcissus"). Of course, the most obvious echoing of the author's name is no echo at all, but repetition. Sui Sin Far places herself into this text, or at least her name, in the character of Sin Far. She also places herself into the text through the title. And finally, she places herself into the text through the offering of the Chinese lily to Mermei; within the space of this fiction, Sui Sin Far (the author) seems to offer her fictive body/blossom to another woman. This offering has the power to make Mermei "forget that she was scarred and crippled" (102). In the presence of one who is like her, and of one who likes (desires) her, Mermei's "deformity," the sign of her aberrant sexuality, may cease to be operative. The author's placement of herself in the text, then, seems to recover a same-sex desire that has been erased or sutured over by heterosexual norms.

So while the overt text insists that it is Lin John who has lost his loved one, that Lin John "loved Sin Far ... and she loved [Lin John]" (104), the covert text suggests something else. It is possible that Sin Far realizes that without Mermei her life is meaningless, empty of a love object. It is possible that she refuses the heterosexual marriage plot and the traditional role of Chinese women, and chooses death instead of life without her loved one (Mermei). And finally, it is possible that Mermei accepts this choice, for she agrees to continue living "in this sad, dark world" without Sin Far (104). Again, a kind of melancholy asserts itself, or perhaps a refusal to grieve that allows Mermei to resume a subject-position as a Chinese woman precisely through the exclusion of her love for another woman. A deconstruction of gender roles seems to be enacted when Mermei (not a man) is described as loving Sin Far (a woman). But the ending may cover over these troubling possibilities through its reestablishment of traditional gender identities; the ending reinscribes homosexual desire into discourse only as a melancholy refusal to mourn that what must be silenced (excluded from the body's boundaries) in order for one to "be" feminine or masculine.

That this story is titled "The Chinese Lily" suggests, however, that it is not about Mermei, or about Sin Far, or even about Sui Sin Far, but about the crossings between these fictive and real women: the crossings of identities, the crossings that finally, if but for a moment, allow an almost unsightable/unciteable desire to emerge. As Annette White-Parks has noted, like Alfred Hitchcock, Sui Sin Far often makes "guest" appearances in her texts.[26] Yet in "The Chinese Lily" Sui Sin Far's name is more than a flicker on the screen—it is actually embedded into the text in an unmistakable way. Sui Sin Far is creating a self that is fictive (that is, in the world of the text), but she is also creating a fictive that is self (a body, a name, an identity that she can, perhaps, wear out of the world of the text into the "real" world). Sui Sin Far's use of her own name in this text dismantles the line between fiction and reality, asking us to read not only the text, but also the author of the text, the author of this fictive world that has also, somehow, become real. Finally, Sui Sin Far smuggles herself into the text, undoing yet another series of binary oppositions: fiction versus autobiography, texts versus the "real" world, stories about a life versus the life itself.[27]

Furthermore, Sui Sin Far's presence as an author within the text asks us to consider not only how categories such as the "fictive" and the "real" actually create each other, but also how we, as readers of texts, create both the texts we read and the worlds in which we reside. Sui Sin Far does not provide one way of reading her texts, but rather encodes multiple, often contradictory, layers of meaning we must finally choose between ourselves. Do we choose to read "The Chinese Lily" as a story of homosexual or heterosexual desire? Do we choose to read it as being "about" a set of fictional characters or about Sui Sin Far herself? Do we choose to read it as concerning the construction of masculine and feminine identities, or their deconstruction? Is it about the formation of racial identities, or their deformation? These choices are complicated, however, by the way the text structures them not as separate options, but as categories implicated within each other. In Sui Sin Far's fiction, the line between author and character, between "masculine" and "feminine" identities, between "heterosexual" and "homosexual" desire, and between identificatory practices that construct "race" and "gender," is never firmly drawn. Characters slip back and forth over the borders of these oppositions, crossing them again and again. This does not mean that these categories are no longer operative, but rather that Sui Sin Far's texts reveal the tenuousness of these categories, how they contain a radical instability that gets sutured over by certain identificatory practices but yet remains as a just-barely-legible trace.

"I do not confide in my father and mother. They would not understand. How could they? He is English, she is Chinese. I am different to both of them—a stranger," Sui Sin Far writes in her autobiography (222). Sui Sin Far was, then, an individual who was constantly passing between various racial and gendered terrains. Perhaps because she remained "a stranger" to the various cultural and racial matrices around her, she also remained a stranger—or at least estranged from—the processes of identity-formation that created stable racial and sexual identities. Sui Sin Far herself crossed races, sometimes being taken for an Anglo-American (224), and sometimes being viewed as a Chinese American (227), but she never comfortably inhabited the category of "Chinese" "woman."

The stories I've discussed consistently indicate that she interconnects racial crossing with crossings of gendered and sexual identities, and that the name is one site where racial and gendered identities collide—and one space where these identities can be remade. In Sui Sin Far's writing, the name itself is the trace of the suturing process that attempts to create stable racial and sexual identities, but it also becomes an enabling occasion for revealing just how this suturing occurs, and how it can be turned on itself to create unexpected possibilities of identity and subjectivity that question the very order the name seeks to institute. Furthermore, Sui Sin Far asks us to participate in this questioning not only by encouraging us to "write" and "rewrite" her texts, to create and recreate them, but also by encouraging us to examine their gaps and fissures for encoded, subversive messages. Yet what we find in these gaps and fissures is not so much a stable version of ourselves, or of our own identificatory practices. Rather, written between the lines of these texts, we find a way of reading the fluctuating, unstable, and encoded sexual and textual matrices that create the fictive self—the fiction of a stable self that somehow exists beyond, or outside, these very sexual, racial, and textual matrices that create it.

Notes

For commentary on this essay, I thank Carolyn Sorisio, Deborah J. Rosenthal, Steve Colegrove, Jennifer Kong [Chunzhen] Colegrove, and Xiaojing Zhou. Research for this project was partially funded by Kent State University's Office of Research and Graduate Studies. This essay is dedicated to the late Amy Ling.

  1. On the subject of Sui Sin Far's own name, see Elizabeth Ammons's argument that it may be meant to have both English and Chinese connotations; *Conflicting Stories* (New York: Oxford University Press, 1991), 119–20 (parenthetically cited hereafter). Also see Annette White-Parks's argument that the author's choice to publish under the name Sui Sin Far in her mature fiction (rather than under her English name, Edith Eaton) demonstrates her sense of ethnic identity; *Sui Sin Far/Edith Maud Eaton* (Urbana: University of Illinois Press, 1995); parenthetically cited hereafter. However, there has been little discussion of either naming or cross-dressing in Sui Sin Far's treatment of her fictional characters.

  2. This essay focuses on how Sui Sin Far's names deconstruct binary divisions such as "Chinese" versus "American" or male versus female, rather than on the particular meanings of her characters' names in either Chinese or English. In "Writers With a Cause: Sui Sin Far and Han Suyin," *Women's Studies International Forum* 9 (1986), 411–19, Amy Ling states that Sui Sin Far did not speak Chinese (414). Therefore, Sui Sin Far's knowledge of Chinese names was probably limited to what she could learn from Chinese speakers living in America. This does not mean, however, that she was unable to manipulate or play with the rhetorical possibilities of the meanings of the names she learned. For example, she clearly knew the translation of the name "Ku Yum" ("miserable person" or "daughter") and used it ironically in "A Chinese Boy-Girl." And there is clear evidence that she manipulated the Chinese meaning of her own name in her texts (see note 20 and my discussion of "A Chinese Lily").

  3. In *Between Worlds* (New York: Pergamon Press, 1990), Amy Ling states that

two of Sui Sin Far's stories ("The Heart's Desire" and "The Chinese Lily") are "suggestive of a lesbian sensibility" (48) but does not develop this point. A few critics have suggested that Sui Sin Far writes in code or is a trickster, but none have applied this idea to her portrayals of gender or sexuality. See, for example, Ammons (*Conflicting Stories*), Annette White-Parks (*Sui Sin Far/Edith Maud Eaton*), and Viet Thanh Nguyen's "Writing the Body Politic: Asian American Subjects and the American Nation," Ph.D. diss., University of California, Berkeley, 1997 (parenthetically cited hereafter). On the concept of the "closet" see Eve Sedgwick's *Epistemology of the Closet* (Berkeley: University of California Press, 1990), 67–90; parenthetically cited hereafter.

4. Judith Butler, *Bodies That Matter: On the Discursive Limits of "Sex"* (New York: Routledge, 1993), 143; parenthetically cited hereafter.

5. Jacques Lacan, *The Seminar of Jacques Lacan, Book II*, ed. Jacques-Alain Miller, trans. Sylvanna Tomaselli (New York: Norton, 1988), 169.

6. A reader who knew Chinese would recognize the gender of other names, such as Tian Shan. According to Steve Colegrove and Jennifer Kong [Chunzhen] Colegrove, Tian Shan can mean either "field mountain" or "field good," both traditional male names (private communication).

7. For a lengthier discussion of racial crossings and tensions in Sui Sin Far's writing, see Carol Roh Spaulding, "'Wavering' Images: Mixed-Race Identity in the Stories of Edith Eaton/Sui Sin Far," *Ethnicity and the American Short Story*, ed. Julie Brown (New York: Garland, 1997), 155–76.

8. My page references to Sui Sin Far's writing normally refer to *Mrs. Spring Fragrance and Other Writings*, ed. Amy Ling and Annette White-Parks (Urbana: University of Illinois Press, 1995) and will be parenthetical hereafter. However, "The Story of Tin-A" was not published in *Mrs. Spring Fragrance*, so parenthetical citations are to its original printing in *Land of Sunshine* 12 (1899), 101–3.

9. In my reading of "A Chinese Boy-Girl" and Sui Sin Far's other stories, I focus on how they blur gender and racial distinctions for an Anglo-American audience, rather than on how they might be interpreted within the context of traditional Chinese culture or by readers familiar with traditional Chinese customs. Like Nicole Tonkovich, I believe that Sui Sin Far's writings "seek to explain Chinese immigrant culture to the dominant white communities in which they lived" ("Genealogy, Genre, Gender: Sui Sin Far's 'Leaves from the Mental Portfolio of an Eurasian,'" *Beyond the Binary: Reconstructing Cultural Identity in a Multicultural Context*, ed. Timothy Powell [New Brunswick: Rutgers University Press, 1999], 239; 236–60). Indeed, Sui Sin Far herself was quite far removed from traditional Chinese culture. Her mother was raised in England, where she learned "English ways and manner of dress" ("Leaves" 219), and her father was British. According to Tonkovich, the fourteen Eaton children—raised in England, Canada, and the United States—"could claim no national citizenship; rather, they exploited the ambiguity of their physical appearance" (239). Tonkovich's recent research indicates that the children were raised and socialized as "white," spoke English at home, and were educated in British and Canadian schools. Most of the children passed for white. Sui Sin Far was the only child to identify herself as Chi-

nese; unfortunately, she was to discover "that most Chinese of 'pure' blood accepted her reluctantly, if at all" (Tonkovich 239). This does not mean, of course, that Sui Sin Far did not consider Chinese-literate readers' reactions to her stories, but it does indicate that her main concern was critiquing the dominant, Anglo-American culture's attempt to enforce categories of race and gender.

10. *Borderlands: The New Mestiza* (San Francisco: Spinsters/Aunt Lute, 1987), 79.

11. See Matsukawa's "Cross-Dressing and Cross-Naming: Decoding Onoto Watanna," in *Tricksterism in Turn-of-the-Century American Literature*, ed. Elizabeth Ammons and Annette White-Parks (Hanover: University Press of New England, 1994), 110; 106–25.

12. For more information on discourses of Chinese American male effeminacy, see Sau-ling Cynthia Wong, "Ethnicizing Gender: An Exploration of Sexuality as Sign in Chinese Immigrant Literature," in *Reading the Literatures of Asian America*, ed. Shirley Geok-lin Lim and Amy Ling (Philadelphia: Temple University Press, 1992), 111–29, and Min Song, "The Unknowable and Sui Sin Far: The Epistemological Limits of 'Oriental' Sexuality," in *Q & A: Queer in Asian America*, ed. David L. Eng and Alice Y. Hom (Philadelphia: Temple University Press, 1998), 304–22; parenthetically cited hereafter.

13. "Spare Parts: The Surgical Construction of Gender," in *The Lesbian and Gay Studies Reader*, ed. Henry Abelove, Michèle Aina Barale, David M. Halperin (New York: Routledge, 1993), 327; 321–38; parenthetically cited hereafter. Garber is, of course, discussing transsexualism, not transvestism.

14. Trinh T. Minh-ha, *Woman, Native, Other* (Bloomington: Indiana University Press, 1989), 100.

15. As I do, Song argues that in "The Smuggling of Tie Co" names work to both construct and undermine categories of identity. However, Song believes that in this story, "racial identity remain[s] fixed" while "gendered and sexual meanings become unanchored" (317). I argue that all these categories of identity become more permeable by story's end.

16. Xiao-Huang Yin translates Tie Co's name as meaning "pitiful" in Chinese. See "Between the East and West: Sui Sin Far—The First Chinese-American Woman Writer," *Arizona Quarterly* 47 (1991), 69; 49–84.

17. For a different perspective, see Viet Thanh Nguyen's argument that in this story "there seems to be no room ... for a homosexual alternative to the homosocial relationship. ... homosexuality itself becomes an even more deeply buried subtext" (70). I disagree with this reading, for the story seems to suggest that Fabian *is* in fact irrevocably changed by his encounter with Tie Co; he continues to ponder "long and earnestly over the mystery of Tie Co's life—and death" (109).

18. As Sedgwick points out, "new, institutionalized taxonomic discourses—medical, legal, literary, psychological—centering on homo/heterosexual definition proliferated and crystallized with exceptional rapidity in the decades around the turn of the century" (2). If Sui Sin Far was aware of these discourses, perhaps this explains her interest in undermining their stability.

19. See "Leaves from the Mental Portfolio of an Eurasian," where Sui Sin Far

says that after an attack of fever she weighed only eighty-four pounds (226). In "Sui Sin Far, the Half Chinese Writer, Tells of Her Career," she also comments that a bout of fever at the age of fourteen "retarded [her] development both mentally and physically," and that throughout her life she suffered recurrent attacks of this "terrible fever" (291). She was never, as she puts it, "big, healthy and contented" (291). Furthermore, like the title character in "The Story of Tin-A," Sui Sin Far never married, describing herself as "a very serious and sober-minded spinster" ("Leaves" 226).

20. In "Edith Eaton: Pioneer Chinamerican Writer and Feminist," *American Literary Realism* 16 (1983), 287–98, Amy Ling calls the name Sui Sin Far "a Cantonese pseudonym" meaning "Water Fragrant Flower" or "narcissus" (287), while in the story "A Chinese Lily" the author herself translates it as "Chinese Lily" or "Pure Flower" (103). However, in "Fanny Fern and Sui Sin Far: The Beginning of an Asian American Voice," *Women and Language* 19 (1996), 44–47, Ning Yu argues the name should be translated as "water immortal flower" (46). And in *Chinese American Literature since the 1850s* (Urbana: University of Illinois Press, 2000), Xiao-Huang Yin translates "Sui Sin Far" as meaning "'narcissus in Cantonese dialect'" (89); also see page 112, note 18, for more information about the connotations of these names. This name also has resonance with the title and title character of Sui Sin Far's collection, *Mrs. Spring Fragrance*. According to Xiaojing Zhou, Sui Sin Far's name means literally "Water Fairy/Immortal Flower" or "narcissus," and since narcissus is an early spring flower, Sui Sin Far's name is "encoded in the title of her collected stories" (private communication).

21. Adrienne Rich, *A Wild Patience Has Taken Me This Far* (New York: Norton, 1981), 17.

22. According to Xiao-Huang Yin, "Between the East and West," Sui Sin Far's friends called her "the Chinese Lily" (81).

23. "Defiance or Perpetuation: An Analysis of Characters in *Mrs. Spring Fragrance*," *Chinese America: History and Perspectives* (San Francisco: Chinese Historical Society, 1987), 148; 139–68.

24. Freud, "The Ego and the Id," in *The Standard Edition of the Complete Psychological Works of Sigmund Freud*, vol. XIX, ed. James Strachey (London: Hogarth, 1962), 46.

25. It is important to note that in the original text of *Mrs. Spring Fragrance*, each page was lightly imprinted with a Chinese-style drawing of (among other things) "a flowering branch of plum" (Ling, *Between Worlds*, 27). Flowers were, then, literally embedded into the "body" of the text (the printed page).

26. See "'We Wear the Mask': Sui Sin Far as One Example of Trickster Authorship," in *Tricksterism in Turn-of-the-Century American Literature*, 7; 1–20.

27. Nguyen makes a similar point, arguing that "the practice of Sui Sin Far's life and writing … are predicated precisely on the inherent instability underlying notions of the 'real' and the 'fake'" (39).

HERTHA D. SWEET WONG

Taking Place

African-Native American Subjectivity in
'A Yellow Raft in Blue Water'

The Multiracial Subject

Ever since "race" and racial categories have been shown to be "socio-historical constructs," entirely artificial and political rather than biological, "historically contingent and regionally specific" rather than essential, scholars of ethnic literatures in the United States have found themselves in a paradoxical situation.[1] On the one hand, there is a kind of liberatory zeal in, what seems to me, a rush to post-raciality, post-ethnicity, post-identity;[2] on the other, there is the very present everyday experience of living in (however artificially constructed) racialized bodies. Michael Omi and Howard Winant advise against thinking of race as either "an ideo-logical construct" or "an objective condition." Rather, they urge academ-ics to examine "the continuing significance and changing meaning of race," in short, to study the ongoing "racial formation process."[3] We may wish to escape the limited and limiting category of race, yet our society is so thoroughly organized by it that it is difficult to imagine our way out of it. In fact, many of us wish to add categories of race (particularly mixed race) to the census to reflect more accurately our sense of ourselves (a move that has been resisted so far by the federal government) and to in-sist on multiracial identity as "central rather than peripheral."[4] By focus-ing on African-Native American subjectivity and literature, this essay ex-tends and corrects a partial (particularly, binary—either "white" *or* "black," "white" *or* "red"—with Caucasians always the invisible center to everyone else's margins) "tradition" of history and literature in the United States. At the same time, however, it perpetuates the very categories we question. What is the good of constructing new racial identities if they merely stabilize society's conceptual structures of race? Is it possible that a "mixed race" category could, by its very heterogeneous capaciousness (who, after all, is not "mixed"?), carry the potential to undermine the general social categories of race? Does a multiracial subjectivity resist or stabilize what Tomás Almaguer refers to as the "enduring significance of race as a central organizing principle of group inequality ... in this country"?[5] Even without clear answers to these questions, a multiracial category that describes an enormous, yet officially unacknowledged, population underscores the complicated historical interactions among diverse groups and shifts the focus from reductive and untenable binarisms to complex and ever shifting pluralisms.[6]

Mixed blood identity has long been a dominant theme of Native American written literature. Most mixed blood protagonists have been portrayed as red-white conflicted unions or conflicts, thus mirroring the dominant political struggle between colonizer and colonized. And while it has been common knowledge that many African Americans are also mixed bloods (due to rape during slavery as well as consensual unions), because of the "one-drop rule," even those with very little African ancestry were defined as "legally" black. Whether the image is of a mixed blood Indian "torn between two worlds" or a "tragic mulatto/a" agonizing about the possibilities of "passing," the focus has been on white and "Other" mixtures.[7] The mixed blood, claims Louis Owens, serves as "a matrix for the conflicted terrors of Euroamerica,. the horror of liminality that is the peculiar trauma of the colonial mind ..."; the mixed blood is "a mirror that gives back a self-image with disturbing implications. ... The instinct of the dominant culture, facing evidence of its own uncontained mutability, is to rewrite the stories, eradicate the witness, and break the mirror."[8] If "authentic" (often associated with "full-blood") Indians are, as some believe, European American inventions, "colonial surrogates,"[9] then mixed bloods, particularly African-Native Americans, have yet to be imag(in)ed.

Even though scholars like William Katz, Daniel Littlefield, Jack Forbes, and Theda Purdue have written about African American and Native American historical interactions, only recently (as part of the multicultural debates and multiracial subjectivity rights struggle) have scholars like Sharon Holland and Jonathan Brennan argued for an Afro-Indian literary history—a provocative move that makes some scholars of Native American studies and African American studies nervous since there continue to be sound reasons for insisting on their distinct histories as well as their intersections. It has been important to understand, for instance, that

while Native Americans, African Americans, Asian Americans, and La-
tino/as have all experienced racial prejudice and victimization within the
United States, each umbrella group has its distinct history of legal, military, and social struggle. To claim an affiliation based on an overly generalized shared victimization risks obfuscating the particular histories and
distinctive cultures of the variety of peoples collapsed into these categories. Ron Takaki's work illustrates the value of what Cornel West has described as "the new cultural politics of difference."[10] Takaki reveals how,
historically, European America racialized various groups; and he contex-
tualizes the historical, political, legal, and economic forces in the process.
Takaki outlines the common patterns of the racializing process in the
United States, but without sacrificing the particularities of each collective
experience. Examining African-Native American subjectivity, one facet of
a more general multiracial subjectivity, then, can be seen as one way to
become aware of the ongoing "process of racial formation," not merely
from dominant social forces, but from those resisting imposed categories
and insisting instead on their own.

The Place of the Multiracial Subject: "The Ground on Which We Stand"

Spatial metaphors for both transcultural contact and mixed race conditions abound: Arnold Krupat's notion of the literary "frontier" where
written life histories reenact the domination of indigenous people; Patricia Limerick's idea of the historical "multiple frontier" where cultural and
racial diversity, not duality, proliferated; Louis Owens's model of the
conceptual "frontier," a "space wherein discourse is multidirectional and
hybridized" in contrast to "territory," which is mapped and controlled;
Mary Louise Pratt's "contact zone," a site of unequal, contested cross-
cultural interactions; Gloria Anzaldúa's "border/lands," in which geographic and political borders become internalized and carried within; en-
vironmental literature's eco-zones and "edge effect," the meeting of two
ecosystems wherein arises fecund diversity (as well as intense competition
for survival); and my "boundary culture," a third new literary/cultural
structure that results from the contested interaction between two cultures, to name a few.[11] Each of these metaphors attempts to articulate a
space, a site of contact, contestation, and interaction. With these spatial
formulations in mind, I would like to ground my discussion of African-

Native subjectivity by linking it to "place," particularly to "home" or homeland. While shifting the focus to geography does not eliminate the categories of race and ethnicity, it offers a way to ground interlocking racial histories.

In *The Lure of the Local: Senses of Place in a Multicentered Society*, art critic Lucy Lippard relates the "American" obsession with finding/creating/understanding our multicultural/racial, transethnic selves to geography:

> The intersections of nature, culture, history, and ideology form the ground on which we stand—our land, our place, the local. The lure of the local is the pull of place that operates on each of us, exposing our politics and our spiritual legacies. It is the geographical component of the psychological need to belong somewhere, one antidote to a prevailing alienation. The lure of the local is that undertone to modern life that connects it to the past we know so little and the future we are aimlessly concocting.[12]

For both Native Americans and African Americans the "problem" of place (origins, home, social standing) is not some generalized postmodern symptom or the "placelessness" that haunts the colonizer. Frontiers, borderlands, contact zones, boundary cultures are not merely spatial metaphors, but sites of contested and cacophonous transcultural interaction. Historically, both groups have been displaced from homelands (cultures, languages), though by different means; certain portions of both groups have survived slavery (though of distinctly different sorts). How does one relate to "home" when that home/land has been stolen or when one has been stolen away from one's home, when one is *dis*placed? Furthermore, generally, in the contemporary American popular imagination, Native Americans are associated with nature, seen as connected to the earth (even while large populations of native people reside in urban centers), while African Americans are seen as linked to urban areas (particularly, inner-city ghettos) and modes of living (even while many who fled the South are returning to more rural roots).[13] In literature, African Americans are urban *or* rural (Richard Wright's city characters or Zora Neale Hurston's folk, for instance), not both. In addition, the language used to describe "place" has come under scrutiny, its Eurocentric assumptions revealed. For many Native people, for instance, terms such as "wilderness," "wild," and "frontier" all reveal a colonizer's point of view (an us/them mentality that rationalizes subduing the dangerous Other—figured as Native—ensconced in those zones).

But such binary oppositions as urban/rural, human world/natural world are not relevant. In many indigenous contexts, nature, always inclusive of animals, plants, earth, celestial bodies, is not conceived of as separate from humans. In fact, "Native American nature," according to William Bevis, "is urban," that is, "the center of human activity."[14] Many Native North American cultures and the narratives they generate both arise from and refer to specific geographic sites that are mapped in a network of social relations (kinship and clan relations, for instance). As Leslie Marmon Silko reminds us, for many Native writers, the land itself is storied. The simplest story of a hunting or fishing expedition conveyed vital information about animal migrations, water holes, geographic landmarks; such stories could literally map a terrain. For a Native person with a long history of residence in one place, stories of place are both personal and cultural. Such links between stories and place figure also for African Americans: stories (told or sung) could convey coded information about escape routes North during slavery; and African myths reimagined in the American South linked people to a faraway (idea of) "home." Perhaps Toni Morrison's notion of "rememory," described by Sethe in *Beloved*, best describes how places can be inhabited by past experiences that can be reinvoked via mere proximity (a kind of sociohistorical haunting that underscores the interlinking of place and story).

But when people are removed from their homelands, partially or completely dispossessed of cultures and languages, stories can help restore such a relationship. This is neither political escapism nor romantic nostalgia. Sharon Holland argues that examining the Afro-Native presence in literature is part of understanding literature as a process of emancipation (of the enslaved black body) and of sovereignty (of the enslaved red nation).[15] Citing Chandra Mohanty, Caren Kaplan writes: "The intersection of a politics of location and a politics of displacement marks a postmodern moment in which mapping and storytelling vie as technologies of identity formation."[16] With the centrality of spatial metaphors in mind, I want to consider "mapping and storytelling" as "technologies of [African-Native American] identity formation" in Michael Dorris's novel, *A Yellow Raft in Blue Water*.

Taking Place: Rayona's African-Native American Return

Almost everything Michael Dorris wrote was concerned with several recurrent themes: the centrality of family relationships and home; the responsibility to renarrate history from Native perspectives; and the necessity for mixed blood individuals to search for and claim their identities and to situate themselves in relation to Indian and non-Indian communities. Just as important as these recurrent themes is Dorris's commitment to disrupt the dominant stereotypes of Native North Americans, to resist the feathered headdresses and beads, the "noble and stoic"/"savage and libidinous" masks imposed historically on Native people by colonizers.

In his multivoiced novel *A Yellow Raft in Blue Water* (1987), Dorris unfolds the interrelated but distinct narratives of three generations of women. Three sections, each narrated by a character from a different generation—a daughter, a mother, and a "grandmother"—are braided deftly together. The story begins with fifteen-year-old African-Native American Rayona, continues with her American Indian mother Christine, and concludes with her "grandmother" Ida (who prefers to be called "Aunt Ida" for surprising and dramatic reasons clarified only at the end of the novel). Each of the narrators repeatedly confirms and contradicts the others. A typical modernist technique, the multiple narrators provide varying points of view, particularly different generational and relationship lenses from which to consider not only what led to Rayona's mixed blood urban experience, but to ponder the disruptions of Native American history generally.

Although mixed blood identity is a common theme in twentieth-century Native American literatures generally, Dorris presents a less explored mixed blood character: a black Indian, more specifically a young African-Native American teenager named Rayona. Rayona's mother, Christine, is from an unspecified Montana reservation, and her father is an African American postal worker named Elgin. Early in the novel, Rayona categorizes the hues of her family precisely. She imagines finding their "exact shades on a paint mix-tone chart. Mom was Almond Joy, Dad was Burnt Clay, and [she] was Maple Walnut."[17] Awareness of skin color remains important throughout the novel.

While Rayona maps family bodies in terms of color lines, others are assessing her too. Because of her "dual heritage" and her height, she is acutely aware of her appearance. She describes herself as she imagines others see her: "Too big, too smart, not Black, not Indian, not friendly. Kids keep their distance, and most teachers are surprised, then annoyed, that I know the answers on their tests. I'm not what they expect" (25). Her mother, Christine, finds it painful that she and her daughter "didn't look more alike" (203). She understands how difficult it must be for

Rayona: "I had to face it, she was the wrong color, had the wrong name, had the wrong family—all an accident, Elgin and me the same place at the same time. But somehow she turned out right" (254). While Rayona's description emphasizes excess ("too ...") and lack ("not ..."), Christine's underscores out-of-placeness (everything bequeathed to Rayona is "wrong") and rightness (even with a complex heritage, Rayona "turned out right"). Both reveal the multiple displacements of and the social challenges for the African-Native American subject.

Returning to the reservation (where she has visited only once as a toddler) is no solution. Throughout she is aware of people's responses to her racial mixture. When she meets Father Hurlbert, he exclaims, "You're so very tall." She notes to herself, "He has not mentioned the color of my skin. I'm supposed to think he hasn't noticed" (37). A similar scene is played out with Father Tom (51). While the characterization of the European American priests critiques a white liberal ignorance, Dorris similarly disallows any naive expectations for a reservation-based "persons of color" solidarity. When she is introduced to her "full-blood" cousin, Kennedy Cree (known as Foxy), he announces: "You're Christine's kid. ... The one whose father is a nigger" (41). At first his crude bluntness is a relief from the "polite" silence of others, but not for long. Rayona's survival strategy is to isolate herself, to act tough. But after several weeks of enduring the teachers' surprise at her academic gifts, the students' disapproval, the comments about her "Coppertone tan" and poor clothes, she is miserable. "I haven't become popular and I haven't turned invisible" (47), she muses as she plans her escape from the reservation.

In his depiction of Rayona, Dorris complicates the generic plot of a Native mixed blood protagonist being torn between two worlds. "Rayona grows up," explains Dorris, "very much an urban, black, Indian kid in a northwest city." When she ends up on the reservation, she is "inappropriate in every respect: wrong color, wrong background, wrong language."[18] But nonetheless Rayona's search, like that of so many other characters in Native American novels, as William Bevis has noted, is for "home," for belonging. The "pull of place" for Rayona includes being drawn to her cultures, history, and family—all of which she needs to find her grounding. Of course, Dorris focuses almost exclusively on Rayona's contested Indianness, only hinting at her African American "identity." Christine, for instance, worries about her daughter during Rayona's infrequent visits with Elgin, wondering whether Rayona is "still Indian" for those hours. Her mother's musings suggest fears that not only might

Rayona "pass" into an African American community, but that Indianness itself is not merely biological; it is where and with whom you live—your place. Christine's thoughts about her daughter's situational identity raise questions also about how to identify the racial (and cultural) ambiguity of multiracial subjects. For Rayona, finding self-acceptance can only be accomplished by realizing that *she* is not inappropriate, not *out of place*; what is inappropriate, *misplaced*, is the behavior of the dominant society (represented in the novel by social workers and priests who try to "save" her) and of "full-blood" relatives who taunt her about her biraciality.

In addition to outlining the vexed state of transracial relations and problems for the African-Native subject in the United States, Dorris maps the twentieth-century history of relocation of indigenous people from reservations to urban centers. The central movement of the novel is a return—from urban Seattle to a rural Montana reservation with an interlude in Bearpaw Lake State Park. This "return," of course, is ironic because Rayona has only visited the reservation once briefly. But like many Indians removed from homelands, Rayona must understand her past to take her place in the present. Certainly the journey to the reservation is a more explicit return for her mother, who left the reservation twenty years before, lured by another powerful "pull of place"—the promise of a place in the urban dream of America—and the relocation program.[19] Displacement, like mixed blood diasporic subjectivity, like African-Indian identity in this novel, is a confusing and contested condition, associated simultaneously with freedom, lack of belonging, placelessness, and loss. As Rayona and her mother drive toward the reservation in a falling-apart Volaré, Rayona thinks about stopping to settle in one of the small towns and imagines that she could "move anywhere be anybody" (26). In a place with no predetermined stories to define her, no rememories to haunt her, she imagines that perhaps she could invent herself anew—a project she tries out when she runs away and makes up stories about herself and her (loving, middle class, two-parent, nuclear, picket fence, and dog-owning) family. But this, of course, is revealed as a discredited American myth of self-invention by a simple act of transplantation. A change of place, after all, is not always or necessarily a change of identity.

Predetermined stories are not just about geographic space, though, but about social place. Dorris makes evident that in Seattle, there are social workers (who recurrently "discover" Rayona's potential), while on the reservation there are priests who, while trying to "save" her, urge her to discuss her "dual heritage." It is ironic, of course, that Father Tom, the priest who tries to sexually molest her, gives her a gaudy, plastic "beaded medallion" made for tourists so she could display her Indianness (presumably the trinket is supposed to make manifest the Indian identity that her African ancestry masks), before abandoning her guiltily in an attempt to cover up his inappropriate behavior.

Dominant stories include those narrated *and* those withheld by the three generations, the silences juxtaposed with popular culture stories on the television and videos, excerpts of letters not addressed to her, and the reports of social workers and priests all mingled in a fifteen-year-old's imagination. As she is falling asleep at the Bearpaw Lake State Park, she thinks: "My brain hums with half-told stories, with pieces that don't seem to fit anywhere, with things I should have said and didn't, and I can't tell the real from the could-be. It's as though I'm dreaming a lot of lives and I can mix and match the parts into something new each time. None pin me down" (80). Because the pieces and places in Rayona's life do not match or meet, she tries to borrow someone else's story, one that seems to her to be a coherent script lifted from a television sitcom (where all problems are resolved at the end of the half hour). But she finally rejects her fantasy of having a "perfect" family like the *Leave it to Beaver*, white middle-class family of Ellen DeMarco, a beautiful and popular camper at the park. Later, when Rayona finally tells her story to Evelyn, the woman who befriends her and provides her a place to stay, it's a relief.

Finally, by returning home and by uncovering her (family) history, she learns how she fits into a much larger story. Although the plot sounds like a romantic search for a lost past, Dorris resists easy answers. Going "home" doesn't necessarily guarantee a warm welcome or a gift-wrapped Indian identity, but it does offer the possibility of gathering pieces of one's story. Rayona's coming-of-age story (only one aspect of the tripartite novel) suggests the problems and possibilities of a multiracial subject who must take not her place, but her places, in a multilocational, transcultural society.

By the end of the novel, Rayona has found her place, a sense of home in a multicentered society: she understands that she belongs on the rural Montana reservation as well as in the urban center of Seattle, to reservation and urban Indian communities; she becomes aware of her own family histories—both her mother's Native American and, to a lesser extent, her father's African American; and she accepts and affirms her multiply positioned place in United States society. Similarly, by the end of the novel, Rayona has moved from being a victim of untold, partially told, or mistold stories to being a speaker of her own experience, from being at the mercy of urban social workers and reservation priests to becoming an active agent on her own behalf.

Dorris often compared his role as a writer and anthropologist—both careful observers and shapers of experience—to those of mixed bloods who, having survived incalculable loss, find themselves, like many anthropologists, outsiders and mediators. As a mixed blood anthropologist writer, Dorris was particularly mindful of his role as one who observes and translates (mediates and shapes). *A Yellow Raft in Blue Water* dramatizes a quest for personal identity and historical accuracy through remembering the past and imaginatively (re)constructing it in the present. In the novel Michael Dorris problematizes and humanizes the formation of racial identities; explores family ties; sets the record straight about Native American history; locates "home" in a multicentered society; and unravels the complexities, ironies, and multifaceted possibilities of African-Native American subjectivity.

Notes

1. Tomás Almaguer, *Racial Fault Lines: The Historical Origins of White Supremacy in California* (Berkeley: University of California Press, 1994), 9, 205.

2. See, for instance, Werner Sollors, *Beyond Ethnicity: Consent and Dissent in American Culture* (New York: Oxford University Press, 1986); David Hollinger, *Postethnic America: Beyond Multiculturalism* (New York: Basic Books, 1995); and the recently formulated journal *Post Identity*.

3. Michael Omi and Howard Winant, "On the Theoretical Status of the Concept of Race," in *Race, Identity and Representation in Education*, ed. Cameron McCarthy and Warren Crichlow (New York: Routledge, 1993), 3. See also Michael Omi and Howard Winant, *Racial Formation in the United States: From the 1960s to the 1990s*, 2d ed. (New York: Routledge, 1994).

4. Darby Li Po Price, "Mixed Laughter," in *We Are a People: Narrative and Multiplicity in Constructing Ethnic Identity*, ed. Paul Spickard and W. Jeffrey Burroughs (Philadelphia, Penn.: Temple University Press, 2000), 179.

5. Almaguer, *Racial Fault Lines*, 213.

6. For a concise discussion of the inadequacy of binary categories (such as insider/outsider, center/margin, etc.), see Trinh T. Minh-ha, *When the Moon Waxes Red: Representation, Gender and Cultural Politics* (New York: Routledge, 1991).

7. Similarly, what has often been called "race relations" in the United States has been discussed predominantly in the binary terms of black and white, savage and civilized. See also Darby Li Po Price who, in a move to subvert the "ethos of tragedy" surrounding multiracial people, examines "constructions of mixed race as comic experiences" (179) in stand-up comedy.

8. Louis Owens, *Mixedblood Messages: Literature, Film, Family, Place* (Norman: University of Oklahoma Press, 1998), 25.

9. The debates about Indian "authenticity" (concerning enrollment, blood quantum, cultural experience, etc.) are contentious and ongoing. The term "colonial surrogate" is from Jana Sequoya Magdaleno, "How? (!) Is an Indian: A Contest of Stories, Round 2," in *Postcolonial Theory and the United States: Race, Ethnicity, and Literature*, ed. Amritjit Singh and Peter Schmidt (Jackson: University Press of Mississippi, 2000), 279–99.

10. See Cornel West, "The New Cultural Politics of Difference," in *Out There: Marginalization and Contemporary Cultures*, ed. Russell Ferguson, Martha Gever, Trinh T. Minh-ha, and Cornel West (New York: New Museum of Contemporary Art, 1990), 19–36; and Ronald Takaki, *A Different Mirror: A History of Multicultural America* (Boston: Little, Brown, 1993) and *Iron Cages: Race and Culture in Nineteenth-Century America* (New York: Oxford University Press, 1990).

11. See Arnold Krupat, *For Those Who Come After: A Study of Native American Autobiography* (Berkeley: University of California Press, 1987); Patricia Nelson Limerick, *The Legacy of Conquest: The Unbroken Past of the American West* (New York: Norton, 1987); Louis Owens, *Mixedblood Messages*; Mary Louise Pratt, *Imperial Eyes: Travel Writings and Transculturation* (New York: Routledge, 1992); Gloria Anzaldúa, *Borderlands: La Frontera—The New Mestiza* (San Francisco: Spinsters/Aunt Lute Books, 1987); Hertha D. Wong, *Sending My Heart Back Across the Years: Tradition and Innovation in Native American Autobiography* (New York: Oxford University Press, 1992).

12. Lucy R. Lippard, *The Lure of the Local: Senses of Place in a Multicentered Society* (New York: New Press, 1997), 7.

13. See, for instance, Carol Stack, *Call to Home: African Americans Reclaim the Rural South* (New York: Basic Books, 1996).

14. William Bevis, "Native American Novels: Homing In," in *Recovering the Word: Essays on Native American Literature*, ed. Brian Swann and Arnold Krupat (Berkeley: University of California Press, 1987), 580–620.

15. Sharon P. Holland, "'If You Know I Have a History, You Will Respect Me': A Perspective on Afro-Native American Literature," *Callaloo* 17, no. 1 (1994), 334–50.

16. Caren Kaplan, "Reconfigurations of Geography and Historical Narrative: A Review Essay," *Public Culture* 3.1 (1990): 25–32.

17. Michael Dorris, *A Yellow Raft in Blue Water* (New York: Henry Holt, 1987), 9; hereafter cited in the text.

18. Bill Moyers, "Louise Erdrich and Michael Dorris," in *A World of Ideas* (New York: Doubleday, 1989), 460–69. Rpt. in *Conversations with Louise Erdrich and Michael Dorris*, ed. Allan Chavkin and Nancy Feyl Chavkin (Jackson: University Press of Mississippi, 1994).

19. The 1956 "Relocation Act … provided funding to establish 'job training centers' for American Indians in various urban centers, and to finance the relocation of individual Indians and Indian families to these locales. It was coupled to a denial of funds for similar programs and economic development on the reserva-

tions themselves. Those who availed themselves of the 'opportunity' for jobs, etc. represented by the federal relocation programs were usually required to sign agreements that they would not return to their respective reservations to live. The result, by 1980, was a diaspora of Native Americans, with more than half of the 1.6 million Indians in the U.S. having been scattered to cities across the country." Ward Churchill and Glenn T. Morris, "Key Indian Laws and Cases," in *The State of Native America: Genocide, Colonization, and Resistance*, ed. M. Annette Jaimes (Boston: South End Press, 1992), 16.

Developing a Kin-Aesthetic

Multiraciality and Kinship in Asian and Native North American Literature

> We are what we imagine. Our very existence consists of our imagination of ourself [sic]. ... the greatest tragedy that can befall us is to go unimagined.
> —N. Scott Momaday, in Vizenor, *Earthdiver*

> When stillness culminates, there is movement. Non-alignment paradoxically means new alliances: those that arise from-with-in differences and necessarily cut across variable borderlines.
> —Trinh T. Minh-ha, *When the Moon Waxes Red*

How do we attain the imagination required to develop "new alliances ... that arise from-with-in differences?" I theorize that profound alliances of this kind can develop through recognition of familial relations. Acknowledging the mixed heritage of the family changes the identities of the monoracial/ethnic individuals who comprise that family. The recognition of the Other as family, as *kin*, cannot but help shift one's own identity. My mother once asked me if seeing me, a person of Chinese and European ethnicities, would make my brother's European American friends see my half-brother, who is entirely Chinese, as "more white." It was when she asked this question that I first began to see the significance of mixed heritage identity as something that lay outside the individual mixed heritage person's "border-crossing" or "trickster" abilities. Rather, within the metaphor of the nation-as-family, people of mixed heritage function as mirrors that reflect back the Other-within-ourselves. In order to establish the complex interrelations of individual, familial, and national identities involved in this exchange, I examine the development of the recognition of the Other as kin, or the "kin-aesthetic," through literature that explores the familial connections between Asian and Native North Americans.

The first step in the process of the recognition of the Other as kin is the stripping away of stereotypes, which so firmly establish "Otherness" and deliberately disallow the possibility of kinship. Homi K. Bhabha articulates the difficulty of renegotiating imagination past the boundaries of binary oppositional stereotypes in "The Other Question: Stereotype, Discrimination and the Discourse of Colonialism." Bhabha explains the complex nature of the stereotype in colonialist discourse, arguing:

> Stereotyping is not the setting up of a false image that becomes the scapegoat of discriminatory practices. It is a much more ambivalent text of projection and introjection, metaphoric and metonymic strategies, displacement, over-determination, guilt, aggressivity; the masking and splitting of "official" and phantasmatic knowledges to construct the positionalities and oppositionalities of racist discourse. (81–82)

Deciphering the true nature of the stereotype is necessary in order to begin strategizing methods to move beyond stereotypes in interethnic interactions. To resist the totalizing effect of the simplification of knowledge generated by stereotypes we must generate not only more information, but also new ways of knowing and new forms of knowledge. In Bhabha's view, "it is a non-repressive form of knowledge that allows for the possibility of simultaneously embracing two contradictory beliefs, one official and one secret, one archaic and one progressive, one that allows the myth of origins, the other that articulates difference and division" (80). But this solution can be difficult to realize when our gaze is directed by the powerful force of media-projected stereotypes.

How do we see ourselves and how do we see each other? When those seeing and being seen are circumscribed by images created with profit rather than truth telling in mind, the apparently innocuous action of "gazing" can become quite damaging. The reality of human relations disappears in the face of binary oppositional structures. But how are we to escape the black/white racial dichotomy that rules even the structure of our language, and certainly the structure of our society? It is only in knowing, personally and familiarly, the disjunction between these false representations and the reality in our own lives that we begin to develop a clearer vision of who "we" are. Consequently, I argue that it is absolutely necessary to begin to see "Others" as "kin"—as sharing identity with ourselves—for us to be able to break through stereotypical relations based on media-induced racial dichotomies. Within literary representation, the attempts by some ethnic writers to represent the utopian vision of coalition politics still struggle with binary oppositional stereotypes.[1] Ultimately, it is a recognition of what I call the "kin-aesthetic"—the understanding of the "Other" as "kin," as a member of the in-group—that moves beyond the logic of binary opposition and thus begins the work of reframing "the gaze."

Theorists such as Frantz Fanon have developed postcolonial theory to examine how people of color see themselves through the dominant gaze.[2] But postcolonial theory is too often merely an oppositional position. When bell hooks "reverses the gaze" to see how African Americans look at "whiteness," she is similarly reversing the relationship of margin to center. "Spaces of agency exist for black people, wherein we can both interrogate the gaze of the Other but also look back, and at one another, naming what we see" (116). So how do ethnic minorities name themselves and see each other? Ethnic literatures have historically dealt with relations between European Americans and ethnic Americans. There is now, however, a developing tradition of representations of interethnic relations, and it is the complexity of these interactions that interest me in the context of constructing identities outside the limitations of the "dominant gaze."

My understanding of the "kin-aesthetic" is developed through an examination of the following texts: Alejandro Morales's *The Brick People*, Gerald Vizenor's *Griever: An American Monkey King in China*, Shawn Wong's *Homebase*, Mei Mei Evans's "Gussuk," and Sky Lee's *Disappearing Moon Café*. In these texts, the crises of meaning created by the logic of binary opposition run on both a larger systemic scale and the smaller one of personal identity. The personal identity crisis and the systemic identity crisis meet primarily around the issue of national identity. National identity in this sense refers to the construction of the individual in relation to the community and political power structure, and vice versa. National identity is also critical in terms of the relationship between the ethnic community and the larger nation to which that group belongs.[3] The conflict inherent in these relationships creates crises of identity. Perhaps it is the in-between places, the fissures and cracks in identity, that open the possibility of alliances across the boundaries of those categorizations that merely catalog our differences from one another. These "fissures" and "cracks" are often embodied in these texts by mixed heritage characters that become the mediators of the "kin-aesthetic." It is not only through them that monoracial/ethnic people can see the racialized "Other" as kin, but often it is they themselves who, in seeing the Other as kin, destroy the racial categorizations that limit relations. The rhetoric that places mixed heritage people as bridges between cultures creates an untenable position. Thus I argue instead that mixed heritage can provide the space in which the process of recognition, that is, the development of a kin-aesthetic, can take place.

Trinh Minh-ha describes the necessary beginnings of this process in the particular case of Asian Americans as the "hyphenated condition":

> It is in having to confront and defy hegemonic values on an everyday basis, in other words, in assuming the *between-world dilemma*, that one understands both the predicament and the potency of the hyphen. Here, the *becoming Asian American* affirms itself at once as a transient and constant state: one is born over and over and over again as hyphen rather than as fixed entity. ... The *hyphenated condition* certainly does not limit itself to a duality between two cultural heritages. ... The multidimensional desire to be both here(s) and there(s) implies a more radical ability to *shuttle between frontiers* and to cut across ethnic allegiances while assuming a specific and contingent legacy. (Trinh 159, my emphasis)

The question of alliances, and the determination to "shuttle between frontiers," takes on a particular urgency when coupled with a national crisis of identity—as in times of war. One of the most profound "crises of identity" the world has ever experienced is that engendered by the horrifying violence of the atomic bomb, and its use against Pacific Islanders and the Japanese people. The atomic age, coupled with the racist nationalist rhetoric, which did not match the multiracial composition of the American nation during the Second World War, brought a heightened awareness of this rupture of meaning to ethnic literature. It is thus the particular crisis of the atomic age that makes the use of postmodernism—always with and inseparable from postcolonialism, feminism, and queer theory—necessary for the study of ethnic literature.

It is difficult, however, to make these analyses without succumbing to a merely oppositional stance. As Toni Cade Bambara says, "The trick, I suspect, at this point in time in human history as we approach the period of absolute devastation and total renewal, is to maintain a loose grip, a flexible grasp on those assumptions we hold to be true, valid, real. They may not be" (Tate 23). I must reaffirm here Homi Bhabha's contention that we must develop a "non-repressive form of knowledge" in order to achieve a "flexible grasp" on our understanding of interethnic representations. Acknowledging, then, that there is no "graspable real," I will begin by documenting first the "unreal," that which is deliberately "fake": the stereotypes with which we have sometimes seen each other.[4]

"The "Enemy Within": Japanese Americans in Other Ethnic Literatures

I will begin "re-framing the gaze" by examining representations of interethnic interactions in the period after World War II, which was, I argue, in many ways critical to ethnic identity development. Given the wartime rhetoric of national identity defined against "the enemy," it is not surprising that the texts in this section respond to this dynamic through representations of Japanese Americans, at the time identified as the "enemy within." The tension around issues of identity and nationalism in the situation of Japanese Americans is revealed in Alejandro Morales's *The Brick People* and Leslie Marmon Silko's *Ceremony*.

'THE BRICK PEOPLE'

Alejandro Morales's first novel in English, *The Brick People*, documents the resettling of Mexicans in a particular Los Angeles barrio to work in an Anglo-American-owned brick factory. Written in the late 1980s, *The Brick People* demonstrates a historical understanding of the multicultural beginnings of Los Angeles. As the Simons brickyard workers dig in the brickyard's clay field at the beginning of the novel, they come upon hundreds of cadavers, which they at first take to be the remains of a Native American burial ground. What they discover instead is a confirmation of a story everyone had assumed was myth. Morales's description of the revelation of the mummified bodies and the truth that was buried with them is itself revelatory of constructions of views of "the Other."

> The many accounts of the massacre had rendered the infamous occurrence a blurry memory in the community's conscience. Most people believed that the Chinese were apt to spin tales against the Anglo Americans and that the story of the massacre was a legend brought from China. (18)

The fact that in this case a multitude of accounts only helped to bury the communal memory of the massacre proves that the volume of information available does not bring the truth to light, but rather that the power of the media's gaze determines how we view information. Particularly interesting is the second part of the quote above, which implies that Anglo-Americans were victims of "a legend brought from China." Like a contagion brought by "aliens ineligible for citizenship," the story of the massacre is reconstructed as a tale, brought from a foreign land, which may somehow disenfranchise the dominant group. Even when there is a possibility of "reversing the gaze," the power of the dominant story can even turn the gaze of the Other back on itself. This reversal of the reversed gaze is powerful enough to bury "hundreds, perhaps thousands of Chinese" (18) from historical memory.

The violence trained on "outsiders" by the power of the gaze is both literal as well as figurative. This memory of anti-Asian violence becomes the myth of a threat, which is once again fulfilled after the evacuation and incarceration of the West Coast Japanese Americans. The incarceration of Japanese Americans places the Mexican American community in danger. This danger is twofold. First, it reprises the time during the 1930s Depression when there had been talk of "repatriation for all Mexicans" (195), and, second, it poses a real danger to the livelihood of Mexican Americans employed to work on Japanese American farms. Arturo feels that "the world had become eerie, strange, and unrecognizable without the presence of the Japanese families. The fields belonged to nobody. The crops would go unpicked, and there would be no job for Arturo" (254).[5] For another member of Arturo's family, Javier, the burning of their house in Simons forces a deeper feeling of "common relationship" with those who have been vilified as America's enemies. Javier, recognizing the real violence represented by this physical division, sees "the blinding flash over Hiroshima" (277) in his burning home. By these gestures of kinship Morales displays the interdependence between ethnic groups linked by, rather than separated by, socioeconomic concerns.

Morales introduces a character that represents the relationship between Mexican Americans and Japanese Americans: the Japanese-Mexican Armando Takahashi Subia. Significantly, this multiethnic character is part of a multiethnic workers union. The coalition meets in a shop described as containing hundreds of "Japanese woodblock prints" (206). A rather mysterious character, one Stewart Josia Teaza, is described moving through the scene. He is both a gambler and a collector of art, and is said to reside in Tokyo. By such signs, he is constructed as someone who might be an Orientalist, but is also possibly a more positive crosser of cultural boundaries. In contrast, Armando Subia's ability to move between fissures is further reflected in his ability to relate to the female union organizer "without male and female formalities, which he believed were obstacles to social progress" (207). His flexibility in this matter serves to reinforce his role as a cultural and "racial" mediator. Yet, ultimately, this move toward recognition of "kinship" through a mixed heritage character is too brief; we will have to wait for Morales's 1992 novel, *The Rag Doll Plagues*, for a fuller treatment of the pivotal role of mixed heritage characters in "race" relations.

'CEREMONY'

Leslie Marmon Silko takes the representation of the mixed heritage character as mediator of race relations as a structuring thematic of her novel *Ceremony*. As the novel opens, Silko writes about the moment of death as revelatory of the insubstantial nature of racial differences. When the protagonist, Tayo, a World War II soldier of European and Native American descent, sees dead Japanese soldiers for the first time, it begins an unraveling of his sense of identity that continues throughout the novel. Tayo's mixed heritage identity causes him to intuitively understand the way in which flesh is made to stand for race as a form of racial stereotyping. "Tayo ... realized that the man's skin was not much different from his own. ... even white men were darker after death" (7). This recognition of the superficial nature of the differences ascribed to "skin color" is complicated by Tayo's situation as a Native American soldier for the United States: Tayo is by definition robbed of his nation by the nation-state he has been called upon to defend. Furthermore, the defense of the nation is predicated upon killing those defined by the nation as its enemies, in this case the Japanese. For Tayo, this situation creates a true psychological identity crisis, for he finds the "enemy" to be too familiar—in the sense of reminding him of family. "That had become the worst thing for Tayo: they looked too familiar even when they were alive. When the sergeant told them to kill all the Japanese soldiers lined up in front of the cave with their hands on their heads, Tayo could not pull the trigger. ... he saw Josiah [his uncle] standing there. ... he watched his uncle fall, and he *knew* it was Josiah" (8). At what level is this knowledge? Tayo's *knowledge* that the Japanese soldier *is* his Uncle Josiah is the knowledge that structures the rest of the novel. It is this *knowledge* of the Japanese as kin—irreconcilable with wartime anti-Japanese propaganda—that causes Tayo to be hospitalized, and causes his mental deterioration throughout the rest of the text. Even the attempts of Tayo's cousin, Rocky, to make Tayo see the government-mandated "truth" of the Japanese as enemy can not win over Tayo's *knowledge* that they are kin.

As in *The Brick People*, the knowledge generated here by an ethnic minority's experience is irreconcilable with the message of the dominant media. Tayo cannot look at the corpse of a Japanese soldier; "Rocky made him look at the corpse and said, 'Tayo, this is a *Jap*! This is a *Jap* uniform!' … 'Look, Tayo, look at the face,' and that was when Tayo started screaming because it wasn't a Jap, it was Josiah" (8). If we read this passage in terms of Tayo's *knowledge*, as opposed to the binary oppositions of media stereotypes, then Tayo's perception is correct, this Japanese soldier is "not a Jap," because a "Jap" is a racist ideological construct that does not exist outside media representation. Tayo has already had to see the Other as kin, because he, as a person of mixed heritage, is always already to recognize himself in the "racial" Other. Tayo's later attempts to restructure family in the city, with his European American girlfriend and the multitribe Native American religious movement, are only partially successful, because he has already destroyed his "family" by killing his uncle Josiah in the bodies of the Japanese soldiers. Tayo's destruction through his participation in the "world war" signals the destruction of a notion of a national family, as represented by the American "melting pot," despite its claims for the construction of both national identity and unity.

The irony of Tayo's "identity," or kinship, with the Japanese as part of a global family is made even stronger as Tayo, a European and Native American U.S. soldier, is identified by subtle signs with the Japanese Americans who were also constructed as "Japs" because of the war's propaganda. Early in the novel Silko establishes this connection through a series of associative structures. Soon after his release from a mental hospital, Tayo finds himself on a railroad platform: "His name was on the tag and his serial number too. It had been a long time since he thought about having a name" (16). Tayo is without "a name" because his sense of identity has been shattered by a nation-state unable to imagine his mixed heritage identity. Immediately after this passage, which echoes for anyone familiar with images and stories of Japanese American families given serial numbers to identify them during the internment process, the function of language to determine identity becomes an issue. "[The Japanese Americans] spoke to him in English, and when he didn't answer, there was a discussion and he heard the Japanese words vividly" (17). These voices, speaking bilingually and finally in Japanese, throw him back into his memories of the war—memories of confusion over identity—and his overtaxed mind and body collapse. Tayo's disorientation regarding his identity is related by parallel images to the disjunction of identity experienced by the recently released Japanese Americans. "The Japanese women were holding small children by the hands, and they were surrounded by bundles and suitcases" (17). The suitcases in this image of the Japanese American women and children echo the suitcase held by Tayo on the previous page—at the same moment when he recognizes the cardboard tag with the serial numbers that identify him in the military context. The suitcase also implies the homelessness to which both Tayo and the Japanese Americans are now subject, and thus implies the connection between the Other and the self. What Silko does here by connecting the alienation felt by a mixed heritage Native American soldier to the alienation experienced by Japanese Americans during World War II is to recognize that "the struggle is always multiple and transversal—specific and not confined to one side of any border war" (Trinh 18).

Native Mixed Heritage Identities in Chinese American Literature

This "multiple and transversal" struggle is certainly more dramatic when the "war" in question is recognized by hegemonic powers and given the weight of recorded history. However, in the works with which my analysis ends, the focus shifts from relations with Japanese Americans who experienced explicit vilification as enemies of the nation-state, to narratives about the relations between Native and Chinese North Americans. Shawn Wong's *Homebase;* "Gussuk," a short story by Mei Mei Evans; and Sky Lee's novel *Disappearing Moon Cafe* come progressively nearer to seeing the ethnic Other as family, and begin a revision of relations between peoples of color. To establish the paradigms through which I will examine the dynamics of interethnic—Chinese–Native North American—interactions, I begin by analyzing Gerald Vizenor's *Griever: An American Monkey King in China* and his depiction of stereotypes and their reversals.[6]

'GRIEVER': "MIXBLOOD TRIBAL TRICKSTER"

Gerald Vizenor's novel *Griever: An American Monkey King in China* uses stereotypes to create unexpected juxtapositions and thereby induce a state of "knowledge" that goes beyond hegemonic discourse. Vizenor's attempts to reframe the "already established" gaze of, and at, Native Americans is accomplished in *Griever* through the mirror of China—that is, China Browne, a Native American woman to whom the protagonist, Griever de Hocus, writes letters from China, the nation-state. China Browne serves as an enigmatic and only partially visible mirror for presumptions about Chinese culture:

> [China] is enchanted with the wild energies of smaller men and she is fascinated with pictures of bound feet. As a child she bound her feet and earned her given name; she folded bright blue bandannas around her toes and moved at night on ceremonial lotus feet to exotic places in the world. (20)

But China Browne's obsession with stereotypical chinoiserie is immediately counteracted by Griever's interaction with a woman he meets on his way to China. Upon learning his destination, the woman asks, "Have you ever seen bound feet?" (14). Griever, the "mixblood tribal trickster" (34), turns the mirror of the gaze upon this woman's presumptions when he replies that he has seen such deformity on their very flight. To the woman's consternation, Griever points to another woman who is not Chinese: "There, that woman with the narrow high heels, see how her toes are turned under?" (14).

This scene with the woman on the airplane is particularly intriguing because it calls into question the meaning of "reality" and "knowledge." Griever says of the woman, "She hauled me back from dream scenes with her narrow realities" (15). Throughout the novel, Griever's "mixed-blood" dreams convey just as much, or more, "real knowledge" as any other source of information. The particular source of information Vizenor critiques the most is the dominant media. Griever says, "imagination is the real world, all the rest is bad television" (28). And of one of the other English-language teachers working with Griever in China, he says she "imagines movie sets when she does not understand a time or place" (46). In a similar vein, Vizenor notes mockingly that "China was discovered twice on television" (203), meaning nothing about China has been understood—or discovered—at all, through the haze of media stereotypes.

This failure of dominant narratives to communicate something vital is the focus of the novel's touchstone scene: Griever's liberation of the chickens in the market (19). He sees the chickens not as meat, but as living creatures with whom he shares the world.[7] This scene, which is referred to repeatedly throughout the novel, gains greater resonance when paired with Griever's memory of the grade school science class trauma of being asked to dissect frogs. Instead, he frees them because he cannot see them as objects of scientific study. A tall blonde science teacher says of Griever:[8]

> The cause of his behavior, without a doubt, is racial. Indians never had it easier than now, the evil fires of settlement are out, but this troubled mixblood child is given to the racial confusion of two identities, neither of which can be secured in one culture. These disruptions of the soul ... become manifest as character disorders. He is not aware of his whole race, not even his own name. (49–50)

Even Griever's grandmother says of him, "His urban mixblood tongue ... 'wags like a mongrel, he's a wild outsider.' Even at home on the reservation he was a foreigner" (42). His mixed blood status, like Tayo's in *Ceremony*, relegates him to perpetual outsider status. He is the "Other within," neither Native nor "white," therefore questionable—and questioning.

However, as Vizenor's novel progresses, more and more characters are revealed to be "mixedbloods," and what is an authentic, "real" identity is constantly questioned. Griever finally becomes involved with Kangmei, a blond Chinese whose "father was an American" (142). She is a mixed blood who is related to the mixed blood translator, Hester Hua Dan, who becomes pregnant with Kuan Yin, Griever's daughter. At the same moment during which Griever is informed by Hester of her pregnancy, a Chinese official is giving a toast "to the revitalization of the Chinese people, [and] to the harmony and friendship between the Chinese people and all the peoples of the world," a harmony and friendship made literal by Griever's sexual transgression (190). In the end, however, Vizenor's development of the kin-aesthetic is cut short by the forced abortion of the multiply mixed heritage child carried by Hester Hua Dan. Furthermore, the fact that it is her stereotypically patriarchal Chinese father who enforces the standards of female sexuality and racial purity only reinforces Hollywood stereotypes about over-patriarchal Asian cultures. "All the peoples of the world" cannot come together so easily, even in fiction.

'HOMEBASE'

In thematic terms, Shawn Wong's *Homebase* is an inversion of Vizenor's *Griever*. As with Griever, Wong's protagonist, Rainsford Chan, is on a journey of self-discovery. Both characters are strangers in a strange land, although Wong's text seeks to locate someone perceived by others to be a foreigner firmly within the American landscape, whereas Vizenor's novel appears to situate a foreigner around the edges of culture and society, mixed blood as perpetual negotiator of culture. Also like *Griever,* Shawn Wong's *Homebase* negotiates, around stereotypes and ancestral knowledge of racial heritage, the kin-aesthetic representation of the relations between Chinese and Native Americans. The protagonist, Rainsford Chan, finally begins to understand his place in the American landscape only through the intervention of a "mixblood" Native American man. As a Native American, the man apparently holds the key to belonging in a nation that has denied that Asians can be anything but "unassimilable aliens" who have no right to own the land. However, it is this Native American man's claim to Chinese blood, and therefore to kinship with Rainsford, that allows Rainsford to feel that he belongs to the land that his grandfather had hopelessly traversed in search of a home. Rainsford, narrating his experience, says, "During Christmas 1969, an Indian man in whom I saw my grandfather showed me my grandfather's face" (81). Seeing his ancestor in this man, whom he had perceived as the Other, is the beginning of Rainsford's development of a kin-aesthetic. Rainsford's meeting with the Native American man is initially fraught with stereotypical interaction. The question "where are you from" is reiterated *ad infinitum.* The Native American asks, "Where are you from?"; "Where are you from originally?"; "How long you been here?"; "How long you been in the United States?"; and when Rainsford responds "All my life" the man insistently questions, "You mean you ain't born in China?" (82–83). But the stereotype of the Asian as perpetual foreigner is counteracted by a kin connection between Chinese American and Native American. Soon, the old man tells Rainsford that he too is Chinese, both by way of a Chinese grandfather as well as by the 30,000-year-old migration from Asia to the North American continent.

This reclamation of history from the dominant narrative of separate racial classifications as marked by color—yellow man versus red man—is enacted further by Rainsford's political action of camping on Alcatraz to support Native American sovereignty. However, the shadow of the European American historical perspective inevitably informs the interaction between the old man and Rainsford, who, because of his own internalization of that perspective, misunderstands when the old man asks, "What are you doing here? This isn't your battle or your land." Rainsford defensively reiterates his desperate plea, saying, "I'm part of this land too." Led by the old man's exhortation to "go out and make yourself at home," Rainsford finally finds himself amid the Chinese American ghosts of Angel Island (84).[9] Rainsford's return to his roots embodies Werner Sollors's theory about the American urge to define identity. As Sollors documents, the figure of a Native American is key to establishing authenticity of identity in America (Sollors 231). Wong, however, goes beyond the mere reiteration of stereotypical associations of Native Americans with "the land" by identifying the grandfather of the Native American man as a Chinese American bone collector. The figure of the bone collector is important in *Homebase* (and also, we shall see later, in *Disappearing Moon Café*) because the bone collector signifies the death of thousands of young Chinese men in the building of the railroad that created the nations—the United States and Canada—from which they would later be excluded. Unlike in Morales's novel *The Brick People*, in *Homebase* the bones of Chinese Americans are not allowed to be buried and forgotten. The figure of the bone collector is metaphoric of Wong's attempt to inscribe Chinese Americans indelibly into the memory of the nation that has tried so hard to erase all memory of their historical presence.

In the final image of the novel, Wong lays kinship claim to the Native American through the overlapping images of the grandfathers, both Rainsford's and the mixed heritage Native American man's. The development of this "kin-aesthetic"—this recognition of a "common relationship"—is inextricably bound up in the development of a sense of belonging to the land and the nation, made possible through the figure of a mixed heritage character. The novel ends with these words:

> We are old enough to haunt this land like an Indian who laid down to rest and his body became the outline of the horizon. This is my father's canyon. See his head reclining! That peak is his nose, that cliff his chin, and his folded arms are summits. (98)

Like the "Indian," Rainsford is saying, his Chinese American forefathers have died in this land and their descendants can thus lay claim to it. Once "the Indian" is established as a symbol of the land, the transference of the Chinese American father's image onto this figure, and onto this land, confers "true, authentic" citizenship upon the son.

"GUSSUK": THE CHINESE NATIVE

Belonging to a nation-state can be a complex and contradictory process. In Mei Mei Evans's short story "Gussuk," Lucy, the Eurasian American health care giver, is torn between her desire to belong to the Native Alaskan community of Kigiak and her inability to "let go" of her "first world" status. We are subtly given to understand that this desire to "relocate" herself (to move and to find herself) is because she does not fit in "at home" in Boston. This sense of dislocation seems to be generated by her mixed heritage identity. Faced with the insistence that she must be Native, Lucy responds by claiming Chinese American identity through a Chinese grandmother. However, the Native woman who questions her, Mercy, recognizes that sometimes appearance can translate into a form of identity. She thus proceeds to insist to Lucy that "you look Eskimo. Now you gotta act Eskimo" (155). Lucy proceeds to make superficial attempts to relocate herself within this group of people, but she ultimately fails to recognize the Other as being enough like herself, thus, by the end of the story, she faces an even greater sense of dislocation.

Despite Lucy's desire to find community with the people of Kigiak, and their acceptance of her based on her physical resemblance to them, particularly to Robert, Lucy ultimately flees to Anchorage. That she does so to escape Robert's persistent courting is particularly significant in terms of the development of a kin-aesthetic. Lucy cannot see what Robert sees—the Other as kin—precisely because of her first world status. Because of her privileged situation in the world she has been overexposed to inimical media stereotypes. Despite her recognition of familiarity (in the sense of family) with Robert, her "sense of her self" as a first world individual prevents their coming together, and once again the issue of the "truth" of hegemonic discourse overwhelms the self-generated *knowledge* that belies media-induced stereotypes.

Significantly, it is around the symbol of national identity building—a Fourth of July party—that many of these conflicting impulses become evident. Lucy's desire to avoid being classified as an outsider causes her to go so far as to reject her national identity as an American at the Fourth of July party, which provides the narrative climax of the story. "Someone suggested loudly that they sing the national anthem, and Mercy nominated Lucy to lead it. ... Lucy protested in embarrassment. 'I don't know the words, honest'" (159–60). The problematics of identifying as an American are politicized when, in her drunkenness, the Native Alaskan woman, Mercy, confuses the Fourth of July with Christmas. Not only "opposite" temporally, Christmas is also a sign of the condescending *gussuk* missionaries who live ever outside the Native community, thus demonstrating the equal foreignness of Christianity and U.S. nationalism. In her drunkenness, Mercy marks the irony of the celebrating the Fourth of July, Independence Day, as a member of a colonized people.[10] She says, "Yeah, yeah, yeah. Freedom and liberty and all that jazz" (161). Similar to African Americans, Native peoples are faced with the bitter irony of celebrating the cessation of their "freedom" in the name of nation building.

During this party, however, Lucy's desire to disassociate herself from an American identity is not completely fulfilled. She sees that "Robert stood beside his wife all evening. For some reason, they struck Lucy as an Eskimo version of that 'American Gothic' painting" (160). Lucy's observation both marks her "Americanness," her nationality, because she uses it as a frame of reference, and marks her difference from Robert and his wife, whom she sees as reproductive of what is to her a foreign "Eskimo" culture. Ironically, her physical resemblance to Robert could place her just as easily into this portrait of "Eskimo" nationality as she places him. Robert recognizes her as kin, and that is why he is so persistent in his courting of her. When they do have sex, her first concern is procreation. Lucy tries to reassure herself, thinking "at least she was reasonably sure that she hadn't risked pregnancy" (161). Had she risked getting pregnant, the identity of her child's father would have drawn her into the community of which she feels she cannot be a part. When she finally dismisses Robert's advances, she is dismissing any possibility of relocating herself, in the double sense of moving and of finding a self that has been lost between monoethnic, monoracialized identities.

In Anchorage, two years later and after Robert's suspicious death by drowning, the Fourth of July party and the identity crises it marks still resonate for Lucy as "a middle aged Native woman approache[s] her" (163). The woman locates Lucy and identifies herself. "I met you in Kigiak. On the Fourth of July … I'm Robert's cousin … He died. Last year. Drowned. … You look even more like him now than when I met you," she says to a discomfited Lucy. When Lucy's current boyfriend, Rick, arrives and questions the woman's identity, Lucy dismisses and generalizes her to evade the specific connection to Robert, a part of herself she has tried to forget. The woman becomes "just some Native woman. I really don't know what she was talking about" (163). Lucy's inarticulate tears belie her disavowal. Each of the pieces of the woman's identification locates Lucy in a particular way. According to Robert's cousin, their resemblance is even stronger now that he has died. What does it mean that Lucy's visual identification with Robert should be intensified after his death? His death seems to symbolize her own inability to integrate the conflicts within her identity, particularly in terms of the "interruption" between her national and personal identities, her position as a mixed heritage person of color within a white-identified nation. Her despondent tears are like the river in which Robert drowns himself, the river in which the salmon return to die: it is the river of memory, of re-location through re-membering history.

'DISAPPEARING MOON CAFE'

Finally, Sky Lee's *Disappearing Moon Cafe* illustrates that a resolution of the conflict between insider and outsider *can* come through the development of the "kin-aesthetic" recognition of the Other as kin. *Disappearing Moon Cafe* is a family's history told through intergenerational and interethnic gazes. Sky Lee's representations of a multigenerational Chinese Canadian family demonstrate the outsider and insider dynamics in kinship relations and how these categories change over time and with changing developments in "knowledge," as in Silko's *Ceremony*. In *Disappearing Moon Cafe* those who do not "fit in" to the community on the level of individual identity are the mixed heritage Chinese-Native Canadian Kelora, her son Ting An, and Ting An's Native-Eurasian son, Morgan. Kelora's interrupted presence in *Disappearing Moon Cafe* "exposes" but also "repeats" the alienation of the "Chinamen" in the land/nation that she, as a Native Canadian, ironically represents. Kelora Chen, the narrator's great-grandmother, is supposed to be the product of the interethnic mixing of the Native woman Shi'atko and the "Chinaman" Chen Gwok Fai. Her parentage begins the Wong family tree, but it is her mate, Wong Gwei Chang, who is the family patriarch.

Wong Gwei Chang, in 1892, is a young man searching the lonely wilderness of western Canada for the bones of fellow "Chinamen." Like the grandfather of the Native American man in Shawn Wong's *Homebase*, Gwei Chang searches for bones in defiance of the binary structure of the dominant narrative, which seeks to erase Chinese Canadian history. Gwei Chang views the land as desolate and "uncivilized." Thus, when he meets Kelora, "he thought she had to be a spirit" (2), while she immediately recognizes him for who he is, because it is also a part of her: "'Look, a chinaman!'[11] She crept up behind him and spoke in his own language" (2). Throughout the exchange she has the advantage of her hybrid identity and the bilingualism and biculturality it provides her. She mocks his presupposition that she is uncivilized when, as a disembodied voice in the forest, she observes, "Ah, so he speaks chinese," but he remains "unwilling to believe what he saw before him" when she emerges from the concealment of the forest and he sees that "she was an indian girl, dressed in coarse brown clothing that made her invisible in the forest" (3). Despite his inability to see her, she claims her identity with him, saying, "My father is a chinaman, like you. His eyes are slits like yours. He speaks like you" (3). National origin, appearance, and language tie them together, but, as for Lucy in "Gussuk," Wong Gwei Chang's sense of national/ethnic identity causes him to reject her proclamation. "'But you're a wild injun.' He spilled out the insults in front of her, but they were meaningless to her. In chinese, the words mocked, slanglike, 'yin-chin'" (3). His rejection falls flat because it is based on the adoption of European stereotypes of Native North Americans, as signaled by his need to use English to convey the insults, while Kelora conversely frames his words through a Chinese worldview. Thus, when Kelora further admonishes, "Ahh, he has no manners" (3), he is the one left feeling

> uncivilized, uncouth; the very qualities he had assigned so thoughtlessly to her, he realized she was watching for in him. ... [H]e was surprised to see that she was wary of him. It emphasized the distance between them, as if she was not a human being as he was, or ... as if he was not a human being as she was. (4)

And indeed, they are not wholly the same. She emphasizes their difference at the same time that she invites him to join her as she says, "My father enjoys the company of his own kind" (4). Thus she claims some distance from him, perhaps somewhat based in gender differences, because the two "chinamen" relate to each other not only as Chinese, but also as men. When he does accept her, Gwei Chang recognizes her actions as similar to those of Chinese women he remembered. Most telling of this gendered-racial difference, however, is that she comes to represent the land, as a female body, and thus fulfills the gendered stereotype of female connectedness to the land, while also fulfilling the racial stereotype of Native North American connection to the land.

Thus, his acceptance by her is figured as an acceptance into the land that she is made to represent. In Lee's description it is "as if the barren wasteland around him had magically opened and allowed him admittance" (4). Later, as their relationship develops, Kelora's association with the land is ironically used as a moment for Gwei Chang's recognition of her "chineseness." "When Kelora took him into the forests of 'the hidden place,' another world opened up. She had a way of murmuring as they walked. Gwei Chang remembered chinese women doing the very same" (13). The fact that this scene could easily be read as a metaphor for sexual intimacy indicates that the implication of that kind of intimacy (and thus the possibility of conceiving children) requires Gwei Chang to seek "identity" with Kelora even at the same moment that he is drawn to her "foreignness." Kelora faces the difficulties of her "in-between" identity not only from the "chinaman" who is drawn to her "civilized" Chinese qualities, as well as her ability to live in the land he finds so barren, which he sees as her "untamed" exoticness (9). She also faces less than total acceptance from her mother's people. Their concern over her identity, however, is manifested in a concern for her progeny, for the family she will create within their community, even though she and her (probable) father always remain slightly outside of it. "Not everybody was sure about another chinaman, but Kelora seemed to prefer it, and that was enough for them" (8).

Ultimately, her identity is defined in negative terms, as "neither chinese nor indian." Gwei Chang sees her as "a strange one, with her own private language" and finally concludes that her identity can only be defined by the land, as he perceives her language as arising "from deep within the wildness of her soul" (14). In the form of a "native informant," Kelora then teaches Gwei Chang "to love the same mother earth and to see her sloping curves in the mountains ... [which] he had once thought of ... as barriers" (14–15). The indeterminacy of pronoun relations in this passage (does "her" here refer to Kelora, or to "mother earth"?) is magnified by the last sentence of this passage, which declares "this beautiful mother filled his heart and soul" (15). Why is it that Kelora's identity can only thus be determined by the land in the very stereotype of a "wild injun" that Lee earlier mocks through Gwei Chang's racist reaction on first meeting Kelora? By maintaining that Kelora's "family on her mother's side was very wealthy, old and well-respected" (7), Lee undermines the "wild injun" stereotype by implying a very complex society with intricate social relations that allow some to be "very wealthy." This image goes quite far, in fact, toward substantiating Kelora's indirect claim that she is civilized, while intimating that, in contrast, Gwei Chang may not be. It is puzzling, therefore, that Lee would take so much trouble to establish the "civility" of both the "chinese and indians," yet revert in her characterization of Kelora to the stereotypical image of Native North American women. Werner Sollors argues that the "squaw" is "the ultimate in American female adoptive ancestors" (Sollors 231), thus perhaps this characterization simply serves the Asian North American "nationalist" agenda of establishing "roots" in this new land.

Multiraciality, "miscegenation," and incest,[12] as figured in *The Disappearing Moon Cafe*, are fragmented and fragmenting identities for both the individual and the "family/community/nation" to which the individual belongs. It is only when the truth of the family's multiracial history is revealed that the multiple crises of identity are resolved. These crises of personal and national identity can only be resolved in the escape from binary oppositional thinking—and its attendant focus on racial purity—that recognition of transracial kinships facilitates. Transracial and transnational kinship alliances are, in this sense, revolutionary. However, Trinh Minh-ha recognizes that in order for the "transnational alliance" to work, our individual identity development must remain flexible and dynamic, rather than stationary and goal oriented. In Trinh's words, "the becoming is not a becoming something; it remains active and transitive" (Trinh 161). The language of categorization, and "naming," is one of the most important locations for enacting this process of "becoming." Ethnic literature has maintained this "active and transitive" process of self-development by problematizing the categorizations imposed by dominant representations.

Conclusion

For ethnic literature, the very structure of categorization (legal definitions, for example) has always been problematic. "Truth" and "authenticity" have been questioned in American ethnic literature because it has been a site for exploring lack of authorization (in the form of documentation), of being "illegal," of the difference between the hegemonic story and that of the Other. The internalization of feelings of "foreignness" and not belonging complicate the negotiation between how visible minorities, and ethnic minorities who appear white, see themselves and how they are envisioned in the dominant media. People of mixed heritage, within family formations, form the junction of these issues by making apparent the cracks in the construction of monoracialized individual, familial, and national identities.[13] For ethnic writers, the personal identity crisis is thus always already a political identity crisis on the national level. How could Chicanos, Latinos, and Asian Americans know they belonged to a nation that saw them/sees us as perpetual foreigners? How do people of mixed heritage complicate these issues, and how can the development of a kin-aesthetic through the representation of people of mixed heritage help heal these wounds? For African and Native Americans, most of whom are now multiethnic through the process of often forced mixing, the question is more profound: how could they belong to a nation when they were not free, from the beginning, to make the *choice* to belong? It is only by seeing our relation with one another that we can solve these dilemmas. But in order to see this, we must find a new way to see each other and ourselves, and through this re-vision—of the history and the present—we can begin to confound racial boundaries and found multi-ethnic coalitions for change.

In the project to re-imagine ourselves and others, the figure of the person of mixed heritage is critical. However, it is not the person of mixed heritage as a lone or isolated figure that is the most significant factor in this struggle; rather, what we must be concerned with is the connections people of mixed heritage make between peoples who had thought they were unrelated and disconnected. As a metaphor, the situation of people of mixed heritage within the monoracialized family structure functions to reflect the dynamics of North American society.

It is the development of the possibly double-edged sword of a "new multi-cultural alliance" that emerges through the development of the kin-aesthetic (Trinh 159). As these feelings of kinship become more complex and prevalent in the work of ethnic writers, we will begin to see real changes in the fixed notions of binary oppositional identities that today rule the politics of identity formation in North America. This lack of fixity is as perilous as it is wondrous.

Notes

1. For example, several of the texts explored in this chapter suffer from a failed attempt to construct a notion of authentic identity.

2. For an examination of Fanon's view of the female postcolonial and her reaction to "the gaze," see Gwen Bergner.

3. Although the scope of this essay does not provide room for an extended analysis of the development of immigrant identity issues, such an examination would be critical for an understanding of the relations of "minorities" and mixed heritage identity with national identity.

4. I realize that the terms "real" and "fake" necessarily invoke Frank Chin's "authentic ethnic identity" theory as expressed in "Come All Ye Asian American writ-

ers of the Real and the Fake" (The Big Aiiieeeee!). Although I do not dismiss Chin, I would argue that our understanding of the "real" is only possible through a process of eliminating that which is known to be "fake." Defining the "real" itself, in positive terms, requires a mirror rather than a microscope.

5. Like Morales's novel, Maya Angelou's memoir, *I Know Why the Caged Bird Sings*, written in 1969, describes a situation in which the economic security of one group is pitted against that of another. Her text records the history of the African American migration to San Francisco at the beginning of World War II. She describes the shift from Japanese American to African American residence in the neighborhood known as the Western Addition as a "visible revolution" (177). As she writes her memoirs, she comments that:

> A person unaware of all the factors that make up oppression might have expected sympathy or even support from the Negro newcomers for the dislodged Japanese. Especially in view of the fact that they [the Blacks] had themselves undergone concentration camp living for centuries in slavery's plantations and later in sharecroppers' cabins. But the sensations of common relationship were missing. (178)

This hindsight recognition of similarity of experience is coupled with an even more profound recognition that the oppositional rhetoric of hegemonic power structures created an atmosphere in which ethnic minorities would appear to benefit from one another's misfortunes. Writing her memoirs twenty years after the circumstances she describes, Angelou exhibits an easy familiarity with things Japanese American in her narration of the "visible revolution"; she mentions "Nisei customers," "tempura, raw fish and *cha*" (178). At the time of the experience, however, her vision of Japanese America was still fogged by the dominant media. Thus she says, "I was unable to tell the Japanese from the Chinese and as yet found no real difference in the national origin of such sounds as Ching and Chan or Moto and Kano" (178). Of course, the names "Chan and Moto" would have been familiar to Angelou not necessarily from any personal experience with Asian Americans, but rather from the popular "Charlie Chan" and "Mr. Moto" movie series of the time. Angelou devotes only two pages to this issue, and though her tone is momentarily apologetic regarding her lack of feeling "common relationship," the main focus of even this brief passage is on the economic advancement of African Americans.

6. As the title indicates, the action of the novel takes place in China, and thus the Native American of the title is integrating with Chinese, and not Chinese Americans. The stereotypes I deal with, therefore, are limited to those that have been expressed toward Chinese Americans as part of the perpetuation of their foreignness and "exoticization." I do not examine the substantial portion of the novel that deals with other stereotypes, such as American images of a communist state, for example.

7. This understanding of animals as a kind of "kin" is also the subject of hapa writer Ruth L. Ozeki's novel, *My Year of Meats*.

8. Like the American Lesbian "Jack" and the racial purist "Hannah," this

blonde female character points to a problematic tendency on the part of Vizenor to locate American imperialism in the bodies of blonde women.

9. Angel Island, like Alcatraz, lies in the San Francisco Bay. Angel Island was the western equivalent of Ellis Island; the difference is that a significant number of the primarily Chinese immigrants who had to stop at the immigration station on Angel Island stayed for lengthy incarcerations—sometimes for up to two years.

10. Audre Lorde, in *Zami: A New Spelling of My Name*, describes a similar sentiment in the young Audre: "I always hated the Fourth of July, even before I came to realize the travesty such a celebration was for Black people in this country" (69).

11. In this text, Lee uses the lowercase for proper nouns of national or ethnic identification.

12. Incest is a critical issue for isolated groups like the Chinese North American communities of this time. Restricted by antimiscegenation laws from participating in exogamy, and by immigration laws from endogamy, these communities were faced with extinction. In this case incest, and the obsession with secrecy it engenders, becomes a metaphor for the process of re-membering history, which the community must undergo to avoid dissolution.

13. The recent scientific confirmation of Thomas Jefferson's having sired mixed heritage children with his slave, Sally Hemmings, is merely another example of the inextricability of America's racial dialogue from our history of interethnic mixing.

Works Cited

Angelou, Maya. *I Know Why the Caged Bird Sings*. New York: Bantam, 1971.

Bambara, Toni Cade. *The Salt Eaters*. New York: Vintage, [1980] 1992.

Bergner, Gwen. "Who Is That Masked Woman? or, The Role of Gender in Fanon's *Black Skins, White Masks*." PMLA 110, no. 1 (Jan. 1995).

Bhabha, Homi K. *The Location of Culture*. Routledge: New York, 1994.

Evans, Mei Mei. "Gussuk," in Shirley Lim and Mayumi Tsutakawa, eds., *The Forbidden Stitch: An Asian American Women's Anthology*. Corvallis, Ore.: Calyx Books, 1989.

Fanon, Frantz. *Black Skins, White Masks*. New York: Grove Weidenfeld, 1991.

Kim, Elaine, Christine Choy, and Dai-silkim Gibson, directors. "Sa-i-Gu." Video recording broadcast on PBS (1994).

Lee, Sky. *Disappearing Moon Cafe*. Seattle: Seal Press, 1990.

Lorde, Audre. *Zami: A New Spelling of My Name*. Trumansburg, N.Y.: Crossing Press, 1982.

Morales, Alejandro. *The Brick People*. Houston: Arte Publico Press, 1992.

Sollors, Werner. *Beyond Ethnicity: Consent and Descent in American Culture*. New York: Oxford University Press, 1986.

Tate, Claudia, ed. *Black Women Writers at Work*. New York: Continuum, 1983.

Trinh, Minh-ha. *When the Moon Waxes Red*. New York: Routledge, 1991.

Vizenor, Gerald. *Earthdiver: Tribal Narratives of Mixed Descent*. Minneapolis: University of Minnesota Press, 1981.

———. *Griever: An American Monkey King in China*. Minneapolis: University of Minnesota Press, 1987.

———. "Socioacupuncture: Mythic Reversal and the Striptease in Four Scenes." In *Out There: Marginalization and Contemporary Cultures*, ed. Russell Ferguson et al. Cambridge, Mass: MIT Press, 1990.

Wong, Shawn. *Homebase*. New York: Plume, [1979] 1991.

Waharoa

Māori-Pākehā Writing in Aotearoa/New Zealand

> Two rivers within me flow
> They have one source
> and that is my heart
> —Apirana Taylor, "Mixed Blood"

> If the existence of certain human beings causes problems for
> certain concepts or systems of categorization, then it is the
> concepts or systems of categorization and not the human
> existants which need to be criticized and changed.
> —Naomi Zack, *Race and Mixed Race*

> It all depends
> on what story
> you hear
> —Keri Hulme, "Headnote to a Maui Tale"

There is a body of interesting and rich literature in Aotearoa/New Zealand[1] by people of mixed race,[2] particularly Māori/Pākehā writers.[3] The size and extent of this body of texts is not yet fully realized because criticism has not consistently acknowledged the multiracial dimension of this literature; however, it is observed that many of the earliest published Māori writers were of dual descent. This discussion argues that considering this dimension of the literature reveals much about the texts themselves, the writers, and the wider social situation. It will attempt to identify issues of multiraciality that are present in the literature by describing their sociopolitical and literary environment, and will then suggest a literary framework through which they may be considered. My motivation for exploring this intersection between multiraciality and literature is rooted in my own identity as Māori *and* Pākehā, and my dissatisfaction with the lack of acknowledgment that current discussion gives my experience. The method by which I approach these texts therefore assumes that multi-raciality is a legitimate ethnic identity. In effect, this means that I write with a bias against the critics who question—or indeed ignore—its exis-tence.

This discussion is situated on the notion of a metaphorical marae on which mixed race writers perform, and attempts to construct a waharoa/ gateway to that place.[4] While it is true that a marae is a "Māori" concept, and that a Pākehā frame of reference might be as applicable as a Māori one, it is arguably the case that in the history of Pākehā/Māori relations, Pākehā constructs have been much less subject to Māori cultural influ-ences—particularly because of the Pākehā position as the "dominant" cul-tural group in Aotearoa/New Zealand—than Māori constructs have been to Pākehā understandings. The marae embraced here contains elements of both, and yet it is a new marae, with its own complex and diverse history and community: writers of mixed race.

The waharoa/gateway is composed of a number of elements. Mixed race writing will be approached first by looking at the construction and maintenance of the taiapa/fence that presently surrounds the marae, and the supporting poupou/posts of the waharoa/gateway. The discussion then moves on to a description of the history and contexts of local mixed race literature, as laid out on the carved kōrupe/lintel at the top of the gateway.

Te Taiapa/The Fence

The first visible feature when approaching our metaphorical marae is the taiapa/fence around its perimeter. This structure performs a double function: it obscures the area from the view of those outside the space of mixed race writing, making serious engagement with the topic difficult; and it can also seek to prevent writers from moving freely between all of the spaces—which would include "Māori" and "Pākehā" as well as "mixed race"—from which they are entitled to speak. The nature of encounters between ethnic groups in Aotearoa/New Zealand—and the different evaluations of these encounters—erected this taiapa/fence. Today it is maintained by the binarism that has developed during that process[5]

Examination of the historical relationship between Māori and Pākehā, and related power differentials, is basic to any discussion about the offspring that result from that relationship. The Māori arrived in Aotearoa at the end of long voyages around Te Moana-nui-ā-Kiwa, the Pacific Ocean. The actual arrival times of the waka (vessels), and the possible number of these arrivals, is a contested issue. The "orthodox" view touts 950 A.D. as a probable time, although different histories, accounts, and traditions offer theories of arrivals up to 1,000 years either side of this date. They are tangata whenua[6] to the group of islands, and were socially organized according to a system of autonomous tribal groups, with related mythologies, dialects, histories, and elements of identity. The European (mostly English, Scottish, and Irish) populations settled in New Zealand following a colonial recipe, beginning in the late eighteenth century but not arriving en masse until at least half a century later. They began to call the place home after a few generations, and the term "Pākehā" was applied to them by the tangata whenua. Orsman defines "Pakeha" in his *Oxford Dictionary of New Zealand English* as "a non-Polynesian New Zealand–born New Zealander esp. if pale-skinned," and it has come to be a term that many New Zealanders of European descent now use for themselves.

Contact between the Māori and Pākehā groups was mediated haphazardly at first, but in 1840 the British government formally annexed the islands when members of both groups signed the Treaty of Waitangi (English version) and Te Tiriti o Waitangi (Māori text), mistakenly believing that the documents conveyed the same meaning. Resulting differences in expectations have been a major source of tension between the groups since then. Te Wai Pounamu/the South Island was officially colonized on different grounds, that of *terra nullius*.[7]

It may be helpful to note at this stage of the discussion that there has never been a defined "mixed race" community in Aotearoa/New Zealand. "That there is no definite set of symbolic artefacts or experiences of people with acknowledged joint Māori and Pākehā ethnicities is undisputed."[8] In some overseas situations, communities of mixed race people have been constructed and maintained, with a shared language, social space, and sense of history. However, while some evaluation of mixed race experiences in the South Island has been attempted, such as Atholl Anderson's *Race Against Time*, there is not a mixed race community as such, and multiraciality does not seem to have been a prominent factor in Aotearoa/New Zealand to the extent of being the basis for the creation of a separate group identity. In nineteenth-century national censuses, for example, "half-caste" individuals were divided into "half-castes living as Māori" and "half-castes living as Europeans," which in turn attempted to subsume them into the two "major" groups. Of course, the absence of a political mixed race community would have been a precursor for the present inability of many critical writers to conceptualize a mixed race identity.

Several "official" theories and policies dealing with te iwi Māori have been implemented by governments and their agencies over the last two centuries.[9] Assimilation replaced theories of extinction when the Māori population began to recover from its all-time low in the 1890s, and prominent "half caste" politicians such as James Carroll (native minister in 1899) and members of the Young Māori Party supposedly demonstrated its potential success. In 1960 the Hunn report, a governmental review of the Department of Māori Affairs since 1861, concluded that assimilation had not been as successful as hoped, and that Māori culture remained "an ongoing part of New Zealand life."[10] The report retained assimilation as a far-off goal, but stated an intermediate objective of integration: "to combine (not fuse) the Maori and Pakeha elements to form one nation in which Maori culture remains distinct."[11] Finally, in the 1980s, the government adopted another framework, that of biculturalism. Although attacked for not acknowledging the presence of other groups (as embodied in the concept of multiculturalism), it reflects an attempt to recognize the dual nature of the basis of Aotearoa/New Zealand's community, as determined by the signatories to the Treaty/Te Tiriti. As Danielle Brown notes, however, this focus on two essential groups was understood to be conceptually incompatible with the existence of members who belong to both. She suggests that "the official government policy of biculturalism seems to be based upon the either/or proposition, disallowing the possibilities of both/and."[12] As any indigenous group is aware, the process of decolonization starts the very moment that colonization does. Leaders and movements appeared in Aotearoa/New Zealand throughout the nineteenth and twentieth centuries with a shared commitment to mana motuhake.[13] The processes of colonization had "legally" usurped land, authority, and natural resources, and had slain a great deal of the population. A national infrastructure that derived from—and depended on—an imbalance of power between the two groups was created, the results of which are reflected in the overrepresentation of Māori in prison occupancy, smoking, mental health problems, single parent families, teenage pregnancy, welfare dependency, educational underachievement, infant mortality (especially cot death), shorter life expectancy, and so on.

A number of movements in the 1970s catalyzed the growing sense of discontent, taking action to facilitate change in the situation and public profile of Māori people. The movements of the last three decades have had a profound effect on Māori and non-Māori identity, both internally and in terms of the wider community. The "rest" of New Zealand was offered the challenge that the famous phrase "he iwi kotahi tātou"[14] was a farce because it failed to recognize the diversity that exists within Aotea-roa/New Zealand society. Further, some were forced to take notice that their claim of harmonious race relations was mythical. In 1981 Keri Hulme described a Pākehā reaction as follows: "They are hurt and bewil-dered and resentful of Māori land protests, Māori rights marches, radical and very vocal Māori militants. ... 'But we've always got on together so well', they say in hurt and bewildered tones. 'Why, some of my best friends are Maoris'."[15]

In 1966 John Harre conducted a study of Māori/Pākehā intermarriage in which he observed that half of the marriages involving at least one Māori partner in Auckland in 1960 were to a Pākehā. However, the high inci-dence of intermarriage revealed in these statistics did not alter the binary way in which ethnicity was viewed, as a number of Harre's interviews re-vealed: "Our children will have a Maori surname and will more than likely be Maori in appearance, so everyone will think of them as Maoris. What would be the use of us telling them that they were Pakehas? That would be a sure way of getting them all mixed up." Harre concluded, "most parents were of the view that their children would be identified ei-ther as Maoris [sic] or as Pakehas [sic] by the community and that it would be unrealistic not to follow this procedure themselves."[16]

In order to pursue the advancement (indeed, the "catching up") of the Māori people, loyalties were galvanized within the two camps. Apirana Taylor, a mixed race writer, recalls "Now the voices divide. The brown to the brown, the white to the white."[17] Individuals were either Māori or Pā-kehā. They could actively support either side, but their personal identity needed to reflect one or the other. Those who were able to claim both heritages as their own would need to make a choice. At present, the writing of Māori/Pākehā mixed race writers is discussed and interpreted by most discourse in a way that continues to suggest a specific singular allegiance to one group or the other. While the literature may indeed be rightly considered as "Māori" or "Pākehā" writing, this binary separation has led to a situation in which those who are currently writing are auto-matically contained within these parameters, and their potential explora-tion from a mixed race model has rarely been considered.

Ethnic relations in Aotearoa/New Zealand have been permeated and shaped by discourses of binarism for two hundred years, and this taiapa/fence has kept the arena of multiraciality securely enclosed. The binary system relies on shared understandings of (mutually exclusive) difference, and so does not easily comprehend—let alone embrace—individuals who claim to be of mixed race.[18] Self-identified "mongrel" writer Keri Hulme explains in her 1981 article, "When the frightened seek to erect a fence between two peoples, we are on both sides of it."[19]

Poupou/Posts

The "Māori" and "Pākehā" literary traditions make up the tall supporting poupou/posts of the waharoa/gateway. Without the strength of either of these, the kōrupe/lintel upon which the story of mixed race literature is outlined would not be securely held. A brief examination of both traditions will assist the visitor when viewing the kōrupe/lintel itself.

THE MĀORI ORAL/WRITING TRADITION

> Before there was a literature of New Zealand, there was a Maori oral tradition of Aotearoa with an ancient history which began in the Polynesian homeland of Hawaiki.[20]

As is typical of nonliterate cultures, the Māori community stores and maintains stories through a symbolic and complex oral tradition. All members of society had methods of receiving and passing on certain knowledges, from ornate and deeply leveled metaphorical whaikorero (formal speeches), to songs and poems taught to children to aid their memory and development and instill a sense of belonging. While this tradition is still practiced throughout Aotearoa/New Zealand to this day, the flexible nature of such orality has enabled many Māori to embrace new methods of storytelling, such as those transported to Aotearoa/New Zealand with print literacy. As argued by McRae, "the oral tradition ... is not simply a precursor to the literature but exists in and alongside it."[21]

Māori adapted and manipulated the new media of discourse, and the technologies of print that support them, for their own communal purposes. Religious, political, and historical material has been printed by Māori since the printing press first arrived in Aotearoa. More recently there has been a proliferation of Māori filmmakers and actors. This indigeniza-

tion of new tools and technologies does not mean that the products are
no longer Māori, and this point forms a central thesis of Witi Ihimaera's
six-volume collection of Māori writing, *Te Ao Marama*:[22]

> Although we may appropriate non-Maori genres and the marvellous bag of
> post-modern tricks, we go back to our own. As often as we go forward or
> outward, increasingly we do so by looking backwards at where we've come
> from, taking our bearings from the past.[23]

The processes of colonization, urbanization, and attempted assimilation
have combined to hasten and entrench this process, and for many Māori
now, written and electronic language is the predominant form of cultural
communication.

Te Ao Marama contains a wide and creative range of writing in English and Māori since 1980, and its editor Witi Ihimaera, along with his
editorial team, claims that "nobody again may have such an opportunity
to say to the present, 'This is how we are,'—to say to the future, 'This is
how we were'."[24] The editors also profess "we maintain our view that
anyone with Maori ancestry is a Maori writer whether they choose to
claim Maori identity or not."[25] There are obvious political implications in
imposing ethnic identities on writers who resist them, even if the fact of
their conscious objection speaks as much about the processes and experiences of the Māori people in general as self-proclaimed "Māori literature"
does. These matters aside, the editors' bold and inclusive embrace of all
writers with Māori ancestry is significant to a discussion of mixed race literature because it is an ostensible claim to embrace those writers as Māori.

THE PĀKEHĀ WRITING TRADITION

> Pakeha you
> Milton directing your head
> Donne pumping your heart
> You singing
> Some old English folk song[26]

The Pākehā literary tradition is more difficult to delineate, based on written sources, than the Māori one. This is not necessarily an indication that
it is richer or more complex, but because of the nature of minority/major-
ity community relations it has received more publishing encouragement
and opportunities, and more academic "air time." Additionally, of course,
the traditions are sourced from a set of dominant histories and cultures
that have been recording and analyzing their literatures in writing for

hundreds of years. Two points about the Pākehā writing tradition are pertinent to this discussion: its historical nature as a cultural import; and its present attempts to address issues of Pākehā, New Zealand, and Aotearoa/New Zealand identity.

Europeans began writing what is currently identified as "New Zealand literature" the moment they burst in upon Aotearoa/New Zealand, and they have been putting pen to paper ever since. The *Oxford History of New Zealand Literature in English* peels the body of works to trace its history through a set of genres: nonfiction, the novel, the short story, drama, poetry, children's literature, and popular fiction.[27] The wide range of writing types and styles makes it difficult to generalize about the character of the writing, but Lawrence Jones remarks on an important aspect of its nature in his chapter about the novel: "As with the history of many New Zealand institutions, this is a history which includes importation and adaptation."[28]

More recent Pākehā literature has continued to grapple with the social and identity issues facing Pākehā culture in general. New modes of conceptualizing Pākehā culture, as well as awareness that such a culture exists, have contested received ways of writing and representation. There have been challenges to practices such as the misappropriation and omission of Māori, gay, women's, and other nondominant groups' stories. In his introduction to the second edition of the *Oxford History*, Sturm considers the thematic and contextual features of contemporary New Zealand literature, and these provide a helpful underpinning of the multiple faces of the body of texts:

> The best of our recent literature is actively engaged in negotiating the multiple, uncertain, contested sites of identity, location, history, both within the geographical entity called 'New Zealand' (or 'Aotearoa') and in its larger, constantly shifting, global relations. Such negotiations are far from context-less, but the contexts which sustained literature in the past—colony, Dominion, Empire, nation—are no longer 'given'. New contexts are having to be invented, in a condition of radical uncertainty.[29]

Kōrupe/Lintel

Finally we arrive at the kōrupe/lintel of the waharoa/gateway, adorned by the stories of mixed race writers because this is their marae. The carved horizontal beam of the waharoa/gateway sits on top of the poupou/posts, and relates a facet of the identity of the tangata whenua group. Two strands are evident on this particular kōrupe/lintel: the mixed-race literature itself, and the criticism that focuses on that literature. This kōrupe/lintel does not attempt to create a sharp distinction between these two, but instead plaits them together, recognizing that the dialogue between the two renders them inextricable from each other.

MIXED RACE LITERATURE

> Two rivers within me flow
> They have one source
> and that is my heart[30]

Some writers draw on both the Māori and Pākehā traditions, not only in terms of language, content, format, and style, but in ancestry, culture, and lived experience. These mixed race writers have stories to tell that are at home within the Māori and Pākehā contexts, but are also influenced by issues of multiraciality. In her article "Mauri: An Introduction to Bicultural Poetry in New Zealand,"[31] Hulme calls them "writers of a double beginning, inhabiting both Te Ao Maori and Te Ao Pakeha, but writing for Te Ao Hou."[32]

It is appropriate that the basis of "classifying" the writers discussed here as "mixed race" be outlined at this point. All of the writers have claimed to be members of both the Māori and Pākehā "communities." I assume no right to project an ethnic label upon any writer, either by ancestry, style, language, culture, or community involvement. This would be wrong for two reasons. Firstly, identity is a personal issue that individuals determine for themselves, with their own whānau/communities. Secondly, the inclusion of texts written by Māori authors who do not explicitly claim to be writing from a mixed perspective would be fascinating, and highlight many issues salient to the mixed race experience and its literature, but it would also raise issues and open doors that cannot be adequately dealt with in an article of this length, and so is outside the scope of this discussion.

Inclusion in Hulme's article identified for the first time the perception that many writers had of themselves as mixed. Many active writers are included in Hulme's discussion: Rowley Habib (Hapipi) has "Ngati Pitiroirangi and Lebanese ancestry"; Apirana Taylor is of "Ngati Porou and English descent"; Brian Potiki is from a "Ngai Tahu and English background"; Henare Dewes is "Ngati Porou and Pakeha"; Harry Dansey is "Te Arawa and Tuwharetoa, and European"; Rangi Faith is "Ngati Tahu and Scots"; Haare Williams is "Te Aitanga-a-Mahaki and Pakeha"; TK Tainui is "Poutini-Kai Tahu and Irish"; and Michael Stevens is "Ngati Tahu and Pakeha."

The language used to describe the writers above is presumably the language they have used to identify themselves and suggests some interesting thoughts about how each writer resolves the dynamic of identity. While the terms "Māori" and "Pākehā" were conceived in the presence of each other, and so reflect the relationship between the two as much as it does the "group-ness" of either one, neither takes into account the complexities of identity *within* each group.

The writers have chosen either iwi (such as "Ngati Porou") or hapū ("Ngati Tahu") to name their "Māori" dimension, rather than the general designation "Māori." This is possible in this context because the discussion is not politicized along the lines of Māori/non-Māori. It also highlights the multileveled nature of ethnic identity, which may result in a change of emphasis within different paradigms of identity according to situation. An individual may be observed—and represent themselves—as non-white to some observers, Polynesian to others, Māori to others, and Te Atiawa (iwi/tribe) to others. Māori identificational protocols offer the individual further "identities" such as "Te Whanganui-ā-tara," tūrangawae-wae/homeplace; "Te Matehou," hapū/subtribe; and "Te Punga," whānau/family. Of course, this specificity of naming is available only to those whose interaction with te Ao Māori has allowed them access to such information, which is becoming more of a luxury as urbanization takes its toll.[33]

Likewise, the manner of denoting the writers' non-Māori heritage varies. Some are quite specific, naming the geographical and cultural home of their forebears: "English," "Scots," "Irish." Others identify with their European-derived ancestry specifically in terms of its Aotearoa/New Zealand context by claiming to be "Pākehā." Apirana Taylor further indigenizes his European whakapapa (genealogical inheritance) by identifying as of "Ngati Pakeha descent" in the biographical details he provides in *100 New Zealand Poems*.[34] The cover of Hilary Baxter's collection of poetry offers details about both of her heritages, avoiding the political resonances of the broader terms "Māori" and "Pākehā": "Hilary is descended, through her mother, from the Taranaki and Whakatohea tribes and, through her father, from the MacMillans of the Western Highlands; she has a strong affinity with these ancestral ties."[35]

In his poem entitled "Mixed Blood" Apirana Taylor explains that

"Two rivers within me flow," but concludes:

> though I am of mixed blood
> it is the darkest
> that runs deepest in me[36]

Taylor explores why many writers identify more strongly with their taha Māori (Māori side/dimension), and although for some it is a result of personal history that denies them familiarity with Pākehā culture, the political implications of belonging to a minority group are frequently a priority. Two commentators from overseas support the role of politics in the writing process:

> [A writer's] works reflect one or more cultural aspects of the intense economic, political, cultural and ideological struggles in a society. ... every writer is a writer in politics.[37]

> All of culture and literature get caught up in movements for political change. Writers tend to be social theorists and activists, as well as writers.[38]

This political role means that writers are often compelled (by themselves and/or their wider communities) to speak on behalf of the minority voice that they represent. Whereas the dominant (Pākehā) discourse in New Zealand has numerous contributors, writers who are members of the Māori community—even if members of the Pākehā community as well—often consider that because the published Māori voice is so weak it needs special emphasis and commitment. These factors do not drain them of a Pākehā voice, but direct their writing toward a Māori focus. Kathie Irwin, an educator and academic, explains why this is so for her:

> My work ... has not been anti-Pakeha or anti three sources of my whakapapa. Rather, it has sought to reaffirm the Maori world so that the gifts could be equally valued by me and the wider community. ... There are very good historical, cultural and social reasons why my Maori tipuna need my professional and personal energy more than my Pakeha tipuna. My tipuna know and understand this. Society is slowly coming to realise it.[39]

Many writers who have been "cast" as Māori writers have asserted their Pākehā heritage as well. Mihi Edwards's two autobiographical works, *Mihipeka: The Early Years* and *Mihipeka: Time of Turmoil/Nga Wa Raruraru*, have been promoted as "Māori" texts—which, of course, they are—and focus on her experience of "passing" for white/Pākehā, a choice made possible because a paternal grandparent was Pākehā. The fiction and nonfiction works by Ngahuia Te Awekotuku, at present professor of Māori studies at Victoria University of Wellington, have been widely used as prominent examples of "Māori" (and, where appropriate, "gay") texts. However, her short story, "Painfully Pink," appears in the Canadian collection *Miscegenation Blues: Voices of Mixed-Race Women*, in which her bibliographic details declare "her tribes include the Te Arawa, Waikato and the Tuhoe peoples. Her maternal grandfather was of French background."[40]

Likewise, the inclusion of some mixed race writers in the *Te Ao Marama* anthology does not implicitly deny their Pākehā side. Cathie Dunsford falls into this category. The editor notes "Cathie Dunsford ... is of Nga Puhi, Hawaiian, Yugoslav and British descent."[41] The relative shortness of time that Europeans have been in Aotearoa/New Zealand means that most Pākehā are still aware of their European roots. For example, Hilary Baxter claims to be from "the MacMillans of the Western Highlands,"[42] and Renee is specifically identified, in the published text of her play *Jeannie Once,* as "born in 1929 of Ngati Kahungunu and Irish/English ancestry."[43]

DISCOURSE ON MĀORI/PĀKEHĀ MIXED RACE WRITING

Very little serious discourse about multiraciality has emerged in Aotearoa/New Zealand, and writing that relates the mixed race experience specifically to literature has been even sparser. Although discourse about identity has become academically highly fashionable, the exploration of mixed identity within this is largely ignored or marginalized. However, an analysis of Māori/Pākehā writing, and of the mixed race experience in Aotearoa/New Zealand, might be usefully informed by the small amount of recent overseas scholarship. Specific issues raised in Australia about Sally Morgan,[44] and in the United States about Louise Erdrich,[45] have been central to the development of arguments articulated in this discussion.

Current debates in Aotearoa/New Zealand, such as they are, have focused on the challenge that multiraciality presents to the prevailing construction of a binary (or, in the minds of some, monocultural) New Zealand literary scene. Much of this critical writing is preoccupied with simply determining the "race" (mixed or otherwise) of the writers, rather than accepting the multiraciality of the texts and approaching the literature itself in those terms. Such contributions are often more fascinating as signifiers of context, in their demonstration of the critics' attitudes toward multiraciality, than in their roles as critical texts.

Many of the mixed race texts have been examined through frameworks of criticism within the academic literary tradition of analysis that draw almost exclusively on Western-derived critical and theoretical discourses, and may be rightfully described as "European" in nature.[46] The methodologies by which Hughes, During, Stead, Ash, and Fee examine Hulme's *the bone people* are key examples of this.[47] An obvious illustration is During's article that he entitled "Postmodernism or Postcolonialism?" His method of approaching the Aotearoa/New Zealand text is inseparable from wider discourses of literary theory. Harding and Brown offer discussions of Alan Duff's writing from similar critical perspectives.

More recently, Māori scholars and individuals have begun to develop ways of "looking" at the texts that are rooted within a Māori paradigm and draw on Māori frames of reference. For example, in her 1985 article "The Politics of Maori Literature," Miriama Evans does not recognize a distinction between internal textual elements and the experience of the communities from which the writers come. Her contribution centers on the difficulties that Māori writers, particularly those who retain a sharp Māori focus, face in publishing: "The criteria for acceptance has worked against Maori writers who have sought to incorporate bilingualism and to integrate Maori and European literary traditions."[48] Evans writes about the publication issues surrounding Hulme's *the bone people*, and offers a comparison of two responses to the book as an illustration of the unique perspective of "Māori literary criticism":

> Maori reviewers alert us to the mauri of a book and the mana of its author. For example, reviews in the *Listener* (12 May 1984) by Joy Cowley and Arapera Blank both extolled *the bone people*, but Arapera keyed in Maori readers: 'Keri's novel has the preciousness of a piece of kuru pounamu.'[49]

Such mixed race texts have been skillfully and honestly treated by both the Māori and Pākehā approaches, and much of what has been discussed by them has been helpful, illuminating, and insightful. This is unsurprising, because the dual Māori and Pākehā identities of the authors potentially place the texts comfortably in either arena. Although both of these frames of analysis are entirely appropriate, they are rooted in the two "sides" of the bicultural divide, and there is a further way in which the texts may (I would argue *must*) be read: a way that embraces their distinctiveness as mixed race literature.

Keri Hulme's "Mauri: An Introduction to Bicultural Poetry in New Zealand" is significant because it is the only article on the topic to date written by someone who actively claims to be of mixed race. Hulme describes samples of contemporary poetry in terms of its biculturality. She explores some topical issues related to poetry by Māori/Pākehā writers, relating the writing to matters of wider social concern, writing "A sizable number of New Zealanders have both Maori and European ancestry, and a large proportion of these 'mongrels' are familiar with both cultures. I am a mongrel myself" (p. 294). Also, "This poetry is literature of contact, of cross cultural contact" (p. 295). The article contains some compelling and instructive comments, particularly in a section where she discusses the predicament in which mixed race writers find themselves: "A dual heritage is both a pain and an advantage" (p. 294). Hulme's methodology presents a picture that suggests that mixed race writing is rooted "essentially" in the Māori tradition. It is true the Pākehā tradition is significantly referenced as a provider of language: "They owe much to Maori thought and mythology and ways of expression; and *because they are written in English* an equally incalculable debt is owed to taha Pakeha, the side that is European" (p. 307). Nevertheless, Hulme's emphasis is on their Māori derivations. After all, her initial subheadings are "The Māori Past," which briefly describes the social history and oral tradition of the tangata whenua; "The Māori Present," which covers urbanization and associated cultural changes that occurred over the last decades; and "Māori Reality, Pakeha Myth," which discusses the myth of harmonious race relations in Aotearoa/New Zealand.

Hulme then proceeds to the heading "Being on Both Sides of the Fence," a surprising move because only one "side" has been allowed a history in her article. Hulme speaks of Māori language loss and recovery before moving to observations of the poetry itself. The sections that follow focus on the Māori dimensions of the poetry. She does not engage the work specifically in terms of its special mixed race character. Her concluding section, "Writing for a Future People, Drawing on the Past," presents a hopeful and considered account of the future and place of this particular group of texts.

Hulme's article presents a strong case for the "biculturality" of these texts, despite her focus on only one of those cultures. While she refrains from creating a way of reading them that incorporates both "sides," her introductory and concluding remarks suggest a new context from which they can be read. The article contains some salient (if underexplored) statements about bicultural writing in Aotearoa/New Zealand.

A number of other critics have attempted to tackle issues of multiraciality in some Aotearoa/New Zealand writing, focusing on individual writers. For example, Danielle Brown ("Pakeha, Maori and Alan")[50] and Bruce Harding ("'Wrestling with Caliban': Patterns of Bi-racial Encounter in *Colour Scheme* and *Once Were Warriors*")[51] consider the issues surrounding Alan Duff's position:

> Duff ... seems to be a "collaborator" with the dominant white regime. His maternal bloodline links him to the Te Arawa tribe (Ngati Rangitihi and Tuwharetoa), but Duff also has a European bloodline and "literary genealogy" via his grandfather Oliver Duff, his father and his uncle, Dr Roger Duff. ... Duff has spoken about "the curse of being half-caste"—that "you're neither one nor the other."[52]

Other dialogues (diatribes?) about mixed race writers in Aotearoa/New Zealand were sparked by a highly controversial article by C. K. Stead, which the Canada-based magazine *Ariel* published in 1985, in which he reacted strongly against the award of the Pegasus Prize for Māori literature to Keri Hulme for *the bone people*. His pronouncements and analyses elicited response from interested academics globally, and a sudden gush of discourse was born in Aotearoa/New Zealand about authenticity, blood, and ethnicity. The local academic community was given a crash course in identity politics, the traversing of which remains to be assessed. Stead's article certainly directs attention to aspects of the literature in question: both overtly, in the issues he raises, and covertly, as a stark revelation of the depth to which such writing—and its controversial "public" reception—challenges comfortable academia.

Stead (perhaps unknowingly) touches on a crucial problematic when he asks of *the bone people* "in what sense is it a Maori novel?"[53] His objection to Hulme's receipt of an award targeted at recent writing "by a Maori" is compelling in its portrayal of group allegiance and inclusion/exclusion. It asks whether writers may benefit from being members of one group if they simultaneously claim membership of another. Much writing has been churned out since addressing Stead's interrogatory "what is a Maori writer?"

Perhaps it *is* significant that Hulme is concerned less with defining group boundaries than with the historical, contextual, stylistic, and linguistic features of the writing itself, and that Stead and his consorts busy themselves conducting border inspections and squabbling over where each writer "belongs." As a mixed race individual herself, Hulme is presumably sensitive to exclusion from certain ethnic communities on the grounds of someone else's definitions.

Looking Inside

Once the waharoa/gateway has been examined, and a sense of history and context has been developed, it is time to venture inside. In-depth discussion and analysis of the activity—both of the writers and their words—that takes place on this mixed race marae is outside the scope of this essay. However, the appreciation for Māori/Pākehā mixed race literature that has been gained while pondering the entranceway surely challenges the reader to carefully consider the way in which the activity inside will now be interpreted. In view of such a realization, a new framework for doing precisely this is suggested below.

Because the methods of examining multiraciality have been rooted in one or the other of the contributing traditions, they still enforce an overriding binarism. It is exactly this preferencing and marginalizing of groups that has restricted literary analysis from adequately conceptualizing multiraciality in literature. A way of reading the texts that is distinctly "mixed race" has not yet been developed. Because a literary construct/theoretical base is essentially founded on the culture of a community, and multiraciality does not (at least in Aotearoa/New Zealand) denote membership in a separate "mixed" community, there is no single theoretical foundation upon which a framework may be based.

Any exploration of mixed race literature must incorporate the values and methods of reading texts/the world from all of the groups represented in those texts. Dual centrality of the Māori and Pākehā worlds is difficult to conceptualize, particularly when most theoretical debate comes from a Western academic framework that has often applauded the conceptualization of social and other realities in terms of binaries and polemics. Despite—perhaps, indeed, *because of*—these inevitable tensions, specific modes of Western academic thinking and of Māori thinking *both* need to be present in a central way to any new method of analysis.

A paradigm for Māori well-being was developed in the 1980s and articulated by Mason Durie in several publications, including a major book on Māori health, *Whaiora*. The conceptual metaphor is composed of four "walls"[54] or "cornerstones,"[55] without the balanced strength of which a house will not stand. These are tinana, hinengaro, whanau, and wairua. These four "walls" also encapsulate major concepts highlighted in Western discourse: the body, self-identity, community, and spirituality, respectively. An advantage of this particular paradigm is that it draws out a more rounded discussion of the writers by including their community and spiritual dimensions: "Tinana is the physical element of the individual and hinengaro the mental state, but these do not make up the whole. Wairua, the spirit, and whanau, the wider family, complete the shimmering depths of the health pounamu, the precious touchstone of Maoridom."[56]

There is a danger in presenting a "model" in which the central emphases of two cultures fall into similar concepts when overlaid. It implies that the two cultures approximate each other sufficiently to suggest assimilation, in which case the mixing of the two would be interesting but not particularly problematic or challenging. Contrary to this, mixed race writing testifies that the experience is far from free of tension, and so supports the hypothesis that there *is* real difference between and within these core emphases after all. Annamarie Jagose writes, "The *mestiza* [mixed race individual] ... demonstrate[s] that the continual transitions of the border which they effect not only obscure the border's demarcation of oppositions but also and equally reinscribe that very demarcation."[57] Rawinia White internalizes the predicament, writing "But your mother is not Maori, she has no language, she has no whanaunga Maori, and many, many New Zealanders have a little Maori blood. You're no different. Just get on with it, forget! I have walked this tightrope all my life."[58] Clearly, the relationship *between* the cultures needs to be incorporated in a dynamic way within the "model."

In her 1986 collection of short fiction, Keri Hulme uses the gaps in language as much as she does the substance of it. According to Heim and Zimmerman:

> Splitting into, or joining together, unmatched parts is only one aspect of the binary principle that pervades the book: what animates the texts is what happens between the two parts or poles. The interaction between the parts tends to gain so much momentum in the course of reading that the oscillatory movement takes precedence over the existence of the poles—which then appear as necessary but provisional abstractions.[59]

The pivotal point in the case of the title *Te Kaihau/The Windeater* is not either of its phrases (which are both rooted securely in the language of either "side"), but the slash in between them. This is the point of negotiation, of contact, of tension, of boundary, and of connection. It represents and epitomizes the mixed race experience: it focuses not on the poles but on the relationship between the two.

> The *function* of the border is better represented not as the single stroke of the dividing line, nor even as the twin categories it bisects, but as a tripartite structure constituted by the line of the border and its flanking binarisms. ... its interposition between categories enables the at times simultaneous opposition, and even coincidence of those categories.[60]

To carry this method of reading into the mixed race texts, a four-part scheme may be envisaged.[61] Pertinent to both the Māori and Pākehā perspectives, its component parts are capable of raising a number of key issues regarding the topic, and also of revealing the tensions with which multiraciality imbues the texts. It is through these four concepts, therefore, that mixed race Māori/Pākehā texts may be explored: tinana/the body; hinengaro/self-identity; whānau/community; and wairua/spirituality. The quadripartite framework allows issues of physicality, personal identity, community, and spirituality that are specific to the authors' multiraciality to be highlighted and discussed.

For example, an investigation in terms of tinana/the body pulls into focus the implications of passing for white in Mihi Edwards's autobiographies: "Maori do not have the same privileges as Pakeha. I have to hide my identity—to better myself."[62] Conversely, Keri Hulme's *the bone people* and a later short story, "He Tauware Kawa, He Kawa Tauware," both examine the complexities of physical appearance when a mixed race individual looks Pākehā and wishes to fit into a Māori group. She writes, "As always, she wants to whip out a certified copy of her whakapapa, preferably with illustrative photographs."[63] And also, "She's proud of that whakapapa. As she's one of the blue-eyed white-blond kind of Maori, she probably feels she needs it, nei?"[64] In the case of Renee's play *Jeannie Once*, the "hinengaro/self identity" aspect of the model draws attention to the importance of the mixed race servant, Martha, whose fascinating shift in identity has remained unnoticed in previous critical writing:

> It is a strange place, the one I inhabit. I am that terrible place we have run from and I am this place. I am the town and I am the Mahia. For a long time I was neither one nor the other but now I know I am both.[65]

Questions of belonging and isolation are more clearly discernable when the whānau/community lens is applied to writing such as J. C. Sturm's poetry, Rawinia White's short fiction, and Alan Duff's novels. Wairua/spirituality has the potential to raise issues about syncretism and the overlaying of spiritual systems, such as in Hulme's *the bone people*. Significantly, however, wairua/spirituality is concerned with concepts that extend beyond dogmatic, "theological" issues. Notions such as reo/language and kawa/protocols are also central to the spiritual dimensions of mixed race texts in different ways than they have been read before. Although this model does not claim to be an exhaustive method of identifying issues that are relevant to the literature of the Māori/Pākehā mixed race experience, it does provide a starting point from which new ways of looking at a group of texts may be attempted.

Conclusion

Filmmaker Merata Mita argues that "identity at any meaningful level cannot be manufactured or manipulated. ... No matter what destructive processes we have gone through and are going through, eventually the taniwha stirs in all of us and we can only be who we are."[66] As long as there are writers in Aotearoa/New Zealand who identify themselves as mixed race, there will be a body of mixed race literature. Recognizing this multiracial nature of Māori/Pākehā literature, a nature that has been downplayed or ignored by the dominant discourses, has the potential to open up new dimensions of the texts.

It is as if the mixed race texts of Aotearoa/New Zealand are rooms that have been lit by two bulbs, the Māori and Pākehā systems of analysis, exhibiting the furniture inside the room in a certain way. Rather than claiming to disclose new or different furniture in the room, the waharoa/gateway to multiracial literature provided in this discussion attempts to light another lamp, which will reveal details and aspects of that which is already present. This further angle of illumination is not in competition to the others, but allows dimensions of the texts that are currently underlit to become visible. The texts would still contain a wealth of meanings, stories, and implications if this new light were not lit, because of the lamps that are already there. The fullest enjoyment and understanding of their content, however, will be limited until this new light is allowed to glow.

Notes

1. "Aotearoa" literally translates as "the land of the long white cloud," and the country was so called by a voyager when Māori first navigated to these islands. The "official" name for the country is New Zealand, as it was called by a voyager when Europeans first came across these islands. It is appropriate, given the history of this place, to use both terms. Perhaps this layering seems cumbersome, but such is the load that a colonized place must bear in all aspects. Where either name is used in isolation in this discussion, it refers to the imagined "nation" or "nationhood" of the relevant group.

2. There are numerous terms in use that describe the groups and experiences discussed here, each of which is loaded with connotative baggage. In the interests of consistency, I have selected certain terms that will be used throughout this discussion, self-consciously mindful of their problematics. I will use "race" as the way to differentiate groups such as Māori and Pākehā, hence "mixed race," "multiracial" (that which is mixed race), and "multiraciality" (a state of being mixed race; literally mixed-race-ness).

3. "Māori" refers to the indigenous group of Aotearoa/New Zealand, and is also the name used to refer to their reo/language. Pākehā is a generic term that refers to nonindigenous white New Zealanders of white/British descent. Throughout this essay, the long vowels of the Māori language have been marked in the standard way, with a macron. In direct quotes from sources printed without this demarcation, I have left the language without macrons, as published.

4. A marae is a deeply symbolic courtyard space in front of a "wharenui," or meeting house. The marae is an appropriate metaphor here because of its centrality to Māori culture, particularly in terms of identity, wairua (spirituality), and community, as well as its functions as a mediator of meetings, a receptacle of community treasures such as whakapapa (genealogies) and stories (sometimes symbolized by carvings and painting), and a site of community expressions of hostility/welcome.

5. Binarism is used in this context to denote anything comprising two component parts, here specifically Māori and Pākehā. Since it is concerned with the distinctness of the two parts, it is unable to comprehend the complexities (or possibility) of dual heritage.

6. Tangata whenua, literally "the people of the land," is an expression of prevailing indigeneity, with an emphasis on a spiritual and communal relationship with the land. It may be used, as it is here, to denote the Māori people as a whole, or it may be used, as later in this essay, to denote the local group associated with a particular marae or a particular geographical area.

7. A dimension of international law that recognizes the "first come, first served" basis of appropriating uninhabited land. Australia was colonized on the same principle, despite being home to at least 260 separate language groups, containing 500–600 dialects, according to Eve Mungwa's unpublished "How the English Language Is Used to Put Koories Down, Deny Us Rights, or Is Employed as a Political Tool Against Us," 2. Clearly, a declaration that their land was

uninhabited would certainly have come as a surprise to the iwi who lived there, including Ngati Mamoe, Waitaha, and Ngai Tahu.

8. Megan Somerville, *Of Shades, Tints and Tones* (MCom diss., University of Auckland, 1997), 41.

9. Although Māori society has always been—and still theoretically is— organized according to the iwi/hapu/whanau stratas mentioned above, Pākehā have conceived of their belonging to one group. Colonization and urbanization have together resulted in a large number of individuals whose identity is fashioned around being "Māori" rather than more specific identifications. This discussion acknowledges the diversity within the Māori group, particularly in terms of "tribal" and regional identities, and yet chooses the term Māori as its central frame of reference. This reflects both the political way in which the identity is shaped as well as allowing the writers a common basis upon which to be considered.

10. Andrew Armitage, *Comparing the Policy of Aboriginal Assimilation: Australia, Canada and New Zealand* (Vancouver: UBC Press, 1995), 145.

11. Ibid., 145.

12. Danielle Brown, "Pakeha, Maori and Alan: The Political and Literary Exclusion of Alan Duff," *SPAN* 40 (Apr. 1995), 77–78.

13. Mana motuhake is a phrase that translates as "self-determination." It implies actively shaping one's own destiny, at "Māori," iwi, hapu, whanau, and personal levels. Most recently, political focus has also been on the words "tino rangatiratanga," in reference to the phrase of Te Tiriti/the Treaty, which guaranteed Māori signatories "absolute chieftainship," or sovereignty.

14. "We are one people," spoken by Hobson as chiefs signed the Treaty/Te Tiriti at Waitangi.

15. Keri Hulme, "Mauri: An Introduction to Bicultural Poetry in New Zealand," in *Only Connect*, ed. G. Amirthanayagam and S. C. Harrex (Honolulu: Centre for Research in the New Literatures in English, 1981), 294.

16. John Harre, *Maori and Pakeha* (Wellington: Reed, 1966), 66.

17. Apirana Taylor, "Whakarongo," in *Ki te Ao: new stories* (Auckland: Penguin, 1990), 9.

18. This discussion does not attempt to dismantle the system of ethnic groups. Instead, it actively confirms the significance of these identities by advocating the negotiation of a model that is capable of acknowledging the mixed race experience while recognizing the importance of retaining group identities, histories, language, and literatures.

19. Hulme, "Mauri," 294.

20. Jane McRae, "Maori Literature: A Survey," in *The Oxford History of New Zealand Literature in English*, ed. Terry Sturm (Auckland: Oxford University Press, 1998), 1.

21. Ibid., 3.

22. Five volumes have been released in book form since 1992. The sixth volume, unreleased as yet, will be recorded on cassette tape.

23. Witi Ihimaera, "Kaupapa," in *Te Ao Marama: Te Torino: The Spiral: volume*

5, ed. Witi Ihimaera (Auckland: Reed, 1996), 17. In the case of Alistair Campbell, this was stretched to include Cook Island Māori communities as well.

24. Witi Ihimaera, "Kaupapa," in *Te Ao Marama: Te Whakahuatanga o te ao: reflections of reality: volume 1* (Auckland: Reed, 1992), 12.

25. Ihimaera, *Te Ao Marama: Te Torino: The Spiral: volume 5*, 17.

26. J. C. Sturm, "Maori to Pakeha," in *Dedications* (Wellington: Steele Roberts, 1996), 50.

27. Terry Sturm, ed., *The Oxford History of New Zealand Literature in English* (Auckland: Oxford University Press, 1998).

28. Lawrence Jones, "The Novel," in *The Oxford History of New Zealand Literature in English*, 119.

29. Sturm, ed., *The Oxford History of New Zealand Literature*, xix.

30. Apirana Taylor, "Mixed Blood," in *3 Shades* (Wellington: Voice Press, 1981), 11.

31. Hulme, "Mauri," 296. The phrases mean "The Māori World," "The Pākehā World," and "The New World," respectively.

32. Hulme, "Mauri."

33. In the 1996 census, one-fifth of all people who identified as "NZ Māori or a descendent of a NZ Māori" did not know the name of their iwi group.

34. Bill Manhire, *100 New Zealand Poems* (Auckland: Godwit Press, 1993), n.p.

35. Hilary Baxter, *The Other Side of Dawn* (Wellington: Spiral, 1987), back cover.

36. Taylor, "Mixed Blood."

37. Ngugi wa Thiong'o, *Writers in Politics* (London: Heinemann, 1981), n.p.

38. Marc Zimmerman, *Literature and Resistance in Guatemala, vol. 1* (Athens: Ohio University Center for International Studies, 1995), 30.

39. Kathie Irwin, "Becoming an Academic: Contradictions and Dilemmas of a Maori Feminist," in *Women and Education in Aotearoa 2*, ed. Sue Middleton and Alison Jones (Wellington: Bridget Williams Books, 1992), 54.

40. Carol Camper, ed., *Miscegenation Blues: Voices of Mixed Race Women* (Toronto: Sister Vision, 1994), 388.

41. Ihimaera, ed., *Te Ao Marama: Te Torino: The Spiral: volume 5*, 149.

42. Baxter, *The Other Side of Dawn*, back cover.

43. Renee, *Jeannie Once* (Wellington: Victoria University Press, 1991), back cover.

44. See, for example, Bain Attwood, "Portrait of an Aboriginal as an Artist: Sally Morgan and the Construction of Aboriginality," *Australian Historical Studies* 99 (Oct. 1992), 302–18; Jackie Huggins, "Always Was Always Will Be," *Australian Historical Studies* 100 (Apr. 1993), 459–64; Elizabeth Reed, "Sally Morgan: A Tall Black Poppy?" *Australian Historical Studies* 101 (Oct. 1993), 637–39; Tim Rowse, "Sally Morgan's Kaftan," *Australian Historical Studies* 100 (Apr. 1993), 465–67; Isabel Tarrago, "Response to Sally Morgan and the Construction of Aboriginality," *Australian Historical Studies* 100 (Apr. 1993), 469.

45. See, for example, Daniela Daniele, "Transgressions in a Native Land:

Mixed-blood Identity and Indian Legacy in Louise Erdrich's Writing," *RSA Journal* 3 (1992), 43–58; Allan Chavkin and Nancy Feyl Chavkin, *Conversations with Louise Erdrich and Michael Dorris* (Jackson: University Press of Mississippi, 1994); Jennifer Shaddock, "Mixed Blood Women: The Dynamics of Women's Relations in the Novels of Louise Erdrich and Leslie Silko," in *Feminist Nightmares: Women at Odds: Feminism and the Problem of Sisterhood*, ed. Susan Ostrov Weisser and Jennifer Fleischner (New York: New York University Press, 1994), 106–21. Leslie Marmon Silko, "Here's an Odd Artifact for the Fairy-Tale Shelf," *Studies in American Indian Literatures* 10, no. 4 (1985), 178–84.

46. The study of New Zealand literature is a recent development in academic programs, and it still remains a relatively marginalized or at least a quiet voice within the wider English programs of Aotearoa/New Zealand's seven universities.

47. Mary Ann Hughes, "Transgressing Boundaries," *SPAN* 39 (Oct. 1994), 56–68; Simon During, "Postmodernism or Postcolonialism?" *Landfall* 155 39, no. 3 (Sept. 1985); C. K. Stead, "Keri Hulme's *The Bone People* and the Pegasus Award for Maori Literature," *Ariel* 16, no. 4 (Oct. 1985), 101–8; Susan Ash, "*The Bone People* After *Te Kaihau*," *World Literatures Written in English* 29, no. 1 (Spring 1989), 123–35. Margery Fee, "Why C K Stead Didn't Like Keri Hulme's *the bone people*: Who Can Write as Other?" *Australian and New Zealand Studies in Canada* 1 (Spring 1987), 11–31.

48. Miriama Evans, "The Politics of Maori Literature," *Meanjin* 44, no. 3 (Sept. 1985), 359.

49. Ibid., 360.

50. Brown, "Pakeha, Maori and Alan," 72–80.

51. Bruce Harding, "Wrestling With Caliban: Patterns of Bi-racial Encounter in *Colour Scheme* and *Once Were Warriors*," *Australian and New Zealand Studies in Canada* 8 (Dec. 1992), 136–55.

52. Ibid., 145. Harding explains in the article that this latter comment by Duff had first been expressed in a radio interview.

53. Stead, "Keri Hulme's *The Bone People*," 101.

54. Mason Durie, *Whaiora: Maori Health Development* (Auckland: Oxford University Press, 1994), 70.

55. Dr. P. Ngata and L. Dyall, "Resource Manual—Turangawaewae Marae 1985," in J. Kent and T. Besley, *He Whakamarama (Human Relationships): A Bicultural Resource* (Christchurch: Canterbury Education Centre, 1990), 50.

56. Durie, *Whaiora*, 71.

57. Annamarie Jagose, "Slash and suture: Post/colonialism in *Borderlands/La Frontera: The New Mestiza*," in *Feminism and the Politics of Difference*, ed. Sneja Gunew and Anna Yeatman (St Leonards, Australia: Allen & Unwin, 1993), 223.

58. Rawinia White, "The Return," in *Te Ao Marama: Te Torino: The Spiral: volume 5*, ed. Witi Ihimaera (Auckland: Reed, 1996), 217.

59. Otto Heim and Anne Zimmerman, "Hul(l)man Medi(t)ations: Inter-Cultural Explorations in Keri Hulme's *The Windeater/Te Kaihau*," *Australian and New Zealand Studies in Canada* 8 (Dec. 1992), 112.

60. Paraphrase of Gloria Anzaldúa, by Annamarie Jagose. "Slash and suture," 213.

61. Of course, the four parts are inextricably plaited together, just as they are divisible into these strands. "The divisions between temporal and spiritual, thoughts and feelings, mental and physical are not as clear-cut as they have been in Western thinking since the advent of Cartesian dualism." Durie, *Whaiora*, 74.

62. Mihi Edwards, *Mihipeka: Early Years* (Auckland: Penguin, 1990), 125.

63. Keri Hulme, *the bone people* (Auckland: Spiral and Hodder and Stoughton, 1985), 112.

64. Keri Hulme, "He Tauware Kawa, He Kawa Tauware," in *Te Kaihau/The Windeater* (Wellington: Victoria University Press, 1986), 92.

65. Renee, *Jeannie Once*, 52.

66. Merata Mita, "The Soul and the Image," in *Film in Aotearoa New Zealand*, ed. Jonathan Dennis and Jan Bieringa (Wellington: Victoria University Press, 1992), 54.

Index

In this index an "f" after a number indicates a separate reference on the next page, and an "ff" indicates separate references on the next two pages. A continuous discussion over two or more pages is indicated by a span of page numbers, e.g., "57–59." *Passim* is used for a cluster of references in close but not consecutive sequence.